The Relational Dynamics of Enchantment and Sacralization

The Study of Religion in a Global Context

SERIES EDITORS
Tim Jensen
EXECUTIVE EDITOR
UNIVERSITY OF SOUTHERN DENMARK

Morny Joy
SERIES EDITOR
UNIVERSITY OF CALGARY

Katja Triplett
MANAGING EDITOR
UNIVERSITY OF GÖTTINGEN

The series, published in association with the International Association for the History of Religions, encourages work that is innovative in the study of religions, whether of an empirical, theoretical or methodological nature. This includes multi- or inter-disciplinary studies involving anthropology, philosophy, psychology, sociology and political studies. Volumes will examine the continuing influence of postcolonial, decolonial and intercultural dynamics, as well as contemporary responses from intersectional studies. They will also address the relevance and application of more recent approaches such as cognitivist, as well as ones concerned with aesthetic culture—art, architecture, media, performance and sound.

PUBLISHED

Philosophy and the End of Sacrifice:
Disengaging Ritual in Ancient India, Greece and Beyond
Edited by Peter Jackson and Anna-Pya Sjödin

The Relational Dynamics of Enchantment and Sacralization:
Changing the Terms of the Religion Versus Secularity Debate

Edited by
Peik Ingman, Terhi Utriainen, Tuija Hovi,
and Måns Broo

Published by Equinox Publishing Ltd.

UK: Office 415, The Workstation,
15 Paternoster Row, Sheffield,
South Yorkshire S1 2BX
USA: ISD, 70 Enterprise Drive, Bristol, CT 06010

www.equinoxpub.com

First published 2016

© Peik Ingman, Tuija Hovi, Terhi Utriainen, Måns Broo and contributors

All rights reserved. No part of this publication may be reproduced or transmitted in any form or by any means, electronic or mechanical, including photocopying, recording or any information storage or retrieval system, without prior permission in writing from the publishers.

British Library Cataloguing-in-Publication Data

A catalogue record for this book is available from the British Library.

ISBN 978 1 78179 474 6 (hardback)
ISBN 978 1 78179 475 3 (paperback)

Library of Congress Cataloging-in-Publication Data

Names: Ingman, Peik, editor.
Title: The Relational Dynamics of Enchantment and Sacralization: Changing the Terms of the Religion Versus Secularity Debate / edited by Peik Ingman, Terhi Utriainen, Tuija Hovi, and Måns Broo.
Description: Bristol, CT : Equinox Publishing Ltd, 2016. | Series: The study of religion in a global context | Includes bibliographical references and index.
Identifiers: LCCN 2016010530 (print) | LCCN 2016034330 (ebook) |
 ISBN 9781781794746 (hb) | ISBN 9781781794753 (pb) | ISBN 9781781794807 (e-PDF) | ISBN 9781781794814 (e-epub)
Subjects: LCSH: Religion—Philosophy. | Secularism.
Classification: LCC BL51 .R34155 2016 (print) | LCC BL51 (ebook) | DDC 200—dc23
LC record available at http://lccn.loc.gov/2016010530

Typeset by Queenston Publishing, Hamilton, Ontario, Canada

Printed by Lightning Source Inc. (La Vergne, TN), Lightning Source UK Ltd. (Milton Keynes), Lightning Source AU Pty. (Scoresby, Victoria).

"This volume brings the study of ritual, religion, and spirituality into full conversation with agency, networks, and materiality. The result is a fascinating and insightful resource that casts new light on enchantment and sacralization, which become in the authors' hands very useful analytical concepts. In a day when traditional notions of 'religion' have lost relevance, a new set of conceptual tools is important to develop. This book makes a splendid contribution."

Professor David Morgan, Department of Religious Studies, Duke University

"This is a wonderful book. It draws on sophisticated cutting-edge theory to provide significant new insights into ritual, enchantment, and religious practice. I particularly enjoyed the creative engagement with contemporary debates about 'religion' that draws us back to empirical studies of the ethical and moral challenges negotiated through the experience and practice of religion."

Professor Douglas Ezzy, University of Tasmania, and President of the Australian Association for the Study of Religion.

"Invoking the previously exorcised 'religious' terms, enchantment and sacralization, this radical volume experiments with re-positioning religion and the study of religion as relational encounters. Facing down some suffocating polemics, the contributors demonstrate what may be achieved by allowing new possibilities to emerge from dialogue, reflection and a willingness to learn."

Graham Harvey, Professor of Religious Studies, The Open University, UK

Contents

LIST OF ILLUSTRATIONS ... ix

1. Introduction: Towards More Symmetrical Compositions ... 1
   PEIK INGMAN, TERHI UTRIAINEN, TUIJA HOVI AND MÅNS BROO

PART I: REVISITING ENCHANTMENT AND ANIMISM

2. Objects as Subjects: Agency and Performativity in Rituals ... 27
   ANNE-CHRISTINE HORNBORG

3. Enchantment, Matter, and the Unpredictability of Devotion ... 45
   AMY WHITEHEAD

4. Empowerment and the Articulation of Agency among Finnish Yoga Practitioners ... 65
   MÅNS BROO AND CHRISTIANE KÖNIGSTEDT

5. Mastery and Modernity: Control Issues in the Disenchantment Tale ... 85
   LINDA ANNUNEN AND PEIK INGMAN

PART II: POLITICAL CONCERNS

6. Recomposing Religion: Radical Agnosticism and Transformative Speech ... 109
   MICHAEL BARNES NORTON

7. Re-enchanting Body and Religion in a Secular Society: Touch of an Angel ... 125
   TERHI UTRIAINEN

8. Marian Apparitions: The Construction of Authenticity and Governance of Sacralization in the Shrine of Our Lady of the Rosary in Portugal ... 145
   NORA MACHADO

9. Protection through the Invocation of Shared Thirds: 165
Sacralization without Iconoclasm

   PEIK INGMAN

Part III: Academic Concerns

10. Enchanted Sight/Site: An Esoteric Aesthetics of Image   189
and Experience

    JAY JOHNSTON

11. From Religion to Ordering Uncertainty: A Lesson from   207
Dancers

    MILAN FUJDA

12. Co-composing a Village History in the Archipelago of South-   231
western Finland

    JAANA KOURI

13. After Dis/enchantment: The Profanity of the Human Sciences   251

    STUART MCWILLIAMS

14. Epilogue: When Things Talk Back   267

    KOCKU VON STUCKRAD

    INDEX   277

List of Illustrations

Cover	"Communal webs composed by the larvae of ermine moths clothe a tree in sun-reflecting silver." Picture taken by Peik Ingman in the summer of 2013, by the river Aura in Turku, Finland.	
Figure 2.1	An illustration by the author, of the ritual space of the *kekunit*.	36
Figure 10.1	Analysis example. From M. Choat and I. Gardner, A Coptic Handbook of Ritual Power. Image reproduced with permission of Museum of Ancient Cultures, Macquarie University.	199

— 1 —

Introduction: Towards More Symmetrical Compositions

PEIK INGMAN, TERHI UTRIAINEN, TUIJA HOVI, MÅNS BROO

Religion is a difficult word. Whenever we deem something religious or non-religious, or when something is compared to "religion," we need to recognize that we are engaging in complex issues and aspects of social, psychological and political life. It is challenging to not lose sight of this complexity while using the same word to refer to such a broad range of practices and from such a broad range of angles, carrying diverse implications. Of course, working with different definitions of the same concept does not necessarily or always have to be a problem. One might argue that what is most important is to be clear about how *we* use the concept in a given study. Unfortunately, precision in defining analytic concepts does not necessarily solve the problem. In fact, it might miss the problem. William E. Paden offers the following analogy:

> Maps of the same city differ radically according to the angle of the subject matter mapped. Picturing any area quite differently would be the charts of the water department, the tourist bureau, political party organizations, cocaine dealers, and church parishes. Again, maps chart only material that is useful and relevant for the purposes of their makers, and ignore all other information as extraneous. Interpretations of religion are like such overlapping, mapped systems existing within the same town. Each makes sense given the selective nature of its data. Each "says" only what it is interested in. (Paden 1992, 112)

While the above description may tempt us to think that the problem is thereby solved, part of the problem seems to be the way in which predefined concepts tend to render our findings predictable and compliant to our theories and criteria. What seems generally agreed on, however, is that there is a pressing need for scholars to think about the implications of when and how we use the "r-word." How are we to study things that look, sound or feel like religion from one angle or for a moment but that from another perspective and in another setting and moment do not? How are we to find ways of being sensitive to the changing face, place, intensity and dynamics of religiosity in the world today? And what are we to make of practices that share an intriguing or uncanny family resemblance with these dynamics, yet are usually not referred to as "religious"? These are the kinds of background questions that motivate the chapters of the present book. Instead of concluding that the issue is merely a matter of happily co-existing perspectives, however, we think that understanding often develops through the productive agonism of bringing different perspectives together.

The story behind the present volume and the questions above goes back to 2010, when the editors were recruited as members of the research project *Post-secular culture and a changing religious landscape* (PCCR, see Nynäs, Lassander, Utriainen 2012; Nynäs, Illman, Martikainen 2015) at Åbo Akademi University, Finland. This project aimed at identifying, describing and analysing the present-day shifting religious landscape, or the transforming and contested boundaries between "religious" and "secular" practices, identities and agencies. In particular, the project had a focus on Finland and the northern countries, but in complex relation to the changing global scene. We were mostly ethnographers, working with interviews and observations on discourses and practices we considered indicative not only of religious change but also changes that realigned or contested boundary areas in interesting ways and thus challenged notions of what was at stake or that are taken for granted. Encountering contemporary people who were engaged in various kinds of healing practices, body pedagogics and personal paths, often simultaneously or alternatingly (more and less) "religious" or "secular," we became increasingly intrigued by the indeterminate dynamics of these classifications and trajectories. The editors of this book were delegated the task of attending to concerns related particularly to the elusive and contested theme of agency. We found ourselves struggling with how to understand and approach this complex field without turning to either individualistic or structural explanations or, alternatively, purely phenomenological description. We wanted to describe and provide accounts of agency and difference, but in ways that would do justice to their complexity.

While the initial question we worked with was whether or not there was something particular about religious agency, as we started inviting scholars from both within and outside religious studies to contribute to the present volume, we gradually found ourselves gravitating towards the concepts of enchantment and sacralization. These terms seemed to provide some traction in allowing for a focus on processes of negotiating the tension between the personal/private and the public, processes that intimately involved actors, but were not thereby only or "merely" subjective. An increasing emphasis on relationality within the humanities had us asking questions about relational engagement. Enchantment and sacralization seemed to provide the necessary focus while providing some leeway from the above preoccupation with the concept of religion. Still, the editors would like to acknowledge that over the long gestation of this project, the volume's overall focus has had various iterations. The construction of its final focus was particularly influenced by the conceptual content of several of the chapters found herein. This includes, in particular, Jay Johnston's emphasis on perceptive co-cultivation, nonhuman and intersubjective agency, Milan Fujda's emphasis on "ordinary ordering practices" that are not arranged through criteria of whether they are religious or not, and Anne-Christine Hornborg's emphasis on the suggestive connection between ritual practices and the contextual agency of objects. Also noteworthy are Jaana Kouri's exploration of the co-composing role of the researcher in ethnography and Christiane Königstedt's and Måns Broo's emphasis on questions of personal responsibility in light of distributed agency. While all of the chapters influenced and contributed to the emerging focus of this book, these authors have been along for the ride from its early beginnings.

How did we end up focusing on the concepts of sacralization and enchantment? In order to answer this question, we need to address some of the problems that have haunted the study of religion throughout its relatively short history and, more specifically, how these problems have led us to conclude that what appears to be needed is a focus on relational dynamics. For reasons that we will elaborate, enchantment and sacralization seem to facilitate such a focus. Moreover, considering that contemporary concerns about the use of religion as an analytic concept involve a postcolonial awareness of said practice's complicity in European imperialism (see Masuzawa 2005; Nongbri 2013; McCutcheon 1997, 2001, 2003; Fitzgerald 2004; as well as the work of Jonathan Z. Smith and Talal Asad), we argue that our discussion concerning the relevance of key terms may prove instrumental in correcting some of the negative effects of an asymmetric anthropology. Let us try to qualify these claims with a brief look backwards.

A Brief History of Some Relevant Controversies:
From the Comparative Method to the Critical Study of Religion

Anthropology, sociology and philosophy have all developed significantly *through* disputes, such as the productive disagreements between Edvard Westermarck and Emile Durkheim, Durkheim and Gabriel Tarde, and Bruno Latour and Pierre Bourdieu. While these, as well as recent debates in religious studies, have admittedly led to and intensified polarization, disagreements also facilitate recognition of important matters of concern that provide direction and help us to reassess our methods.

Consider the anthropologist and moral philosopher Edvard Westermarck (1862–1939), one of the champions of the comparative method, a system steeped in naturalist presuppositions about the evolutionary theory of culture. According to Olli Lagerspetz, Westermarck's scholarship was haunted by the sharp criticism he received from Durkheim and other functionalists. In his memoirs he noted, indignantly, that he certainly did "see the weak points of the comparative method without the need of reminders from others" (Lagerspetz 2016; Westermarck 1929, 300). He wrote:

> [S]ocial phenomena are not isolated facts, but are largely influenced by local conditions, by the physical environment, by the circumstances in which the people are living, by their habits and mental characteristics. And all these factors can of course be taken into account much more easily when the investigation is restricted to a particular group of men than when it comprises things that are common to widely separated peoples or to mankind in general. (Westermarck 1929, 298–299)

Lagerspetz notes how the problem was taken up in the late 1950s by the American philosopher Peter Winch in his influential *The Idea of a Social Science and its Relation to Philosophy* (1958). As Lagerspetz summarizes, "the question, whether two practices count as *the same* thing, must in the first instance be a question directed to the individuals and institutions who perform it or live with it" (Lagerspetz 2016). He quotes Winch: "[A]lthough the reflective student of society, or of a particular mode of social life, may find it necessary to use concepts which are not taken from the forms of activity which he is investigating, [...] still these technical concepts of his will imply a previous understanding of those other concepts which belong to the activities under investigation" (Winch [1958] 1990, 89). Lagerspetz concludes, "the social scientist's theoretical description must in the last analysis be something that can *connect* with the ideas of the agents" (Lagerspetz 2016). Here we have the main ingredients of a dispute that is far from settled.

Introduction: Towards More Symmetrical Compositions

The Canadian religious studies scholar Russell McCutcheon's more recent dispute with his distinguished colleague Robert Orsi about who should have the right to define the significance of religious practices echoes the concerns raised by Winch and Lagerspetz, concerns that were evidently central already for Durkheim, Westermarck and their contemporaries.[1] In 2004, Orsi reviewed McCutcheon's book *The Discipline of Religion: Structure, Meaning, Rhetoric* (2003) in rather unfavourable terms, asking

> Do the theorized have any voice to speak back to the italicizing theorizer? Can they challenge the assertion that they are in need of theorization or this construal of their lives? Can they protest being made into a theoretician's 'fair game'? If they do, McCutcheon never says so, which is a serious omission: the data remain silent, as one might expect of data. (Orsi 2004, 88)

McCutcheon responded with an article exploring "the limits of the humanistic study of religion and the costs of saving Others from themselves" (2006). In the article, McCutcheon explains his rebuttal as follows:

> [W]hen it comes to those Others whose differences can easily be tolerated or overlooked with little or no cost, scholars in this tradition deploy a different sets [sic] of tools than when their work focuses on Others for whom they feel little affinity and whose interests conflict with their own. Failing to understand all scholarship as necessarily involved in acts of translation and redescription—acts that are all equally removed from some posited authentic source—the essay ends by suggesting that we risk the future of our field when we employ different methods for different people, all based on the degree of our personal identification with our subject matter.
> (excerpt from the article abstract)

Although we take issue with the idealist and representationalist underpinnings of McCutcheon's claim that all translation and redescription are equally removed from some posited authentic source, as well as with the rather scientific notion that employing the same method would provide a solution to this problem, his concern about researchers speaking on behalf of informants is a concern we share. We agree that scholars "should be a little more careful of the tales we choose to tell and in whose voice they are being told," but not because "all representation is inevi-

---

1. Actually, this controversy has involved quite a number of distinguished scholars within religious studies, including Thomas Tweed, Ann Taves and Stephen Prothero. Interestingly, Orsi was *also* criticized for arguing for scholarly neutrality (by Prothero), which it seems McCutcheon would like him to exhibit more of.

tably a form of falsification—regardless of who is doing the storytelling" (McCutcheon 2006, 745). This is because we do not think that scholarship needs to be about representation.

McCutcheon accuses Orsi for the crime of acting like an

> Eliadean cross-cultural comparativist who understands local practices as a disguised instance of an otherwise uniform sacred presence, one that is manifested in the actions and artifacts of a diverse collection of others, *whether or not* these people themselves understand their behaviors to be but one relative node in a cross-cultural system of signification.
>
> (McCutcheon 2006, 741)

A problem here is that McCutcheon makes it sound as if he would be concerned with faithfully representing the views of informants. Actually, his solution to this problem is not that we should take the descriptions of informants at face value, nor does he appear to be arguing that we should need to be particularly concerned when the descriptions of scholars contradict the descriptions of informants. His solution is that we should not even try to do what he understands as creeping into the informants' minds, as if "language and [our] interests are coterminous with reality, allowing [us] unimpeded access to the grieving widower's heart" (McCutcheon 2006, 745). What really seems to bother McCutcheon is that Orsi appears to be engaging in metaphysics. Critical sociologists like McCutcheon tend to insist that we need to focus on social inequalities from a vantage point that generally fails to consider the relevance of its own values, its own metaphysics.[2]

Yet McCutcheon helps us to focus in on this tension between "us and them," a tension that is evident not only in the differentiation of the religious and the non-religious, but that of modern and pre-modern, social constructionism and realism. While all scholarship involves translation, this does not mean that our only solution is to abide by a method whose merit lies in being uniformly rigid and indifferent to the concerns of those it studies. Quite the contrary, we think that we need methods that are adaptable enough to follow the innovations of a myriad of particular practices, including the critical practices of sociologists and the metaphysics of scientists. But let us continue with our brief history. Now we move backwards in time, once again to find controversy.

From Construction to Composition: Towards an Infra-language

According to Bruno Latour, one of the most influential sociologists of the last decade, a seminal chain reaction was put into motion in the late 1960s and early 1970s when science—or, more precisely, scientific practices—

---

2. See Boltanski 2012, chapter 3, for a good critique of critical sociology.

came under investigation by a newly founded discipline. (Note that this was around the same time as *The Social Construction of Reality* (1966), the landmark work by Peter Berger and Thomas Luckmann, which inspired a humanistic sociology of knowledge, was published.) It was within this new discipline, aimed at studying science, technology and society (STS), that many of the weaknesses and troubling implications of the use of the concept of "construction" in social construction—understood as originating in human meaning-making, interpretation and anthropocentric projection—were discovered.[3] For contemporary scholars involved in new materialisms, these weaknesses are glaringly obvious by now. According to Latour, it was when sociologists studying scientific practices began looking into the actual "making of science"—including how certain instruments actively contextualized how science was made—and not just discursive, human-to-human aspects, that they noticed how strange it is to attempt to understand *any* kind of practice without taking into account the formative influence of elements that are not human. Before this happened, however, scientific practices were first subjected to the same treatment that other practices were being subjected to by social constructionists. When scientists undertook the work of studying other scientists, initially using the standard sociological methods applied at the time, something interesting occurred, something that relates directly to the dispute between McCutcheon and Orsi. As Latour put it:

> [R]eligious people never screamed in anger when they were "socially explained." Who would have listened to them anyway? If anything, their sobs would have been further proof that they could not stand witnessing their fanciful and archaic illusions explained by the cold glare of hard social facts. And the same would have happened if politicians, the poor, workers, farmers, and artists had whined at being "put into a social context." Who would have listened to the three-century long string of objections raised by tropical worshippers accused of fetishism? They might have grumbled and shrugged, but never did they bite *back* at the sociologist's proofs. (Latour 2005, 98)

When social scientists finally began studying other scientists, the situation was different:

> [F]or the first time, social scientists had to study something that was *higher, harder,* and *stronger* than them. For the first time, the *explanandum* resisted and grinded the teeth of the *explanans'* cogs to mere stumps. Not only that, but the screams of those being studied could be heard loud

---

3. This is not to say that such discoveries were only made there. Similar conclusions were made, for instance, within Women's/Gender Studies, notably by Donna Haraway.

and clear—and they were not coming from Bali, the ghettos, TV studios, corporate board rooms, or the US Senate, but from departments next door, from colleagues in the very same hiring and grant committees.

(Latour 2005, 98)

STS, along with its offshoot Actor-Network Theory (ANT), was compelled to devise new ways of describing practices, in part because scholars no longer had the option of ignoring the objections of those they studied. These new ways of describing practices involved not only an increasing recognition of the formative influence of nonhuman agents, but also the recognition that "following the actors" proved much more interesting, providing insights into how concerns emerge in practice and are dealt with in practice, than explaining those concerns (away) with theoretical concepts that were taken to be more real than the vocabulary of the scientists.

ANT produced description after description of various practices by tracing complicated, interlinked networks of associated actors. The meaning of their behaviour was not revealed by unravelling the beliefs they projected onto a meaningless, inaccessible world, or the "social mechanisms" at work, but by understanding the matters of concern that actors struggled with as emerging from their entanglement with networks of human and nonhuman actors. Non-intentional and nonhuman actants were shown to direct the course of events in concert with intentional actors. Not presuming a distinction between them proved useful in providing descriptions of practices that traced the productive relationships among actants. The implications, however, were that if science was to be able to maintain its status, a way was needed to negotiate the dichotomy of discovered versus fabricated, a dichotomy that also overshadows the dispute between Orsi and McCutcheon, as we have seen. STS and ANT demonstrated how scientific facts were not exactly discovered, showing how much work was done to achieve the effects scientists wanted to "find." The revolutionary claims that emerged from decades of ANT research were not that scientific facts had been revealed to be socially constructed, but rather that even the highest, hardest and strongest of objects in the modern world (facts) were the emergent results of complex compositions that involved the agency of nonhuman actors—or, in other words, that said practices could not be adequately explained while maintaining a divide between "the social" and "the natural." For natural scientists, nonhuman actors have to be able to speak; otherwise, how could their practices of fabrication be at all differentiated from fabrication considered to be *solely* the result of human meaning-making? Scientists, like religious people before them, objected to the ways in which their practices were portrayed as if they were merely acting on behalf of social forces, but this time the social scientists could not simply dismiss the objections. Once the realization sunk in that the hard sciences actually needed to acknowledge the influence of nonhuman agency in order to legitimate their practices, the great divide between fact and fetish no longer appeared as a given. To underline this ambivalence, Latour eventually coined the term "factish" (see Latour 2010, 2011). Once this pillar of modernity no longer served to maintain the great divide, the question of "belief" was opened anew (see, for instance, Morgan 2009).

Let us now return to the dispute between Orsi and McCutcheon. As noted above, the dispute allegedly concerned the tension between the descriptions of informants and the descriptions of scholars, yet we suggested that the dispute was really about whether or not there is such a thing as a non-metaphysical vantage point from which to engage in research. By bringing in the relevance of nonhuman actors, this issue is broadened and thereby recognized as present even in natural science: is it the object or the scientist that is achieving/fabricating fact? Are objects probed through various methods and techniques in order to provide them with the means to "speak" to us, akin to how an informant may be addressed with the appropriate questions—a practice that is thereby rendered vulnerable to the accusation of "leading the witness"? Whose story becomes authoritative? Are natural scientists speaking on behalf of objects or are they artfully setting up the means by which objects can both respond as well as provide new questions? ANT researchers did not conclude that we have to decide between the stories of the informants and the stories of theorists. They concluded something else.

Latour insists that there is something distinctive about ANT in relation to how we usually understand theoretical concepts. Latour explains:

> Whatever metaphors we want to cling to, they do nothing more than help us counterbalance the weight of social inertia. They are part of our infra-language. Once again, everything happens as if ANT did not locate social theory at the same level as sociologists of the social. What the latter means by theory is a positive, substantive, and synthetic view of the ingredients out of which the social is fashioned—and those accounts may often be very suggestive and powerful. With ANT, we push theory one step further into abstraction: it is a negative, empty, relativistic grid that allows us *not* to synthesize the ingredients of the social in the actor's place. Since it's never substantive, it never possesses the power of the other types of accounts. (Latour 2005, 220–221)

Here Latour is referring to such ANT terms as translation, mediation or centres of calculation. His point is that the terms are such that they could never be used to *replace* the innovative action of actors-in-relation.

To a large extent, the problem with using religion as an analytic concept seems to revolve around practices of replacing compositionally complex, relational dynamics involving heterogeneous actors, usually both human and nonhuman, with this ambiguous and politically loaded term. Timothy Fitzgerald, for instance, has argued that there is no non-theological reason for scholars to use 'religion' as an analytic term. He provides examples of cases where its analytical deployment has served to obscure the subject matter, and he argues that abandoning the term is no great loss, given that we have access to much more useful ones, such as ritual, politics, soteriology, and so forth (Fitzgerald 2003). One could argue that enchantment and sacralization are no less vulnerable to being used indiscriminately.[4] However, the point is not that enchantment and sacralization would be more neutral terms than religion. The point is that "whatever metaphors we want to cling to," we need to make sure that they are not introduced in ways that silence or ignore the innovative action of the actors, the matters of concern they struggle with and give rise to. We need to make sure that they do not *replace* this complexity; instead, they may allude to it. While much is resolved through the emphasis on symmetry found in the strong programme developed within the sociology of scientific knowledge (SSK), Latour's notion of an infra-language allows us to go even further. The options are not limited to either the actor's own metaphysics being reduced to the scholar's or the scholar not being allowed to use any terms except those used by research participants. Neither is it a solution based only on establishing symmetry between knowledge claims. Rather, it is about appreciating the benefits of an "empty" theoretical language that only directs attention and encourages curiosity. It is this "only" that we suggest might address some of the concerns McCutcheon raises, but without arguing that adherence to some scientific method and under the banner of neutrality we might manage to avoid getting our hands dirty.

Enchantment and Sacralization as Analytic Concepts

We think that "enchantment" and "sacralization" may be able to do just that. As noted, it is perhaps not so much the concepts *per se* that are either appropriate or inappropriate as much as the way in which they are deployed in explorative description. This brings us to the emphasis on dynamics. There are no universal templates that can be applied

---

4. Indeed, as Stuart McWilliams notes (this volume), words such as enchantment and magic have been used precisely to position oneself in relation to the calculative ideals of modernity. After all, disenchantment became, after Weber, a label for the state of rational moderns. Likewise, to call something sacred can not only serve to induce reverence; it can also be used to intentionally ridicule.

Introduction: Towards More Symmetrical Compositions

to local or particular practices. However, something is universally true: actors are situated. Exploring situatedness as involving sacralization and enchantment does not oblige us to posit an Eliadean sacred realm. Insofar as the terms sacralization and enchantment succeed in directing our attention towards matters of concern relating to risky, precarious compositions—matters of concern that pertain to relationships that are not given but open-endedly composed—they may prove instrumental in achieving descriptions that "can *connect* with the self-understanding of the agents" (see Lagerspetz on Winch, above) without necessarily coinciding with them. The aim, after all, is not only to learn "their" language but to achieve meaningful and ethically defensible transactions between (non-neutral) academic concerns and the concerns that involve and relate to particular practices.

Latour's experimental metaphysics is instructive in its eschewing of reduction. The problem with instances where religion is treated as a self-evident force is that the interaction and relational dynamics involved are thereby delineated beforehand. We already supposedly know what religion is. As Milan Fujda (this volume) argues, this tempts us to take for granted a focus on certain objects but not others, that is, objects that are "religious." Deciding beforehand what "counts" and what does not is, hence, to a large extent the problem. What about our alternative terms, then? What about enchantment and sacralization? We chose these terms for this volume because we found it necessary to revisit the disenchantment story in order to assess and evaluate our presuppositions, our modern metaphysics. We are not denying that enchantment or sacralization can be vulnerable to the same kind of reductions that the use of the term religion has been accused of. However, we suggest that these terms serve to shift our attention towards practices and dynamics, towards events and encounters, towards a social that circulates, in ways akin to Malory Nye's suggestion to utilize the term "religioning" (Nye 2000). Sacralization involves doing something, such as actively participating in the regulation of relationships and boundaries. Enchantment, likewise, immediately calls to mind not only a state, but an event: to be enchanted is to be enchanted by something. Enchantment is about doing and being done to. Furthermore, given contemporary interest in new materialism (e.g., Coole and Frost 2010, Rieger and Waggoner 2015, Crockett and Robbins 2012) and new animism (e.g., Harvey 2005, 2013), it is no longer a given *how* we approach these terms: investigating sacralization and enchantment can no longer afford to take for granted who or what the participants of these dynamics are or can be. We suggest that these terms may be instrumental in complicating the categories of "religion" and "secularity" without sacrificing the insights garnered along the way, pertaining particularly to the ethnographic study of practices. Moreover, we suggest that these terms are especially felicitous for attending to political matters of concern, considering how much politics involve the negotiation of boundaries of what is important, what is worth protecting, and who or what is allowed to influence decision-making.

Although these terms have been used to exoticize and mystify the concerns of others, contemporary recognition of their value serves less to glorify non-Western practices than it serves to *correct* previous usages of these terms; here "correct" implies that sticking with these terms and getting rid of problematic usages is a better course than abandoning useful notions on the grounds that they have a troubled/troubling history. This argument is based more on the recognition of the potential relevance of enchantment and sacralization, regardless of whether or not we understand ourselves as secular or not, than on their universality. The claim, in other words, is not that these terms are always relevant, but that these terms may be relevant regardless of distinctions between the secular and the religious. Magic, enchantment and eventually even religion are terms that have been used to separate the modern from the pre-modern, two groups of people whose identity (for Moderns) hinges on their stance in relation to these concepts via a logic of progress. Noting then that it is not possible to conclude *a priori* that concerns regarding sacralization and enchantment are more or less prevalent among people, depending on whether or not we consider them modern, we would argue that *for this purpose* these terms have ceased to convince. However, the question that this volume poses is whether or not these terms might fruitfully serve other purposes. Might they serve to direct our attention to relational dynamics, and might they do this in ways that challenge and correct—and perhaps to some small extent even heal—the ways in which they have been implicated in European imperialism?

Revisiting the Disenchantment Tale

Since at least the 1990s, Latour has been engaged in an ongoing project he sometimes refers to as the anthropology of the Moderns. Indeed, this is the sub-heading of his most recent book (2013), while the original French title of *We Have Never Been Modern*, published in 1991, already had the sub-heading *Essai d'anthropologie symétrique*, alluding to his central point that the modern self-image is built up around a distinguishing, but complexly asymmetrical contrast to the pre-moderns. They lived in an enchanted world, while we are disenchanted; they had fetishes, we have facts. As noted, Latour takes issue particularly with the notion of fetishism. His argument is basically that the pre-moderns can be understood as having acknowledged their (inter)dependence, engagement and entanglement

Introduction: Towards More Symmetrical Compositions

with objects and forces that were not entirely in their control. This is one way of understanding living in an "enchanted world." The moderns, on the other hand, saw/see themselves as tool-users, bravely domesticating the world for human purposes (i.e., disenchanting it). Disenchantment was essentially the consequence of understanding ourselves as the active components in all relations—the users, the makers and, above all, the masters.

Latour has endeavoured to argue that actually "we have never been modern" (Latour 1993), in that we have never ceased to be conditioned and "made to act" by the objects we engage with (voluntarily or not). Our tools "make us act," but not necessarily in the sense of enslaving us. In other words, we have never ceased to live in an enchanted/enchanting world. It is our idea of ourselves, our insistence on being masters of passively manageable objects, that has served to convince us that the world has become disenchanted. While in actuality the very concepts (now understood as objects among other objects) we deploy to map and render the world more manageable actively loop back and influence us, *as moderns* we cling to the notion of "projection" in order to mark ourselves as the ones in control. The implication here is that, just as people who self-identify as religious do not necessarily do so at every turn, neither do people who self-identify as modern.[5] According to Latour, mastery is the innovative illusion that characterizes the moderns, and superstition and magical thinking are the illusions we insist we have liberated ourselves from. More and more, however, this notion of mastery is failing to convince us. The archaeologist Ian Hodder, for instance, provides an alter-tale to the tale of human progress as tool-users. He notes that "our relations with things are often

---

5. Thomas Tweed's anthropological theory of religion (2006) emphasizes the spatial tropes of dwelling and crossing and shows how practices of boundary maintenance or transformation understood as pertaining to religion change in intensity and how such practices can become both part of making home and identity as well as an integral element and vehicle of changing place and transforming life. Likewise, the notion of being modern and doing things in a modern way are not always invoked equally intensively by people who might consider themselves modern. On the basis of his ethnographic observations on contemporary British Christian activities, Martin Stringer (2008) notes how horoscopes would become a topic for his research participants. Horoscopes would not be simply *either* religious *or* not religious for the people he studied. Instead, horoscopes *might become* religious messages or devices in *some* situations and moments—in particular, critical moments in life—and then again they might not be religious or they could cease to be religious at other moments. When horoscopes did become religious, they might fall into what Stringer calls "coping religion," that is, religion as it works and is used in caring for important everyday life issues and problems, such as children, health and family economy. Similarly, we can see how self-identifying as modern becomes relevant for people in particular circumstances, such as when they encounter practices they would like to be able to dismiss by calling them superstitious.

asymmetrical, leading to entrapments in particular pathways from which it is difficult to escape" (Hodder 2014, 19).[6]

The claim that "we have never been modern" could hence be translated into the claim that "we have never been disenchanted." The disenchantment tale appears then as a tale that has allowed modern people to self-identify as emancipated, albeit harbouring nostalgia for a sense of connection that clinging to their role as masters in the story no longer provides access to. This nostalgia has come in the wake of insisting that objects were (our) tools and, thereby, non-enchanting. We could enchant them, but we should resist such backwards practices, lest we risk regressing. Meaning-making was seen as the result of projecting anthropocentric meaning onto a meaningless, indifferent world. Philosophers and social constructionists told us—and the notion is still propagated, for instance, by McCutcheon and Craig Martin (2012)—that we do not have access to anything *but* our *conceptions* of the world and that *these* are purportedly (and reductively) human. In part, this can be understood as having conflated causality with responsibility: while we are responsible for our concepts, this does not mean that we are their creators or that we remain their masters. Hence, the moderns' self-image appears to have been driven by the glorification of liberation from superstition.[7] Indeed, modernity may be understood as a kind of over-reaction to the threat of the political power of superstition.

A non-modern perspective would entail distinguishing between the stories we tell about our agency and vulnerability, on the one hand (Broo and Königstedt, this volume), and theorizing on the effects of our entanglement with whatever objects that are "drawing us in," on the other.

---

6. Hodder provides examples where human dependency on objects has become veritably impossible to escape, thereby challenging the notion of material objects being "ours":

    From the first moment when, as *Homo faber,* we invested in stone axes, we found we could do more, and yet we found ourselves entrapped in the needs and demands of things and their limits and instabilities. It proved difficult to make things entirely social—they seemed to have lives of their own that we could not predict or control. [...] We depend on the sweetness of the sugar, and the milk in the cereal, and the electricity grid to light the shops and streets. But in order to produce this ready-to-handedness, this everyday expectation of stability and order, a vast apparatus of humans and things has to be mobilized on a global scale. To get the sugar to the table, to maintain the electricity grid, and to assure supplies of slippers, smartphones and bikes, a massive mobilization of resources, humans, dependencies is involved. Things have lives of their own that we get drawn into, and society depends on our abilities to manage this vibrancy of things effectively, to produce the effect of stability. We often manage to live relatively unaware of the full complexity of what and who provides for us, but we are nevertheless deeply entangled in the vitality of things and the assemblages of their relations. (Hodder 2014, 21)

7. See McWilliams (2012), as well as his chapter in this volume, for a discussion on the awkward but influential relationship between academia and magical thinking.

Introduction: Towards More Symmetrical Compositions

We may like to think that we are tool-users, but once in a while we become aware of our entanglements as being uncanny—as forcing upon us deliberations about more complicated forms of causality. Religious individuals, not unlike experimental scientists, often actively seek out experiences in which they commune with objects and become vehicles and extensions of forces that are not entirely in their control. Reductive interpretations insist that the objects to which they partially surrender their agency are produced by their imagination. Actor-network theorists and object-oriented philosophers working in the wake of the "speculative turn" (Bryant *et al.* 2011; Harman 2010; Reid-Bowen 2011) emphasize instead that any object that has an influence is "real." The point is that if an object—be that object "supernatural" (e.g., an angel), tangible or discursive—is related to in a way that significantly frames an individual's agency, the question of who or what is the producer of said object, while interesting for other reasons, has no bearing whatsoever on the question of *whether or not* they were made to act (or enchanted) by it.

As Timothy Morton has argued, this flips things around. Is it not really our habitual, ordinary world—the one we take for granted and gradually relate to as something un-enchanting—that is perplexing (Morton 2013, 15)? This taken-for-grantedness is not something we achieve by ourselves. Quite a complicated apparatus must be at work in order to achieve the aesthetic effect of an ordinary world that does not kick back. A non-modern perspective allows us to be more symmetrical in our descriptions of how attachments make people act—be these attachments to supernatural objects, ritually empowered objects, conceptually/discursively vitalized objects or scientific facts. We may conclude that experiences of what is experienced as extraordinary and what is experienced as ordinary are both composed, albeit not by any single actor's imagination alone. Indeed, it may be just as fascinating to investigate how a sense of ordinariness can be achieved in order to cope with everyday life as it is to investigate how such a sense may become disrupted by the awareness of something "uncanny" (for instance, when we experience jet lag, to use Morton's example):

> In the state of jet lag, things are strangely familiar and familiarly strange—uncanny. Then it hits you: this is the default state of affairs [...] Your regular house in your regular street is really like this. In truth, their smooth functioning is merely an aesthetic effect to which we have grown accustomed. The smooth world is the illusion! (Morton 2013, 15)

While jet lag may serve to disrupt the aesthetic effect of "the ordinary," we may of course also purposefully seek out experiences of "the extraordinary." In both cases, the effects are what we call compositionally produced and, thereby, they are open to investigation.

Embodiment, Relational Situatedness and Repetition

In his book *Religious Objects in Museums: Private Lives and Public Duties* (2013), Crispin Paine describes what can happen when mostly secular museums all over the world display objects that for some people—and/or under some circumstances—are sacred or alive. The museum world today is becoming increasingly reflexive about the fact that the status and significance of the objects that they store and display can change and vary tremendously, depending on where and when the object is displayed, how it is handled and has been handled before, by whom it is encountered and interpreted, and so on. An object (which can be anything ranging from human remains and artefacts to pieces of ancient wood or stone) may, for instance, respond to the ways in which it is handled by either losing or gaining power or charisma. Its power is hence intimately determined through its attachments, attachments that are spread out over space and time. Regardless of whether or not they were sacred, religious or in ritual use before entering a museum, objects can sometimes, for often unpredictable reasons, become regarded as such by interlocutors who begin to behave accordingly. In extreme cases, religious practices and interpretations can even transform the museum into a sanctuary. The opposite is also possible, and there are many cases where aboriginal people have had their sacred objects repatriated from museums, having argued that these objects, outside of a traditional setting, have lost their capacity to act/affect in the way they were meant to. In a similar way, items of any "religious" tradition and practice can lose or (re)gain in their power to enchant or affect (see Utriainen, this volume).

Paine summarizes something important when he writes, "What matters is how people feel about things" (Paine 2013, 48). Feeling, affect and emotion are important—perhaps even indispensable—in the dynamic processes of sacralization and enchantment (see Riis and Woodhead 2010). The past decade has seen an increase in scholarship focused on affect (e.g., Gregg and Seigworth 2010). Although affects have been approached through various theoretical perspectives that are not entirely compatible with one another, perhaps the most exciting aspect of recent scholarship is the emphasis on how the study of affect concerns the study of the *effects* of attachments and relations—effects which may be surprising in light of what objects are involved. While drives are typically considered to have specific aims and objects, affects can be connected to almost anything. As Eve Sedgwick put it: "Affects can be, and are, attached to things, people, ideas, sensations, relations, activities, ambitions, institutions, and any other number of other things, including other affects" (Sedgwick 2003, 19). This has profound implications for the study of enchantment. If emotions and affective processes typically considered "religious" are seen as the emergent effects of attachments and encounters—as emerging through engagement in spaces (or "atmospheres"), events and relations—and the participating "things" cannot be delimited beforehand, it may be virtually impossible to predict beforehand what kinds of assemblages could potentially produce affects that coincide with some or several definitions of "religious."

The study of affects involves the study of "a different kind of intelligence about the world." As Nigel Thrift has emphasized, "previous attempts to either relegate affect to the irrational or raise it up to the level of the sublime are both equally mistaken" (Thrift 2008, 175). Thus, while the objects participating in the emergence of affects may not be decisive, we should avoid concluding that they do not matter. The mistake would be to abstract the issue too much, thereby missing the ways in which materiality and corporeality are in play (Utriainen, this volume). Instead, to study affects is to cleave "to an 'inhuman' or 'transhuman' framework in which individuals are generally understood as effects of the events to which their body parts (broadly understood) respond and in which they participate" (Thrift 2008, 175). In other words, an individual may engage with an affective "atmosphere" or an affective relation and find their situated agency emerging as a product of such engagement. Recognizing this allows scholars to pay attention to the artful ways in which actors go about attempting to modify, attune and align their capacity for being affected for and through certain practices, for instance, through yoga practices (Broo and Königstedt, this volume) and West-African drumming (Annunen and Ingman, this volume). It also allows us to pay attention to how such vulnerability may become politically exploited, a concern that is intimately linked to the concerns involved in the process of disenchantment (see McWilliams, this volume; Stengers 2010, especially chapter 3).

In many ways, the study of affect would seem to do much that is done in this volume under the rubric of enchantment. Enchantment can be understood both in terms of the ability to enter a state of enchantment and in terms of the ability to enchant. Yet enchantment can also be understood as an event "considered as an encounter between the affected body and a second, affecting, body."[8] Many of the descriptions of enchantment

---

8. Brian Massumi's Notes on the Translation of Deleuze and Guattari's *A Thousand Plateaus* is often referred to in order to define affect:

    AFFECT/AFFECTION. Neither word denotes a personal feeling (*sentiment* in Deleuze and Guattari). *L'affect* (Spinoza's *affectus*) is an ability to affect and be affected. It is a prepersonal intensity corresponding to the passage from one experiential state of the body to another and implying an augmentation or diminution in that body's capacity to act. *L'affection* (Spinoza's *affection*) is each such state considered as an encounter between the affected body and a second, affecting, body (with body taken in its broadest possible sense to include "mental" or ideal bodies). (Massumi 1987, xvi)

found in this volume resonate with work on affect. For instance, Amy Whitehead (this volume; see also 2011, 2013) describes how the aliveness and vitality of a religious statue is connected to the ways in which an adherent engages (with) it. Spending time with it, dressing it and caring for it facilitates an emerging relationship. This involves repetition and the cultivation of familiarity and anticipation. As Anne-Christine Hornborg notes, a person can be familiar with what counts as a ritual object—and engage with it accordingly—without being familiar with the precise script or aim of a ritual. Linda Annunen and Peik Ingman, however, suggest that enchantment often appears to involve the deliberate suspension of belief or expectation, emphasizing instead the facilitation of surprises. Similarly, Milan Fujda discusses how people who are ill often disregard the relevance of whether a cure is "scientific" or not. What matters is getting better or coping better. Worrying whether or not something is scientific or *how* a cure is supposed to come about may, in other words, come across as a privilege people who are gravely ill do not feel they can afford. Opening up to "whatever works" can hence be a matter of cultivating acceptance towards a stance that allows for things to get better through "miracles"—where the term signals the absence of a complete explanation or the significance of having a strategy. In turn, Jay Johnston considers the benefits of allowing ourselves to go beyond a Kantian, disinterested gaze to one that actually takes into account how the senses can be cultivated and perceive on a much broader spectrum than is often acknowledged in academia. All of these perspectives emphasize the relevance of practice for attaining certain experiences. While a particular aim may be in sight, getting there demands some form of "surrender" to a process that exceeds the direct effects of volition.

Often many different forms of practice intersect and complicate one another. Rituals are "ways of disconnecting sufficiently from other worlds to create breathing spaces within practices" (Law and Singleton 2012, 10). Intersecting practices can involve multiple and conflicting agendas. Rituals can be seen as effective ordering practices (to use Fujda's term) that create space for something else by disconnecting from these agendas. Studying rituals can hence be approached by paying particular attention to the tension and differences created through the ritual, between the enacted practices, and the identities they enable and what they disconnect from. The differences enacted may involve tension between the sacred and the profane, but working out what that means in specific cases demands more than a proclamation that we are here dealing with "religious practices." It is here that we may be tempted to jump to use theory in ways that risk "explaining away" complexity. If we instead acknowledge that we find rituals of disconnection almost anywhere where there is a need to create "breathing spaces" for something else, and that they are ways to alter already existing "identity-machines" in order to produce alternatives, we might better recognize how multifaceted the concerns involved can be (Law and Singleton 2012). Pointing this out is not aimed to romanticize the issue; Nora Machado, for instance, discusses how deliberate repetition can also be harnessed as an act of control by the powers that be.

Giorgio Agamben's recent discussion of the term 'profanation' (2007; see McWilliams and Ingman, this volume) is quite in line with our arguments for a shift from explanatory analytic concepts to the utilization of an infra-language. Agamben emphasizes how rituals not only sacralize; they also profane. Rather than take as a given that there is a boundary between the sacred and the profane, we can pay attention to the complex contestations between multiple and often simultaneous processes of sacralization and profanation. One person's or group's sacralization may be another's profanation and sacrilege (Ingman and Utriainen, this volume). Or, if we interpret it differently, we may find no sacrilege at all, only misunderstandings (Norton and Ingman, this volume).

Rituals engage because they situate actors in relation to other actors as participants of relational dynamics. Thus situated, the world looks different than from a view-from-nowhere (Haraway 1988). The philosopher of science Isabelle Stengers emphasizes the crucial relevance of situatedness not only for concerns about a researcher's reflexivity (Kouri, this volume), but for understanding what research that involves immersion demands:

> If subjectivity is to escape the critical clutches that signal the modern territory, immanent critique must present itself as an ingredient of the assemblage, not as critically examining/dismembering the assemblage itself. Referring for instance to William James' remark, that in case of fright, it is hard to decide if it was caused by something frightening, or if that something was perceived as frightening because of our fright, the point is not to address this indecision, but to inhabit the undecided situation, and to learn what it may demand. (Stengers 2008, 44)

As several chapters explore, entertaining the situatedness of others opens up very different kinds of understandings of practices than evaluating such practices by means of a method that presumes to know beforehand what is real (and relevant) and what is not, as well as who/what is acting on who/what. Instead, these alternative perspectives explore and speculate on the particular challenges of various forms of situatedness, while appreciating that "agency is not something that a human being has, but rather the diffused potential for action present in a social and material setting" (Kouri, this volume).

Graham Harvey's *Animism: Respecting the Living World* defines animism as follows: "animists are people who recognize that the world is full of persons, only some of whom are human, and that life is always lived in relationship to others. Animism is lived out in various ways that are all about learning to act respectfully (carefully and constructively) towards and among other persons" (Harvey 2005, xi). What we, the editors, learned while co-composing this book is that the point is not that everything is agentic, but that *how* something is agentic emerges as an effect of entangled networks of relational dynamics. Enchantment and sacralization emerge in these entangled networks as effects that may be welcome or disturbing and as efforts to contain and care for the character and quality of relations.

Outline of the Book

This explorative volume brings together a wide range of heterogeneous practices which, in diverse ways, display, reflect and complicate the relational dynamics of enchantment and sacralization. "Religious," "spiritual," "esoteric" and ritual as well as therapeutic practices, visual art, language, dance and improvisation, ethnographic fieldwork, science and museums—just to mention some most obvious aspects—are investigated through critical relational lenses as complex networks of action and agency.

Structuring this volume proved to be a challenge, as the issues addressed tend to be interrelated. However, in the end we opted to begin with chapters that manage to elucidate the practical implications of revisiting animism and enchantment, particularly in terms of relational challenges for practitioners engaged in maintaining dynamic traditions. Although virtually all of the chapters address questions concerning how we understand enchantment, some of the chapters go on to explicitly address concerns about how we (scholars) understand politics and academic endeavours. The second part engages the political implications of the tension between secularity and religion, particularly in terms of how this tension characterizes modernity, while the third part considers contemporary challenges of scholars who recognize themselves as co-composers of their subject matter. Concluding the volume is an epilogue by Kocku von Stuckrad, who graciously accepted our invitation to assess the achievements and possible shortcomings of the volume.

Acknowledgements

The editors would like to thank Peter Nynäs, who headed the Centre of Excellence in Research project *Post-Secular Culture and a Changing Religious Landscape in Finland* (PCCR), Albion M. Butters for excellent proofreading, Russell Adams for production and copy-editing, Morny Joy for encouragement and constructive criticism and Valerie Hall and Janet Joyce at Equinox for editorial guidance along the way.

References

Agamben, G. 2007. *Profanations.* Translated by Jeff Fort. New York: Zone Books.

Berger, P. and T. Luckmann. 1966. *The Social Construction of Reality.* London: Allen Lane.

Boltanski, L. 2012. *Love and Justice as Competences: Three Essays on the Sociology of Action.* Translated by C. Porter. Cambridge, UK: Polity.

Bryant, L., N. Srnicek and G. Harman, eds. 2011. *The Speculative Turn: Continental Materialism and Realism.* Melbourne: re.press.

Coole, D. and S. Frost, eds. 2010. *New Materialisms: Ontology, Agency, and Politics.* Durham, NC: Duke University Press.

Crockett, C. and J.W. Robbins. 2012. *Religion, Politics, and the Earth: The New Materialism.* London: Palgrave Macmillan.

Deleuze, G. and F. Guattari. 1987. *A Thousand Plateaus: Capitalism and Schizophrenia.* London: Athlone.

Fitzgerald, T. 2004. *The Ideology of Religious Studies.* Paperback. Oxford: Oxford University Press.

———. 2003. "Playing Language Games and Performing Rituals: Religious Studies as Ideological State Apparatus." *Method & Theory in the Study of Religion* 15(3): 209–254.

Gregg, M. and G.J. Seigworth. 2010. *The Affect Theory Reader.* Durham, NC: Duke University Press.

Haraway, D. 1988. "Situated Knowledges: The Science Question in Feminism and the Privilege of Partial Perspective." *Feminist Studies* 14(3): 575–599.

Harman, G. 2010. *Towards Speculative Realism: Essays and Lectures.* Hants: Zero Books.

Harvey, G. 2005. *Animism: Respecting the Living World.* Kent Town: Wakefield Press.

Harvey, G. ed. 2013. *Handbook of Contemporary Animism.* Rickmansworth: Acumen.

Hodder, I. 2014. "The Entanglements of Humans and Things: A Long-Term View." *New Literary History* 45(1): 19–36.

Lagerspetz, O. 2016. "Westermarck, the Comparative Method and the Question of Context." In *Evolution, Human Behaviour and Morality: The Legacy of Westermarck,* edited by O. Lagerspetz, J. Antfolk, Y. Gustafsson and C. Kronqvist. London: Routledge.

———. 2016. "Westermarck and the Emergence of Twentieth-Century Social Anthropology." In *Evolution, Human Behaviour and Morality: The Legacy of*

Westermarck, edited by O. Lagerspetz, J. Antfolk, Y. Gustafsson and C. Kronqvist. London: Routledge.

Latour, B. 2013. *An Inquiry into Modes of Existence: An Anthropology of the Moderns.* Translated by C. Porter. Cambridge, MA: Harvard University Press.

———. 2011. "Fetish-Factish." *Material Religion* 7(1): 42-49.

———. 2010. *On the Modern Cult of the Factish Gods.* Translated by H. MacLean and C. Porter. Durham, NC: Duke University Press.

———. 2005. *Reassembling the Social: An Introduction to Actor-Network-Theory.* Oxford: Oxford University Press.

———. 1993. *We Have Never Been Modern.* Translated by C. Porter. Cambridge, MA: Harvard University Press.

Martin, C. 2012. *A Critical Introduction to the Study of Religion.* Sheffield: Equinox.

Massumi, B. 1987. "Notes on the Translation and Acknowledgements." In *A Thousand Plateaus: Capitalism and Schizophrenia,* edited by G. Deleuze and F. Guattari, xvi–xix. London: Athlone.

Masuzawa, T. 2005. *The Invention of World Religions: Or How European Universalism was Perceived in the Language of Pluralism.* Chicago, IL: The University of Chicago Press.

McCutcheon, R.T. 2006. "It's a Lie. There's No Truth in It! It's a Sin!: On the Limits of the Humanistic Study of Religion and the Costs of Saving Others from Themselves." *Journal of the American Academy of Religion,* 74(3): 720–751.

———. 2003. *The Discipline of Religion: Structure, Meaning, Rhetoric.* London and New York: Routledge.

———. 2001. *Critics Not Caretakers: Redescribing the Public Study of Religion.* New York: State University of New York Press.

———. 1997. *Manufacturing Religion: The Discourse on Sui Generis Religion and the Politics of Nostalgia.* Oxford: Oxford University Press.

McWilliams, Stuart. 2012. *Magical Thinking: History, Possibility and the Idea of the Occult.* London: Bloomsbury.

Morgan, D. 2009. *Religion and Material Culture: The Matter of Belief.* London: Routledge.

Morton, T. 2013. *Realist Magic: Objects, Ontology, Causality.* Michigan: Open Humanities Press.

Nongbri, B. 2013. *Before Religion: A History of a Modern Concept.* New Haven, CT: Yale University Press.

Nye, M. 2000. "Religion, Post-Religionism, and Religioning: Religious Studies and Contemporary Cultural Debates." *Method & Theory in the Study of Religion* 12: 447–476.

Nynäs, P., M. Lassander and T. Utriainen, eds. 2012. *Post-Secular Society.* New Brunswick, NJ: Transaction Publishers.

Nynäs, P., R. Illman and T. Martikainen, eds. 2015. *On the Outskirts of 'the Church': Diversities, Fluidities and New Spaces of Religion in Finland.* Zürich: LIT Verlag.

Orsi, R.A. 2004. "Fair Game." *Bulletin of the Council of Societies for the Study of Religion* 33(3–4): 87–89.

Paden, W.E. 1992. *Interpreting the Sacred: Ways of Viewing Religion.* Boston, MA: Beacon Press.

Paine, C. 2013. *Religious Objects in Museums: Private Lives and Public Duties.* London: Bloomsbury.

Reid-Bowen, P. 2011. "Vital New Matters: The Speculative Turn in Religion and Gender." *Religion and Gender* 1(1): 44–65.

Rieger, J. and E. Waggoner, eds. 2015. *Religious Experience and New Materialism: Movement Matters.* London: Palgrave Macmillan.

Riis, O. and L. Woodhead. 2010. *A Sociology of Religious Emotion.* Oxford: Oxford University Press.

Sedgwick, E. Kosofsky. 2003. *Touching Feeling: Affect, Pedagogy, Performativity.* Durham, NC: Duke University Press.

Singleton, V. and J. Law. 2012. "Devices as Rituals." <http://www.heterogeneities.net/publications/SingletonLaw2012DevicesAsRituals.pdf> [Accessed 16 February 2014].

Stengers, I. 2008. "Experimenting with Refrains: Subjectivity and the Challenge of Escaping Modern Dualism." *Subjectivity* 22: 38–59.

Stringer, M. 2008. *Contemporary Western Ethnography and the Definition of Religion.* London: Continuum.

Thrift, N. 2008. *Non-Representational Theory: Space, Politics, Affect.* London: Routledge.

Tweed, Thomas. 2006. *Crossing and Dwelling. A Theory of Religion.* Cambridge, MA: Harvard University Press.

Westermarck, E. 1929. *Memories of My Life.* London: Georg Allen & Unwin Ltd.

Whitehead, A. 2013. *Religious Statues and Personhood: Testing the Role of Materiality.* London: Bloomsbury.

———. 2011. "Gift Giving and Power Perspectives: Testing the Role of Statue Devotion in England and Spain." *DISKUS (BASR)* 12:24–37.

Winch, Peter. 1990 [1958]. *The Idea of a Social Science and Its Relation to Philosophy.* London: Routledge.

About the Authors

Peik Ingman is a PhD candidate in Comparative Religion at Åbo Akademi University. He is currently working on a doctoral thesis with the working title "Sacralization and the Gift: Queer Family Members in Christian Families." His research combines actor-network theory, philosophy of science and object relations theory.

Terhi Utriainen is Docent and Acting Professor in the Study of Religions at the University of Helsinki. Her research and teaching interests include ethnography of lived religion, gender and embodiment, ritual studies, death, dying and suffering. She is co-editor of *Post-Secular Society* (2012) and *Between Ancestors and Angels: Finnish Women Making Religion* (2014).

Tuija Hovi works as University Lecturer in Comparative Religion at the University of Turku. She is specialized in qualitative methods such as ethnography and narrative inquiry. Her research interests include contemporary popular religiosity and anthropology of Christianity, focusing on the cultural accommodation of global Neo-charismatic influences in Finland.

Måns Broo Måns Broo works as University Researcher in Comparative Religion at Åbo Akademi University. His publications include critically acclaimed translations of Sanskrit texts into Swedish and Finnish. At present, his research interests focus on yoga, both in its classical and modern forms, as well as on modern Hinduism and ritual studies.

PART I

Revisiting Enchantment and Animism

— 2 —

Objects as Subjects:
Agency and Performativity in Rituals

ANNE-CHRISTINE HORNBORG

In ritual theory, objects have mostly been discussed in terms of symbols and interpretations. However, material objects that are employed in rituals are not merely passive carriers of attached cultural meanings. In this article, I will discuss how objects not only become animated in rituals but as such are also ascribed agency, whereby they further animate the ritual field. As ritual agents they achieve important performative functions in the field of transformations. The smoke of burning sage in a ritual setting is not everyday smoke but sacred, and it not only symbolizes a purification process for the participants, but—as a performative agent—it "actually" cleanses them of bad spirits. In attributing objects personhood and agency, it is thus more useful to discuss the phenomenology of animism and ritual objects as forms of relational epistemology than as cases of epistemological fallacies indicating a childish or "primitive" worldview.

In this chapter, I will first briefly explore other ways of understanding indigenous peoples' cosmologies than as "primitive" and ask whether these ways might allow us to understand animism, not as a failed epistemology but a relational one (Bird-David 1999, 67). This initial discussion of animistic worldviews will serve as a background for a further discussion of circumstances under which objects are ascribed agency with performative qualities. Do objects in modern society similarly appear to transform into "persons" and, as such, relate to other "persons" around

---

Keywords: Ritual objects, animism, agency, performativity, relational epistemology

them (for example, to human beings)? To further discuss this question, I will make use of Roy Rappaport's definition of ritual (1994, 24). Rappaport offers a very promising means of analysing forms of enchantment and animation that happen in and through rituals, but I will add to his definition of "the sequences of formal acts and utterances" the use of *ritual objects*, since they are afforded important agency and performative functions in the performance. Thus, rituals seem to be a potentially valuable point of entry for a discussion of the phenomenology of objects, animism and agency. Finally, I will use an illustrative example to show how material objects can be attributed agency in rituals: the *kekunit* (godparent ritual), performed among one of Canada's First Nation groups, the Mi'kmaq in eastern Canada.

Are Stones Persons?

When the anthropologist Irving Hallowell did fieldwork among the Northern Ojibwa in Canada, he was intrigued about the way in which they attributed personhood to other entities than humans. In his classic article from 1960, "Ojibwa Ontology, Behavior, and World View," Hallowell discusses personhood and cultural differences between a Western worldview ("Cartesian") and the worldviews of indigenous cultures, in this case that of the Ojibwa. Hallowell realized that he had found a radically different outlook on the world and on how a "person" was defined. While he read in *Warren's Dictionary of Psychology* that the Western definition of a "person" was a "human organism regarded as having distinctive characteristics and social relations," he discovered that the Ojibwa included animals, natural phenomena (e.g., thunder), spiritual beings and inanimate matter (e.g., stones) in their concept of person. Significantly, animals, stones, stars and thunder were not classified as humans, but as "persons." Being a human was only one way of being a person—with a specific bodily construction that formed the limit for that specific being's agency. The key to understanding why objects among the Ojibwa were also treated as living "persons" with agency was, according to Hallowell, to be found in the ontology of that culture (Hallowell 1960, 43-45).

The Ojibwa cosmology can be seen in terms of what Edward Tylor has characterized as an animistic worldview. According to Tylor, we are all animists, although in Western modern society some animistic traits only reflect a previous state of thinking and are maintained as "survivals" (Tylor 1871, 15). Until recently, Tylor's concept of animism was treated by scholars as obsolete and derogatory, a value-laden word with roots in thought on the evolutionary origin of religion. Today it is highly debated in new forms and interpretations, under the umbrella concept of neo-animism (Bird-David 1999; Descola and Pàlsson 1996; Hornborg 2008,

2006; Ingold 2000; Viveiros de Castro 1998).

Hallowell learned that stones in Ojibwa language are grammatically animate, but when he asked an old man if all stones are alive, the man replied: "No! But *some* are!" (Hallowell 1960, 24). Every stone was not automatically perceived as alive. Being animated as a "person" seemed to depend on whether or not the objects on special occasions had been proven to accommodate power:

> Whereas we should never expect a stone to manifest animate properties of any kind under any circumstances, the Ojibwa recognize, *a priori*, potentialities for animation in certain classes of objects under certain circumstances … The stone was treated *as if* it were a 'person', not a 'thing', without inferring that objects of this class are, for the Ojibwa, necessarily conceptualized as persons. (Hallowell 1960, 25)

To discuss Hallowell's statement "*as if* it were a 'person'," we have to return to the title of his chapter. He is not only examining Ojibwa ontology, but also Ojibwa *behaviour*. I think that a closer look at Ojibwa behaviour may provide an important clue in the discussion of personhood and the animate/inanimate qualities of objects. Hallowell clearly states that the Ojibwa are not "animists" more than he is, since they do not think that all stones in general are alive. But under *certain circumstances*, stones can come alive and establish a relationship with other beings in the world. Hallowell was told by his informant, for example, that some stones possess the ability to move during a ritual.

Ritual activity thus seems to be important for determining which objects are perceived as dead matter and which objects can become persons, animated and agentic—and how. In the above case, the Ojibwan informant referred to stones that came alive in the Midewiwin ceremony. When his father was performing the ritual, he saw a "big round stone move" (Hallowell 1960, 25). The stone seemed to follow the man, and its movements were also confirmed by other participants. But it is also important to note that the informant didn't consider these movements a voluntary act by the stone itself. The movements were an effect of the sacred power of the Midé (medicine man) in the ceremony.

There were also other big stones among the Ojibwa that in distant times had been associated with the Midewiwin ceremony and ascribed animate properties. Hallowell's friend Chief Berens was the owner of one, but he said that this particular stone had lost such qualities. Therefore, the potential to become animate could be lost, and stones that earlier had been powerful could lose their power. Thus, animation and potential "personhood" must be put in a context where objects relate and have interacted with the larger environment *under certain circumstances*. Or, as the anthropologist Tim Ingold interpreted Hallowell's field notes: "[T]he liveliness of stone emerges in the context of their close involvement with certain persons, and relatively powerful ones ... whether a stone is alive or not will depend upon the context in which it is placed and experienced" (Ingold 2000, 97).

Ritual as "Certain Circumstances"

How can the "things we live with" become enchanted in certain practices, such as rituals? The impact of rituals on material objects has been studied in many cultural contexts. The historian of religion Tord Olsson has explored the notion of objects as persons with agency in his study of the Bambara people in Mali (Olsson 2010, 122–124). He observed that among the Bambara it is common to attribute personhood to artefacts such as fetishes (*boli*) and masks, especially in rituals. A close relationship can be found between the fetish and its owner. This also includes the fetish's relationship to other fetishes, such as when a new one is incorporated with others in a household. This relationship is established and manifested in rituals by smearing blood from roosters or goats on the fetishes. After this ceremony the fetish is treated as a person with respect and care. If the owners go on a trip, they bring their fetishes with them, or at least tell them that they are going away for a while.

As in the case of the Ojibwan stones, Olsson also discusses "potentialities for animation": the relationship between the object (stone/fetish/*boli*) and the quality of being a person. Olsson noticed that the fetishes, when not in use, could be treated like any ordinary thing. People sat next to them and talked without taking notice of them; they could be examined, even their insides, and it was possible to take pictures of them (Olsson 2010, 132). It was being ritually smeared with the blood of a sacrificed animal that activated the living power of the fetishes; this was when they achieved the qualities of a person. The Bambara hold that an animal's blood carries a life force (*ni*), and it is this *ni* which animates the *boli*. Olsson explains: "The fetish object appears, during the ritual act, in fact as a person. It is spoken to and treated as a person and it is, by itself, a ritual agent that communicates with the human agents" (Olsson 2010, 125, my translation).

Both Hallowell's observations among the Ojibwa and Olsson's among the Bambara imply that rituals seem to be a key for discussing objects and agency, since perspectives *on* and relations *to* the world, society and individual are framed in alternative terms than those used in everyday life. Rituals are thus not only a way of displaying the world, they may also change one's outlook on the world: "Ritual can be a very creative act that does not just express or represent but actually does something;

it can alter understanding, bodies, or the world itself, as understood by human beings" (Bovin 2009, 7). In these changes of perspective, ritual objects play an important role. Being both symbols and parts (indices) of the cosmological order (the all-embracing "Agent"),[1] they have, as do their imagined source, agency and performative qualities. The stone of a statue of the Hindu god Shiva is just a piece of earth, but when it has been consecrated it comes alive and is subsequently treated with respect. From then on, it not only symbolizes the deity itself, but has an indexical relation to the god (Bell 1997, 156). Worshippers not only meet a symbolic representation of Shiva, but the earth has also been transformed into an index of the god, whereby it participates and channels Shiva's power. It provides an avenue for the devotees to establish a closer relationship with sacredness. When the devotees approach the statue of Shiva, they also come close to the god. Ascribing sacredness to the statue provides this ritual object with a performative function in its collaboration with the devotee.

Ritual objects can thus be read as signs, communicating properties that are simultaneously both symbolic and indexical of the signified. As signs, they play an important function in human communication, and there is a point to making distinctions between different kinds of signs in studies of ritual (Rappaport 1999, 66–67). In Charles Peirce's well-known studies of signs, an index is defined as "a sign which refers to the object it denotes by being really affected by the Object"—like smoke is an index of fire (Buchler [1955] 2011, 102). A symbol is a different sign and, according to Peirce, "a Representation whose Representative character consists precisely in its being a rule that will determine its Representation" (Buchler [1955] 2011, 112). Compared with an index, which has closeness to what it represents, a symbol is conventional. A symbol is thus a culturally defined sign, like a green light means "go" or a piece of earth shaped in a certain way stands for Shiva.

The difference between signs as symbols and indices, discussed in semiotics, has also been important in ritual studies. In Victor Turner's analysis of rituals, he defines symbols as "the smallest units of ritual which still retain the specific properties of ritual behavior" (Turner 1967, 19). He found that certain symbols played a key role in the liminal phase and were important for participants, both for their transformation from one

---

1. In the case of Native American people and the characteristic of Amerindian ontology, Viveiros de Castro speaks of a unifying order to which everything has an indexical relation ("cosmological deixis"). Being parts (indices) of this order is the ground of being "persons." It should be noted that "Amerindian" in Viveiros de Castro's analysis refers to his Amazonian studies. See Hornborg (2006) for an application of Viveiros de Castro's concepts to the Mi'kmaq ethnography.

social status to another and for experiencing this transformation. These ritual symbols possessed a bipolarity, which he named the normative or ideological function and the sensory or "orectic" function, respectively. In Turner's scheme, the normative function of the symbols in ritual is to transfer the cosmological, social or moral order; the sensory function appeals to the participants by provoking and triggering their sensuous way of being-in-the-world. Let us consider an example: in the Orthodox Easter Mass, the lighting and extinguishing of candles' flames have a clear symbolic meaning—but simultaneously the candles admit the participants access to be part of a cosmological order that is enacted anew and experienced through their bodies, by affording an experience of both darkness and the light from the candle flames (Olsson 2000, 17).

The relationship between objects and participants in the ritual is thus twofold. It is symbolic, but also indexical. Bodily experience allows the participants to partake of/re-enact the miracle in a sensuous way. The culturally arbitrary sign/symbol (in this case a candle) not only touches the world of intellectual interpretation, but offers sensuous feelings of being-in-the-world in another way than in daily life. Turner's analysis of symbols and objects can be discussed further. As carriers of symbolic and indexical signs, ritual objects take on a life of their own in the ritual process. These signs transform the ritual objects from being just "things" into being "persons" with qualities of their own. Adopting this new status of being "persons," they also have the capacity to "act" independently of the participant's intentions. For example, when bread and wine are consecrated by ritual utterances during communion, these enchanted ritual objects in the Catholic Mass literally become a "person." From then on, the bread and wine are not "common food," but symbols and indices of the cosmological order and, as such, transmitters of blessings and salvation to the participants. And it is not only the performative utterances that tell the participants that the bread and wine are sanctified and transformed. The tolling bell also "speaks," further signalling that the miracle is repeating itself here and now.

Another similar phenomenon is the Sioux's use of the calumet: "the act of smoking it as respiration for the entire universe may seem to assimilate the smoker into *Wakan-Tanka*" (Rappaport 1997, 301). Rappaport refers to these key ritual objects as "sacra": "[I]n the mere fact of their material existence, [they] may substantiate, or make material, aspects of enduring canonical orders, and at the same time, in their manipulation relate the enduring order to the particulars of the contemporary situation" (Rappaport 1997, 145). Objects as sacra materialize messages that are both symbolical (or, as Rappaport would put it, canonical) and indexical (self-referential) in the ritual.[2] For Rappaport, the canonical quality of ritual acts and utterances was highly important, since canonical messages are reliable in transmitting social messages in spite of the worshipper's intention (Rappaport 1999, 31).[3] But it was the self-referential messages in the performance that tightly bound the participants to the ritual context here and now—or, to repeat his words above—"relate the enduring order to the particulars of the contemporary situation." The ritual object thus establishes a relationship with the participant, similar to a dialogue between two "persons."

However, the interpretation of ritual symbols has been a tricky question among scholars of religion. Turner's work—and later on that of Clifford Geertz (1973)—has been questioned and criticized (Asad 1983). It is far from certain that the symbolic meaning (canonical message) of the object is fully or even at all understood by all participants (see Fujda, this volume). Individuals can participate without having full knowledge—or even any knowledge—of the canonical and symbolic meaning of different ritual acts or ritual objects. Instead, they can be enchanted just by participating, moving their body, using the objects and interpreting their participation in their own, personal way; nonetheless, they may experience intense feelings of transformation (Humphrey and Laidlaw 1994, 89). Familiarity with ritual objects, ritual acts and performance seems to be enough for creating the "sense of ritual"—and furthermore, if ritual rules of conduct are followed, the performative function of ritual acts, utterances or ritual objects can still "work." Thus, it seems that a closer look at the *use* of and *relation* to ritual objects is necessary to fully understand the delicate questions concerning the way in which objects gain agency in a ritually composed, animated universe. To have agency here implies having a performative function, which is to some extent independent of the partner's will in dialogue. To examine how this agency comes into play in rituals, I will analyse the components of a performance of a newly invented ritual, which lacks any tradition of previous performances and conventions. I will focus on ritual acts and the use of objects rather than on how symbolic language or canonical messages are individually interpreted by the participants.

Ritual Objects and Agency in the Kekunit

In order to discuss the relevance of familiarity and a *sense* of ritual, I will now examine a ritual in which I participated in 2000, during a period of fieldwork among the Mi'kmaq, a First Nation group in eastern Canada.

---

2. Compare with Turner's normative and orectic pole of the symbol.
3. Language opens up for lies, but ritual by its construction is a safe language. In fact, Rappaport describes ritual as the "basic social act" (1997, 31).

The Relational Dynamics of Enchantment and Sacralization

Since the 1990s, I have regularly visited the Mi'kmaq, initially in order to finish a thesis on their traditions and rituals (Hornborg 2001). Here I have chosen a newly invented rite, a *kekunit*, or godparent ritual, to show the importance of using ritual objects when inventing traditions. But first let me provide some historical data regarding the context in which the *kekunit* ritual was performed.

The Mi'kmaq were formerly hunters and gatherers, and in the 17th century, they had regular contact with European missionaries. Most Mi'kmaq today are Catholics, and some of them are also Catholic traditionalists, combining Catholic faith with traditional or pan-Indian traditions such as sweat lodges, sacred circles, and pow wows. In 1970, a small but important group of neotraditionalists chose to "walk the traditional way." Some of them fiercely rejected Christianity, proclaiming that it was not their faith and tradition. But it was difficult to gain acceptance on the reserve as a "true, traditional" Mi'kmaq. Some of those who let their hair grow and dressed in buckskin clothes were met with comments such as "Wow, you look like a real Indian." It was easier to foster a sense of community and identity through rituals, which, as noted, can be powerful means for learning new (or old) ways of being in the world. In addition, the neo-traditional rites offered strategic benefits—simply performing them was often demonstrative of how things *should* be.

However, old Mi'kmaq culture was an oral culture, and the only documents of Mi'kmaq history and practices that we have were written by Europeans: missionary reports, documents from merchants, and adventure stories. For this reason, some of the 1970s neo-traditional rituals were pan-Indian or borrowed from other native groups (primarily the Lakota); some of them, like the sweat lodge, are only briefly mentioned in historical sources from the 17th century. Concerning the historical Mi'kmaq rituals, there are nearly no complete descriptions of how they were performed. The performance of a *kekunit* ritual is not mentioned at all in historical documents.

When I arrived from Sweden in the fall of 2000 at one of the Mi'kmaq reserves on Cape Breton Island, I was invited to be part of a *kekunit* ritual in the afternoon for a fourteen-year-old girl, Melinda. A *kekunit* is defined by the Mi'kmaq as a person

> to whom the parent turns to seek advice and help with the raising of the child. The relationships are fostered with love, attention, gifts, and sharing of time together. At each milestone in a child's life, s/he has parents and his or her own special set of godparents to share birthdays, holidays, and their spiritual growth. A godparent will be there always, even when there is breakdown in the family, or when at adolescence a youth seeks his or her own independence. (Battiste 1997, 150–151)

Although establishing godparent relationships has obvious associations with Christianity, the Mi'kmaq ritual leader, who was a firm neotraditionalist, presented it as a purely traditional ritual. However, I'm fairly sure it was the first time that this rite was performed in this way. Billy and Shirley, visiting friends from Kahnawake (Mohawk territory), would also be joining in the ritual: Billy as a godfather and Shirley (like me) as representing one of the four directions. In addition, a Mi'kmaq woman would be initiated as the godmother.

But how is it possible to simultaneously invent rituals and refer to them as "tradition"? Although all rituals are taught and learned, they are not meant to be performed as products of purely human imagination or creativity. An invented ritual always runs the risk of totally failing and becoming just a charade and a source of embarrassment for the participants. Thus, in order to discuss ritual invention I will make use of Rappaport's definition of ritual as "the performance of more or less invariant sequences of formal acts and utterances, not entirely encoded by the performers" (Rappaport 1999, 24). Rappaport's statement that ritual acts and utterances are "not entirely encoded by the performers" is important in performing rituals, especially invented ones, as I will show below. I would also add to his definition the use of *ritual objects*, since they are afforded significant agency and performative functions in the performance. Also included are the performative utterances and ritual acts which are "not entirely encoded by the performers." In the examples that follow, I will stress that ritual objects, their agency and use of materiality are of the utmost importance in achieving a ritual event and "tradition." A ritual thus needs more than only human actors.

The Use of Objects in Framing the Ritual

One of the most important acts in framing a ritual is to make space for a sacred place. Sacred places can be staged anywhere—in nature, in a living room or in a building, such as a church—but there must be ritual-like actions that consecrate this space by separating the profane from the sacred. Ritual objects both visually display the sacred and animate the space through their presence. Since the *kekunit* ritual would be performed in an ordinary living room with a sofa, recliners and TV, we prepared for framing the ritual space by picking cedar twigs. To begin, the twigs were laid on the floor to form an inner circle, in which Melinda would be seated. A larger cedar circle was then built outside this circle, and the four cardinal points were marked as places for four participants. Other twigs were boiled in a large pot and the hot water was poured into a bathtub to become Melinda's purification bath.

The Relational Dynamics of Enchantment and Sacralization

After the bath, Melinda was dressed up and some twigs were attached to her ankles and wrists. The cedar twigs on Melinda's body rendered her an extension of and participant in the sacrality of the sacred circle. By being attached to Melinda's body, ordinary cedar twigs were no longer ordinary; they now served to transform her body into a ritually purified body with an altered relationship to the world. Since we ran out of twigs for closing the big circle, Melinda's mother, Francine, asked me to go out to get more. But picking cedar twigs for the *kekunit* was no longer a profane enterprise, as it had been earlier. She now told me to finish the picking by saying "all my relations" (*mitakuye oyasin*, from a Lakota prayer) and offering the tree some tobacco. The ritual had established a special relationship between the cedar tree and the imminent performance, as well as between the tree and the performers. As a "person," it now provided the participants with gifts that had purifying and performative powers, including the transformation of a profane living room into sacred space. Framed by this ritual context, my offering of tobacco was as a gift-giver to the tree "person." Upon returning, I closed the circle with the newly picked cedar twigs and everyone went to their appointed places.

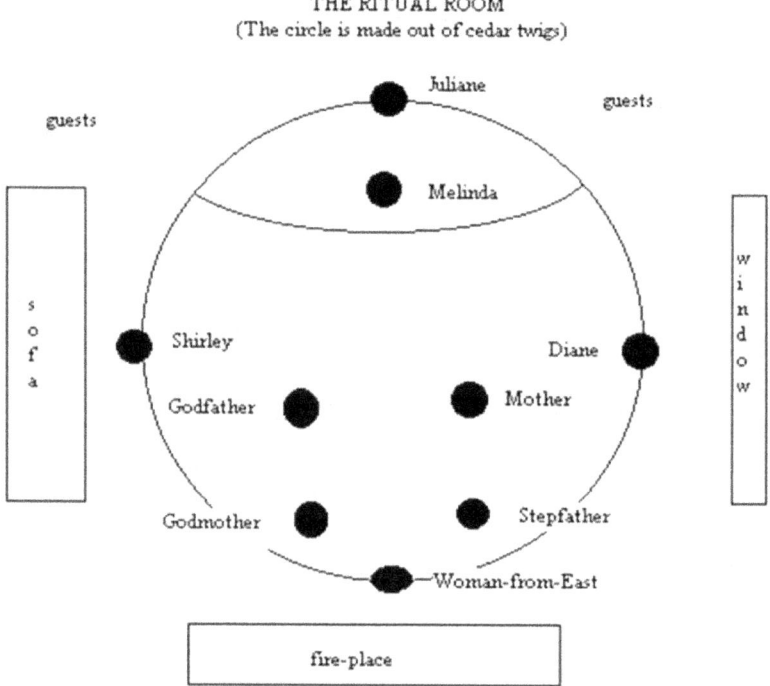

Figure 1   An illustration by the author, of the ritual space of the *kekunit*.

When the ritual space was set up, the performers accepted that they had established from that point on a relationship with that animate universe. The cedar leaves were ascribed important performative functions to protect the space—a sacred, animate universe of transformative powers—during the performance. We solemnly entered the sacred room and sat quietly, waiting for Melinda's stepfather Paul, the pipe-carrier, to begin the *kekunit*. Juliane and Diane (two sisters, friends of Melinda who were 13 and 11 years old) joined the circle to represent the two remaining four directions.

Each of us received new ritual objects: a bundle of tobacco and a cloth symbolizing the four directions (as "Woman-from-East," I got a yellow one, representing the sunrise). Sage was burned; in this context, its smoke was holy and could cleanse the space of bad spirits. The smoke of the pipe carried prayers to the Great Mystery. Without the ritual objects (carrying canonical messages as parts of the tradition) and indexical messages (embedded as sensuous reminders of being part of the cosmological order materializing here and now), this newly invented rite could have lost its ability to enchant. The ritual objects became subjects in activating more than the intellect, since they were also connected to the participants by awakening bodily senses, like the smell of the sage and the taste of tobacco in one's mouth. This relationship also included the object's status of acting by itself, having performative functions in the process of transformation. It is also important to note that, since this was a newly invented rite, most of the objects used are also employed in other rituals. The use of already defined and familiar ritual objects "not entirely encoded by the participants" marked their recognition as carriers of tradition, visually contributing to the ritual not being entirely invented.

The use of objects to enchant new ritual settings has been studied in other contexts. In describing the materiality of sacralization among modern goddess worshippers, the historian of religion Åsa Trulsson has noticed how everyday activities in homes can be seen as practicing sacralization (e.g., by keeping a house altar). A mundane place, such as a kitchen, thereby becomes in its daily use an enchanted place. Even if new objects are introduced from a variety of traditions, one enchanted object does not change: the altar. By being placed on this well-known ritual space, defined as a holy table and used since ancient times, other ritual objects become animated with power (Trulsson 2010, 365). Similarly, in her study of Pentecostal groups in contemporary Stockholm, the scholar of religion Jessica Moberg describes (2013) how materiality is crucial in cultivating piety. Pictures of Jesus, icons, small crosses and Bible quotes on the walls are used to fill the homes of Pentecostals with power from a sacred realm, reminding the individual of how to be a Christian in everyday life. Hence, the use of ritual objects from a "traditional box" almost appears as a prerequisite to maintain a sense of ritual and to visually display that canonical messages are acting in this new ritual context.

Returning to the Mi'kmaq neotraditionalist context, use of the calumet and pipe ceremonies are frequently found in pow wows and sweat lodges. The cedar leaf is classified as a sacred herb and often employed in ceremonies and prayers. The use of sage is also found in other rituals in order to purify and protect participants. Using only totally new paraphernalia would be confusing, since there would be no basis of familiarity on which a relationship could be built between the participants, the ritual and the new ritual object. Even if a new ritual object in an invented ritual were to be verbally defined and used, it could in the best-case scenario be a way of introducing new symbols, but only as an intellectual enterprise, since an efficient use of it and sensuous associations demand more than an intellectual introduction to build acquaintance. The little yellow bag with tobacco that I received as the Woman-from-the-East was a new ritual object, but honouring the four directions and the use of tobacco was not.

It seems safe to say that many participants in ritual are not fully acquainted with the symbolism of different acts and objects; they are familiar with just performing the acts, using the objects, experiencing the smell of the sage and the smoke from the pipe, and singing traditional songs. This familiarity with the objects and how they are used in other rituals, including embodied memories of them, is of utmost importance. As mentioned above, one of Turner's points in his analysis of symbols is the importance of the interpretation of cultural meaning in order for the individual to experience their transformation. As noted, this also appears to be a weakness in his theory. We need to recognize that there may be objects that the participants are not familiar with, at least in terms of how traditional symbolical meanings are encoded. Instead, what they are familiar with is the use of those objects, and by simply using them as they have done before—or have seen others do before—in other ritual contexts (not to forget the sensuous parts of remembering the smell of tobacco, the scent of sage, etc.) clearly signals that they are partaking in a traditional ritual. It is thus not the interpretation of a canonical or cultural meaning that is of utmost importance for the participants' experience of the ritual process, but the *use* of familiar ritual objects and the performance of the ritual acts that engage them.

Interritual Objects with Agency

The *kekunit* ritual opened with Paul's words of welcome, which blended with the scent of the sage and the smoke from the pipe, sensuously reminding the participants of the ritual context. Paul explained why we all had gathered. Since it was a new ritual, we were told not only the meaning of the ritual but also how it was to be performed. The obvious associations with the Catholic godparent rite, familiar to the Catholic Mi'kmaq, were to be downplayed. In this neotraditionalist setting, the ritual needed to be infused with Native American traditions. Objects like sage, the calumet and tobacco testified to the fact that the ritual belonged to the "traditional" Mi'kmaq culture, not the one overlaid by Christianity.

Smoking the calumet is not only a formal act (and used in many pan-Indian rituals), its smoke is also ascribed animate properties: it brings protection and conveys messages to the "Great Spirit," and the smoke breathed from the participants communicates with the "Great Breath." There are also sacred stories of how the calumet was given to the people: in the Pawnee tradition it was a gift from the sun, and in Sioux tradition it came from White Buffalo Calf Woman. Since the calumet is a messenger and its smoke makes prayers to the Creator, the smoke from the pipe acts as an agent. It transforms the participants from being part of everyday life into being part of the sacred realm (the canonical message of the smoke). It also provides a sensuous feeling in the body: tasting it allows the participants to feel a bodily connection to this sacred cosmos (the self-referential message). Thus, the calumet is more than just an object; it has the ability to communicate in the ritual as a person.

Paul interlaces his speech with ritual acts that are familiar from other pan-Indian or Mi'kmaq ceremonies: the pipe ceremony, the prayers performed in the circle, greeting the four directions, burning sage, and singing the Mi'kmaq Honour Song. Re-used in the *kekunit* ritual, these acts function as scattered quotes. As they include texts and cross-references, they could be understood through the concept of intertextuality, but in a ritual context we might call this *interrituality.* By these interreferences, the *kekunit* performance becomes embedded in a larger context, which appears in the Mi'kmaq reserves today as Mi'kmaq tradition. Therefore, it is not only the explanations but also the bodily actions of the participants and the use of specific objects that tell us what it is to be a traditional Mi'kmaq today. Choosing ritual acts from ones that already are familiar as embedded in a larger corpus of pan-Indian rituals appears to be a way of legitimizing and authorizing new traditions. In this interrituality, I have also included the interritual use of objects. As Rappaport stated in relation to ritual acts and utterances, the ritual objects in this *kekunit* are not "entirely encoded by the performers." Being objects with canonical messages, they become agents or "persons" in the *kekunit* context, and even if the canonical messages are not fully understood, one message is clear: ritual objects tell the participants that this particular performance is not entirely a made-up event, and that it is grounded in Mi'kmaq tradition.

When I observed the two young sisters, I noticed how carefully they were listening to Paul's explanations and how familiar they were with some of the ritual acts and objects, since they had participated in other neotraditionalist ceremonies. This was obvious in the way they used the pipe. The older sister, Juliane, puffed it three times. The younger sister, Diane, knew that she was too young to smoke. She just took the pipe and touched her left shoulder with it, then her right, before handing it to the next person. The children's use of the calumet displayed how they had learned from other rituals that it must be treated with special care, respect and movements. Probably they were not fully or even partly aware of the symbolic meaning, but that is not of outmost importance here. The *kekunit* performance, in which different ritual acts and objects are combined, both traditional and invented, involves bodily engagement embedded in a prior familiarity with objects that are experienced as sacra and not as mundane objects. In this engagement, the performers related to the objects as respected "persons," not inert matter.

Paul continued to mix his speech with ritual acts, performative utterances and the use of ritual objects. He turned to the godparents and told them how important it is for a Mi'kmaq child to have many close and caring relationships. Then he turned to Melinda and said: "Something might happen to me, and it is good for us parents to know that people we fully trust can replace us." He then addressed the godparents with the most important and central performative utterances of the *kekunit* ritual, "Are you, the godparents, willing to take your responsibilities as second parents?" "Yes, we are." At this point everyone rose and Paul began to beat the drum, singing the Mi'kmaq Honour Song, familiar from pow wows and other Mi'kmaq traditional gatherings. The beat from the drum filled the room. The song told the participants to respect the Mi'kmaq people highly, to come together, to be proud to be a Mi'kmaq, and to follow the Creator's intentions that people take care of each other. But the beat from the drum was also "speaking." As one Mi'kmaq told me, the beat of the drum is similar to the beat of your heart, similar to the cosmos; as the beat of your heart gives you life, the beat of the drum reminds you of the beat of the cosmos, which brings life to creation. In this way, the drum gains both a symbolic meaning (the all-embracing rhythm of the cosmos) and an indexical meaning (the beat of the drum, which can be heard here and now as part of the pulse of the cosmos).

But it is the *use* of the drum that enchanted the ritual, not the drum itself.[4] The use of the drum closed the *kekunit*—no words were needed.

---

4. This Mi'kmaq friend also brought his drum to my house, just casually leaving it in a corner. But he also told me to not disrespect it by stepping over it, since it had sacred qualities and as such it belonged to the category of sacra.

When the drum stopped talking, the performance was over, and the twigs were taken away. With no cedar twigs remaining as guardians of the sacred place, the place was disenchanted and returned to being a common living room. The calumet was put aside and the drum went "to rest," its potential to come alive waiting for the next ritual, when hands would pick it up, beat it and allow it to "talk."

Summary

In this article I have examined how rituals can animate objects into being "persons" with agency and performative qualities. This animation is a quality that makes them into "persons," since the way in which these "persons" act in rituals is not "entirely encoded by the performers." With such qualities, they are not bound to the intentions of the performers in the specific ritual, but they have their own agency and messages to bring and to embed in the performance. The fetish needs blood to come alive, bread and wine need performative utterances in order to change into a holy body, and the drum must be used in a ritual setting to be able to "talk." Outside the ritual field the objects may lose their agency, but in some cases they still maintain the potential to become animate again. The interritual use of objects also weaves different rituals together, and even if the participants are not familiar with the canonical messages embedded in ritual objects, those objects are nonetheless familiar signs that signal a ritual setting. Since the use of ritual objects in many cases also appeals to other senses than vision—like the taste of wine, the beat of the drum or the smell of sage—they establish a manifold relationship with the participant in what might otherwise only be an intellectual enterprise. The ritual objects thus become "persons" with the ability to speak both intellectually to the mind as symbols and sensuously through the bodies of the participants in the performance.

Hence, the animation of objects needs to be analysed as a relationship to the world that is established in certain contexts—here, in ritual settings—rather than being discussed in terms of the object itself being "alive." If animism is defined as a specific relationship between objects and humans under certain circumstances, like rituals, then we may be said be animists through participation in these enchanted moments.

References

Asad, T. 1983. "Anthropological Conceptions of Religion: Reflections on Geertz." *Man*, New Series, 18(2): 237–259.

Battiste, M. 1997. "Structural Unemployment: The Milonaq Experience." In *The Mi'kmaq Anthology*, edited by R. Joe and L. Choyce, 135–161. East Lawrencetown, Nova Scotia: Pottersfield Press.

Bird-David, N. 1999. "'Animism' Revisited: Personhood, Environment, and Relational Epistemology." *Current Anthropology* 40: 67–79.

Boivin, N. 2009. "Grasping the Elusive and Unknowable: Material Culture in Ritual Practice." *Material Religion: The Journal of Objects, Art and Belief* 5(3): 266–287.

Buchler, J. 1955, *The Philosophical Writings of Pierce*. New York: Dover.

Descola, P. and G. Pàlsson, eds. 1996. *Nature and Society: Anthropological Perspectives*. London: Routledge.

Geertz, C. 1973. *The Interpretation of Cultures: Selected Essays*. New York: Basic Books.

Hallowell, A. I. 1960. "Ojibwa Ontology, Behavior, and World View." In *Culture in History: Essays in Honor of Paul Radin*, edited by S. Diamond, 19–52. New York: Columbia University Press. (Reprinted in *Reading in Indigenous Religions*. Edited by Harvey, G. 18–49. London: Continuum. 2002.)

Hornborg, A-C. 2008. *Mi'kmaq Landscapes: From Animism to Sacred Ecology*. Hampshire: Ashgate.

———. 2006. "Visiting the Six Worlds – Shamanistic Journeys in the Canadian Mi'kmaq Cosmology." *Journal of American Folklore* 119(473): 312–336.

———. 2001. *A Landscape of Left-Overs: Changing Conception of Place and Environment among Mi'kmaq Indians of Eastern Canada*. Lund Studies in History of Religions 14. Lund: Almqvist & Wiksell International.

Humphrey, C. and J. Laidlaw. 1994. *The Archetypal Actions of Ritual*. Oxford: Clarendon Press.

Ingold, T. 2000. *The Perception of the Environment: Essays in Livelihood, Dwelling and Skill*. London: Routledge.

Latour, B. 1993. *We Have Never Been Modern*. Translated by C. Porter. Cambridge, MA: Harvard University Press.

Moberg, J. 2013. *Piety, Intimacy and Mobility: A Case Study of Charismatic Christianity in Present-Day Stockholm*. Södertörn doctoral dissertations, nr. 74, Avhandlingar utgivna vid institutionen för litteratur, idéhistoria och religion, Göteborgs universitet, nr. 30, Huddinge: Södertörns högskola.

Olsson, T. 2010. "Den dubbla blicken: en berättelse om konsten att frammana rituell närvaro hos bambarafolket i Mali." In *Den rituella människan - flervetenskapliga perspektiv*, edited by A-C. Hornborg, 115–150. Linköping University Electronic Press, <http://urn.kb.se/resolve?urn=urn:nbn:se:liu:diva-58921> [Accessed 18 February 2013].

———. 2000. "De rituella fälten i Gwanyebugu." *Svensk religionshistorisk årsskrift* 9: 9–63.

Rappaport, R. 1999. *Ritual and Religion in the Making of Humanity*. Cambridge: Cambridge University Press.

Trulsson, Å. 2010. *Cultivating the Sacred: Ritual Creativity and Practice among Women in Contemporary Europe*. Lund Studies in History of Religions 28. Lund: Lund University, Department of History and Anthropology of Religions.

Turner, V. 1967. *The Forest of Symbols*. Ithaca, NY: Cornell University Press.

Tylor, E. 1871. *Primitive Culture: Researches into the Development of Mythology, Philosophy, Religion, Art, and Custom*. London: Murray.

Viveiros de Castro, E. 1998. "Cosmological Deixis and Amerindian Perspectivism." *Journal of the Royal Anthropological Institute* 4(3): 469–488.

About the Author

Anne-Christine Hornborg is Professor in the Department of the History of Religions, Centre for Theology and Religious Studies, Lund University, Sweden. Her thesis, *A Landscape of Left-Overs: Changing Conceptions of Place and Environment among Mi'kmaq Indians of Eastern Canada* (2001), is grounded on extensive fieldwork conducted on Cape Breton Island, Canada. She has also carried out fieldwork in Tonga and in the Peruvian Andes. In a number of articles, Hornborg has documented the life-world of the Mi'kmaq, including their traditions, rituals, environmental engagements and the phenomenology of places. She has published several articles about indigenous cosmologies, animism, the phenomenology of landscape, ecology and religion, ritual practices and new spirituality. Hornborg was also granted a four-year appointment in ritual studies and in recent years has in a productive way studied new ritual contexts in late modern Sweden.

— 3 —

Enchantment, Matter, and the Unpredictability of Devotion

Amy Whitehead

Both "enchantment" (as concept and experience) and "material religion" (as concept and practical evidence) are currently receiving academic attention. Combining these two fields of enquiry, the "materiality of enchantment" (as distinct from the "enchantment of materiality") can be more clearly understood through that which takes place in moments of devotional encounter with religious statues. Relational in nature, "enchantment" conceptually provides a framework which reflects a quality of encounter that expresses the intimate relationships that people have with religious statues when they are both *in situ* in shrines and temples, as well as on the move during processions. Consequently, theories of "enchantment" are informed by such encounters with religious materiality. Using a contemporary, vernacular form of Catholic Marian Andalusian statue devotion, the chapter builds on the work of Curry (2012), Harvey (2005), Ingold (2011a, 2011b) and Scott (2006) (among others) to test the "dynamics" of enchantment. Since the dynamics of enchantment cannot be tested without some orientation toward the project of modernity, the chapter will also argue that "enchantment" provides a theoretically fluid middle ground to still-productive dualisms that inform Western cultural discourses. Thus, this chapter will bring "enchantment," "material religion," and "the new animism" (as well as the "fetish") into dialogue with contemporary Catholic statue devotion to argue that enchantment is an unpredictable and relational "happen-

---

Keywords: enchantment, materiality, Virgin Mary, Andalusia, animism, vernacular religion

ing," which takes place in moments of encounter, here exemplified through encounters with religious statues.

The Case Study

The Virgin of Alcalá de los Gazules sits in her own shrine on the outskirts of the village of Alcalá in Andalusia, Spain. The shrine consists of a complex of which the Virgin is the owner. "Her" name is on the deeds, and she is powerful. The Virgin is not only powerful because she is a land owner and generates revenue for the *hermandad*[1] and the village; according to devotees, she is powerful because she has the ability to grant miracles, favors, and wishes. This power is also seen in the visible testimony of the material culture found at the shrine. At any given time during the year, one can see *ex votos*[2] and offerings. If one closely examines the *ex votos* on the walls of the shrine, blood-stained hospital bandages, locks of hair, military medals, and pictures of what appear to be family members are in abundance. Flowers, too, occupy special places in the shrine. Of these places, the Virgin has her favourites. If one is permitted by the shrine caretaker to visit the Virgin in her chamber, one can see "up close" that her fingers often bear rings of gold (usually family heirlooms holding sentimental value) and precious gems. All of these objects are given in devotion, either for prayers/requests petitioned, or in thanks for those granted. Whatever the case, it is common knowledge in and around Alcalá that this statue "works" with and for her people.

Research and time spent in and around Alcalá between 2007 and 2011 revealed that vernacular, *lived* forms of Catholicism consist of devotions and practices that quite comfortably sit outside of doctrinal norms. The vibrancy and passion with which devotions to the Virgin of Alcalá are carried out are unequalled to anything I had experienced previously in more northerly parts of Europe. They are mainly seen in the lively, colourful, emotive processions of the Virgin, which take place around her territory. Having observed and participated at the shrine on several occasions, I had the opportunity to speak with statue caretakers and devotees. In particular, I formed a relationship with the shrine *santero*,[3] who was kind enough to take me in, introduce me to the Virgin, and not

---

1. *Hermandad* is the Spanish word for "brotherhood," here referring to the organization that manages the finances and events that take place at the shrine of the Virgin of Alcalá.
2. *Ex votos* are pictorial offerings of gratitude that either demonstrate or request miraculous intervention, in this case that of the Virgin.
3. Santero is translated as "one who works with the saints," and in this case it refers to the steward or guardian of the shrine and statue of the Virgin of Alcalá.

only tolerate my presence but welcome it. Long conversations led me to a better understanding of the nature of not only his everyday relationship with the statue, but others—locals, devotees, and tourists—many of whom are not Catholic, or even Christian. In my fieldwork encounters I was told that the Virgin of Alcalá is particularly powerful when it comes to healing. She appears in the moments after accidents, and she is particularly helpful when it comes to curing problems of infertility in couples. For this reason, people come from all over Spain, as well as from many parts of Europe, to venerate her. The successful results of those venerations are visibly present throughout the shrine (e.g., dummies, baby shoes, and baby jewellery are commonplace offerings on display around the statue). However, accounts of instances when the Virgin "did not want something to happen" can also be heard. The "will" of the Virgin is usually discussed outside her doctrinal position in the theological hierarchy, where the Virgin Mary is *theotokos*, the mother of Jesus, and an intercessor. In these matters, with her mantle darned in gold and her fine European features, the Virgin of Alcalá is referred to as being inherently powerful in her own right.

Time spent around the shrine also led to encounters with a group called the *camaristas*.[4] These women form an elite group within the cult of the Virgin of Alcalá, and they are responsible for the ritual bathing and dressing of the statue body of the Virgin. Their name is based on the place where the Virgin sits in the shrine, which is called the *camara* or "chamber." From interviews conducted with three *camaristas* in January 2008, I learned that they are local women who are chosen because of exhibiting certain virtuous qualities within the community. These qualities often concern marital status (to *not* be married is desirable, but not required) and reputation. The three *camaristas* that I met varied in age. One of them, Fracisca Jiménez Fernández (called "Paqui"), was a woman in her 50s. The other, Yolanda Quintero Díaz, was a mother of two who appeared to be in her mid-thirties. The third *camarista*, who wished not to be named, appeared to be somewhere in her 40s. When I formally interviewed and recorded the *camaristas*' experiences with the Virgin, I was told from the beginning that certain things to do with "her" (the Virgin) are secret and cannot be disclosed, such as the way in which the statue is shaped beneath her petticoats. They did, however, tell me that she wears handmade white undergarments, which they wash and iron. Knowing more than this is out of bounds for an outsider. More specifically, they told me that the only man who has ever seen the Virgin disrobed is the village priest, and that not even the *santero* (the person who spends the

---

4. *Camarista* is translated as "one who works in a chamber," in this case the chamber within the shrine where the Virgin sits.

most time with the statue) was permitted to see her. When I asked about these protocols, I was told that this protection of the Virgin's modesty is due to her virginal status.

Although it is taboo for someone outside of the group to see the statue undressed, the *camaristas* were happy to talk with me about their intimate interactions with the statue during the ritual changing and washing of her clothes. They each provided different accounts of their encounters with the Virgin, but commonalities were identified, such as the singing of devotional songs to the statue (sung for me during the interview, in order to give an example). Other common interactions included speaking to/with the statues of the Virgin and the infant Jesus during their bathing and dressing, as well as the notion of a trance-like state, during which time was purported to take on a different quality. For example, Paqui shared that they say things such as "*Que guapa estas hoy!*" ("Aren't you beautiful today!"); when changing the statue of the baby, Paqui reported that she would say things like "Hold still and stop squirming, son! How can I change you if you keep moving?" Furthermore, Yolanda said that hours passed during their "work," but it often felt like 20 minutes. Paqui and the *camarista* who wished not to be named agreed. All three women told me that the experience is beautiful for them and extremely feminine and intimate. Yolanda said, "The experience is very special. You can't explain it." Paqui told me that three different *camaristas* have seen a tear on the Virgin's face during the process and that she was one of them. She said, "Me and others, we have seen a tear on the Virgin's face." While Paqui was conveying her account, she got goose-bumps, and her eyes welled up with tears.

Based on the personal accounts shared with me during the course of research in and around Alcalá, this chapter explores the dynamics of enchantment as they take place in relation to and with religious material culture specifically. Bringing modernity into conversation with enchantment, as well as with ideas that surround more recent critical approaches to animism and the fetish (here understood as a subset of the new animism, particularly for understanding the powerful roles of objects), this chapter is concerned with understanding the volatile actions and interactions that take place in relation to religious statues such as the Virgin of Alcalá as an exemplary (even exaggerated) form of how enchantment "works" in relation to so-called objects. In relational theoretical discourses such as "new animism," and "the fetish," emphasis is not only placed on the nuanced interactions of "the moment," but on a particular quality of "encounter." As Martin Buber says, "All actual life is encounter," which results in "queer lyric-dramatic episodes" (1996, 62–67). Employing the works of Patrick Curry (2012, 2013), Graham Harvey (2005), Bruno Latour (1993, 2010), Tim Ingold (2011a, 2011b), and

Colin Scott (2006) (among others), Buber's "episodes" will be explored here as "enchanted" episodes, the practical nuances of which will be examined and exemplified through the relationships (both private and public) with, and ritual performances that surround, this specific statue of the Virgin Mary.

Of course, the Virgin of Alcalá is one of thousands of Marian statues in Spain. Yet it is through an examination of vernacular expressions of religion, where the "universal" idea of Mary sits in apparent contrast to her local, traditionally specific forms, that the "treatment" of statues such as the Virgin of Alcalá (e.g., how she is cared for, venerated, dressed, bathed, maintained, and protected), as well as the power of her matter, can lead to an advance in discussions about enchantment. Last, since modern ideas surrounding "representation" and "agency" typically form the bedrock of how material cultures are understood within various social scientific disciplines in the academy (where they are often relegated to the status of metaphor), the chapter will provide relational, creative approaches to these categories based on lived accounts given by participants/devotees, in order to provide an expansion of dualistic constructs. This will create a space for different understandings of enchantment to emerge, which, after all, is relational by its very nature. As it will be demonstrated, the category of "enchantment" (which is paradoxically non-categorical) works particularly well when examining unpredictable roles of especially powerful, vernacular religious matter.

The Dynamics of "Modern" and Religious Enchantment

So what is enchantment? First, it must be said that enchantment is not static. It does not necessarily work as a place in which events can be boxed or categorized. It is an active, fluid and volatile relational possibility, and its potentiality exists in any intersection, at any place, and at any time (and, of course, within any*thing*). Furthermore, it is through relationships that enchantment is coaxed out of its hiding place and brought into being. Enchantment cannot exist without fertile ground having been prepared for it to come or without conditions being supportive for its spontaneous arrival. In other words, enchantment is an occurrence, an emergent quality of a moment, and a continual relational possibility. Let us unpack this further. Gestures, whether religiously orchestrated or not, can set the stage for enchantment's arrival, but this arrival is not guaranteed. Curry (2012, 3) tells us that enchantment is *wild*. In its wildness it differs from the formulaic principles that comprise much of what can be considered within the category of magic (defined in many ways, this polemic will not be fully addressed here). This can be compared with the work of an artist: excellence of technique does not guarantee an enchanted audience.

In terms of material culture specifically, human beings have always had relationships with the "objects" that inhabit their environments, whether those things be mobile phones, cars, computers, certain buildings, or even clothes and food, denial of which remains a wholly modern problem. Being stigmatized as unstable, or even a lunatic, is what is at stake for the modern who admits that he/she enters into active, knowing (vocal or otherwise) relationships with mere things. For this reason, the status of *modern* objects (religious or not) is better addressed after a brief discussion of "disenchantment." Curry's insightful understanding of Max Weber's "concrete magic" aids in understanding both where and how the discursive processes of so-called "disenchantment" began, as well as how "magic" and "mystery" became separated from matter.

> He [Weber] famously contrasted this [*concrete magic*] with 'the disenchantment of the world' resulting from modern bureaucratisation and intellectualisation, which splits experience into the 'iron cage' of causality on the one hand and ineffable mysticism on the other. The point here is that enchantment is always and necessarily both 'material' and 'spiritual': that is, precisely circumstantial—embodied and embedded—and simultaneously deeply mysterious, undelimitable and unmasterable.
> (Curry 2012, 2–3)

This reflects the modern project and how magic (here comparable with enchantment), which at one point was purportedly fused with or immanent in nature (and matter), got pushed out and made separate from the world, resulting not only in the idea that religion and superstition would eventually give way to scientific, secularized rationality, but also a denial of the possibility of enchantment. Enchantment, however, requires us to be "unstable." It can only make an appearance in moments where modern constructs such as "subject" and "object" or even the "sacred" and the "profane" are no longer applicable, and this is often the case where relationships with religious objects take place.

But was there ever a time when "magic" was purely embedded in nature, or in "matter"? In Platonism and Christianity, the "split" between magic and the material world had begun long before (Curry 2012). By the time of Descartes and the influence of the Enlightenment (which was inextricably bound up with Protestant anti-matter, iconoclastic antics), it had already formed a profound part of the European cultural psyche (especially in countries that experienced the Protestant Reformation and interrupted Catholic devotional practices). Furthermore, in many parts of Europe, representation became the dominant discourse concerning religious objects. This was due to what Peter Pels refers to as the Protestant "fear of matter" (Pels 2008) and the modern prizing of mind and/

or spirit over matter. In other parts of Europe, in countries such as Spain and Italy (despite modernity having occurred there, too), "matter"—religious matter such as amulets, relics and statues —remained valuable and viable, playing significant roles in religious communities.

Let us consider once again the actions of the *camaristas*. In *On the Modern Cult of the Factish Gods*, Latour's (2010) theoretical suspension of "belief" asserts that the idea of modern "mastery" over the world and nature is misguided and that both facts and fetishes—or "factishes"—are human constructions that are mistaken as "truth." As with Latour's example of the "fetishist" who is aware that he/she is creating the gods that he/she then gives power, a contradiction is taking place. The *camaristas* are aware that they are having relationships with a "statue," a piece of cedar that has been carved into a small human effigy, and that what occurs in these moments of active devotional relating defies commonly accepted understandings of modernity (where "subjecthood" is relegated to the status of mere metaphor). Here, the experience of "encounter" with the statue (where enchantment is a potentiality) pushes to their limits the dualistic confines often found in concepts such as "representation," as well as in Enlightenment thinking, rationality, and "modernity." As Latour (1993) and others have indicated, modernity is an idea that does not and cannot be used to adequately describe who we are and what we do, especially in terms of the lived realities of religious experiences. This, it would seem, makes modernity an obsolete category. Yet for our purposes here, "modernity" must be entertained in order to get the most out of relational theories. Devotees and other shrine visitors (such as tourists) will have different relationships with the statue. Some of these will hold modern conceptions (meaning that they will encounter and translate the statue as a piece of wood or religious art, whereby the statue's relational status is denied), while other encounters, such as those accounts given by the *camaristas*, will hold other, *non-modern* conceptions. Non-modern conceptions clearly contain more relational possibilities than modern ones, but what is at stake is a denial of reason and rationality. It seems as though enchantment and modernity cannot, then, exist in the same place. Curry frames modernity and enchantment thus:

> In a modernist universe, all subjects are incompletely analysed inanimate objects and therefore ethically inconsiderable potential resources to be manipulated as part of a project of the rational mastery of nature (including human nature). In a relationship, in contrast—and enchantment is nothing if not relational—by definition, neither party is in complete control; issues of ethics, negotiation, and etiquette are therefore paramount. (Curry 2013, 469–470)

According to Curry, modernity is about *control*, while the emphasis of enchantment is *not being in control*. Yet what is not addressed here is what happens when a Western religious statue, such as the Virgin of Alcalá, which is doctrinally relegated to the status of "representation," is engaged—not only as a person, but as a powerful person. What are the dynamics of enchantment under these particular circumstances? As Curry indicates, "etiquette" is important when dealing with enchantment; yet further questions can be raised and explored. From the case studies, it is understood that the Virgin is approached with particular forms of ritual etiquette. It is also known that devotees negotiate with her. Is etiquette significant once enchantment has already emerged, or is etiquette essential for inviting enchantment? If enchantment cannot be controlled, then etiquette must be a significant factor in the honouring of its arrival.

Enchantment is not, however, without its problems. According to Curry, the problematic nature of enchantment is demonstrated by the fact that scholars have neglected the category of enchantment as being non- or anti-categorical. He writes,

> Although enchantment is ubiquitous in human life, it has largely been overlooked by scholars. (The reason is to do partly with the nature of the experience, which doesn't lend itself to articulation or analysis, and perhaps partly the rationalist formation of the academy itself.)
>
> (Curry 2012, 76)

How can one "quantify" experience, especially when it is of a religious and/or "irrational" nature, and especially when that relating involves addressing, praying to, loving or negotiating with statues? More recent approaches to vernacular religion are helping to close this gap. Making "vernacular religion" a category for understanding "everyday" religion (Primiano 1995) has provided a vital shift toward emphasizing the significance of personal, private and unique experiences as they relate with space, place, architecture, communities, objects, texts, and/or all things "sensual" and religious. Therefore, the concepts of vernacular religion and enchantment work particularly well with material religious objects, such as the statue of the Virgin of Alcalá, to emphasize the "whole package" of devotion. Arguably, "magic," modernity, enchantment, disenchantment and re-enchantment all take place simultaneously. Moments of encounter mean that enchantment is a momentary action. One can be enchanted one moment and disenchanted the next. Thus, enchantment relies on "active relating," "active relationships" and relationality. The unpredictability of enchantment is further addressed by Curry (2012), who, in exploring the nature of enchantment, explains that:

enchantment also partakes of a non-anthropocentric animism, or what Plumwood called 'active intentionality', in which subjectivity (the quality of being a subject) manifests in ways which transgress the official boundaries between human/ non-human, animate/inanimate, as well as spiritual/material. (Curry 2012, 3)

Furthermore, the non-anthropocentric animism referred to by Curry complements new animism's engagement (discussed below) with potential "object persons"—or better still, "statue persons"—whereby "treatment" (Harvey 2005) is one of the prime indicators that animism is "taking place." The Virgin of Alcalá is treated as a person of high and honourable standing by her devotees. That said, can she be considered an "object" at all? This is where theories of "enchantment" can aid in advancing relational discourses with regard to religion. "Enchantment," unlike the category of the sacred, permeates, fuses, and flows between the sacred and the profane, immanence and transcendence, rendering Weber's idea of "concrete magic" a more volatile status dependent upon momentary acts and encounters. After all, active relationships are the binding forces that make such encounters "work."

The Nuanced Dynamics of Enchantment

It has been established that enchantment is relational. But how does it work specifically in relation to religious objects? Using animism and the fetish, this section will explore the nuances of enchantment, how it works in public and private spheres, and if it is spontaneous or dependent upon etiquette, as Curry suggests (2013, 69)? In addition, it will explore the idea of "treatment" being part and parcel to enchantment. Does the wilfulness of matter, as discussed in the section on the fetish, interfere with enchantment, or does matter have the power to enchant?

The accounts provided by the *camaristas* in relation to the statue of the Virgin of Alcalá raise several questions in terms of identifying the religious dynamics of enchantment. First, how does enchantment work when "religiously" motivated individuals enter into relationships—indeed, relational practices—with the statue? Do they carry a set of doctrinally influenced or learned protocols into said interactions, which influence whether or not enchantment takes place? Can religious statues such as the Virgin "trigger" an episode of enchantment? Another question concerns whether or not enchantment is spontaneously possible in the context of religious devotion where protocols and devotional etiquettes exist. Many of these questions may never be answered, but practices at the shrine of the Virgin are, for example, steeped in generational, collective and traditional customs, which may or may not interfere with the potentiality of enchantment to "happen." The "wildness" of enchantment makes it unpredictable. Another consideration concerns the desires of the Virgin. Does giving the Virgin what she purportedly wants (e.g., particular flowers, gold) guarantee enchantment? The answer here is no, as it may be the case that enchantment, despite all the "right ingredients" being present or ritually prepared, still decides not to manifest, or it may occur in the most decidedly inappropriate moment. In other words, enchantment is conditional, but the conditions can be elusive.

Enchantment can take the form of a Durkheimian "collective effervescence" (1912) or group excitement, which can lead to swathes of devotees falling under the sway of the charisma of the Virgin. In times of celebration, such as processions, the Virgin of Alcalá becomes a public figure. Orsi tells us that what constitutes "public" also changes during processions, and it proves to be as relationally responsive as the statues themselves, rendering enchantment a possibility in public interactions as much as in private ones. Orsi (2009) writes:

> In the places where Mary is encountered, where the transcendent not only breaks into time, but also gets involved in the nitty-gritty of people's affairs, the boundary between the private and public experience is blurred. (Orsi 2009, 215–16)

Here, too, enchantment has the power to test the boundaries between "public" and "private" domains. Thus enchantment can be a public "event" as much as it can be a private one. Whole groups can be enchanted. Orsi says the following about processions:

> A heightened sense of intimacy exists among people, even among strangers, a sharpened awareness of vulnerability, exposure, and dependence. The boundaries of single subjectivities dissolve in these potent environments of desire and need, conscious and unconscious.
> (Orsi 2009, 216)

In moments of procession, religious statues such as that of the Virgin of Alcalá can be considered "multi-relational." They not only relate to individual devotees, but to a wider public, with whom they have distinct relationships which are influenced by generational devotions and local customs. Although Orsi says that "single subjectivities dissolve in these potent environments" (2009, 215), it can be argued that the "single subjectivities" of individual devotees remain intact. They simply take on another, more complex dimension that involves an entire crowd of "single subjectivities" under the same "spell" of the Virgin. Vocal utterances, gestures and songs are, however, orchestrated by vernacular religious traditions (e.g., there is protocol regarding what devotees *should* and *do* say in these moments). For example, when the Virgin of Alcalá is involved in a procession, devotees throw flowers onto her bier with repeated shouts of *Viva! Viva la Virgen!*[5] The Virgin can be said to inspire and evoke passionate responses, such as these at public events. Objects, it can then be argued, have the power to inspire and thus enchant moments of group or public encounters. Yet the question remains: would the statue of the Virgin be able to enchant if religious "set and setting" were not in place, or if vernacular acts, protocols and processional etiquette were not in place beforehand? Perhaps the best way to answer this question is to turn once again to Curry, who argues that there is an unavoidable conflict between ritual and enchantment—indeed, between religion and enchantment. He writes:

> every religion cannot but try to flesh out the experience of enchantment in a particular way, to dictate and maintain its meaning in a way that accords with its own soteriological programme. Any such programme, being systematic, is necessarily disenchanting. (Curry 2012, 11)

Yet religion, as described by Curry, does not refer to the vernacular kind, but to the category of religion generally. Prescribed religious rituals or protocols of behaviour when a devotee is in the presence of the Virgin certainly exist. But research has found that individuals bring their own personal ideas, beliefs and nuanced relationships into private encounters with the Virgin as much as they bring them into wider public events.

The "New Animism" and Enchantment

The accounts given to me by the *camaristas* exemplify "enchantment" through encounters, and these encounters are "animist" in nature and in quality. I am not, however, referring to Tylor's (1913 [1871]) animism, which emphasizes belief in spirits, but to the "new animism" (Harvey 2005), which emphasizes respectful engagement with a living world that is full of "persons," some of whom are human and others are "things." The relational nature of the new animism helps to broaden understandings of "enchantment." Harvey's (2005) *Animism: Respecting the Living World* offers a different perspective on the debate. Harvey says:

> The newer usage [of animism] refers to a concern with knowing how to behave appropriately towards persons, not all of whom are human. It refers to the widespread indigenous and increasingly popular "alternative" understanding that humans share this world with a wide range of persons, only some of whom are human. While it may be important to know whether one is encountering a person or an object, the really

---

5. Literally translated "Live! Live the Virgin!"

significant question for animists of the "new" kind is how persons are to be treated or acted towards. (Harvey 2005, xi)

The idea of "other-than-human persons" comes from Hallowell's (1960) interpretation of the Ojibwe "worldview" that "persons" are all around us, and that some are human and others are other than human. This is not to say that objects are "living" all the time, every day. They are, however, "alive" when they are participating in relationship. This is not because spirits take up residence in matter, although they may do this, too, depending on epistemological frameworks. Enchantment is not a fixed status, but relationally dependent upon encounters, whether those encounters are between humans, humans and animals, humans and places, or humans and "things." An example of this can be found in the interactions with the Virgin described by the *camaristas*. Here the Virgin is entreated, implored, spoken with, sang to, dressed and bathed, and generally treated as a person. As mentioned above, the difference is that she is treated as a person who is potentially more powerful than the *camaristas* and others who maintain her. This would suggest that the types of enchantment that may occur when devotees are interacting with the Virgin of Alcalá (discussed in greater detail further along) can involve power relations.

Scott's (2006) idea of ontological emergence shares many similarities with the new animism, and it can assist in this discussion about the relational dynamics of enchantment. In reference to the Cree understanding of the world, Scott writes "The attribution of life to the non-living is not what occurs in a world perceived as so many different modalities of life, but of emergence" (2006, 61). Furthermore, Scott views personhood thus:

> The idea that relationships of sharing and mutual responsiveness between human and other-than-human aspects of the environment constitute 'personhood,' I think, is fundamental both ontologically and epistemologically. (Scott 2006, 53)

This idea shares characteristics with those of Hallowell's (1960) idea of personhood. Of course, Hallowell, Harvey and Scott are writing/have written about different Amerindian (Ojibwe and Cree) perspectives. Yet the fact that these perspectives are not "Western" and normative in terms of culture make them all the more valuable in terms of re-thinking ideas that highlight the areas where modern dualisms such as "subject" and "object" do not necessarily work. Let us explore this further.

Scott's idea of ontological emergence and personhood is simultaneous and relevant to place, time and location, indicating that ontological emergence shares some similarities with the emergent nature of enchantment. Scott writes:

> The attribution of life to the non-living is not what occurs in a world perceived as so many different modalities of life, of emergence. In such a world, figurative practice is rather to understand the differences among beings in the world as variations on the underlying themes of life in community. For my Cree interlocutors, the world is a place of deep vitality, sometimes restful, sometimes dynamic; pregnant with possibility; a place of emergent, often orderly, sometimes surprising phenomena. Life in this sense, *pimaatsiiwin*, was translated to me as 'the continuous birthing of the world'. (Scott 2006, 61)

The Cree idea of "the continuous birthing of the world" is reliant upon relational engagement. Scott's idea of ontological emergence indicates a simultaneous coming-into-being of persons and things. Arguing for a relational epistemology, Scott uses Nurit Bird-David's (1999) "discussion of Nayaka talking with trees" to exemplify his point. Bird-David writes:

> In the interaction of a human with a tree, intelligence lies not "inside the head of the human actor, let alone inside the fabric of the tree. Rather, it is immanent in the total system of perception and action constituted by the co-presence of the human and the tree within a wider environment." (Bird-David 2006, 53)

According to Scott, however, both Bird-David and Tim Ingold suggest that the attribution of personhood comes *after* the engagement with the tree (i.e., after epistemological value has already been attributed). In contrast, he argues that engaged responses are simultaneous, immanent "and mutually reinforcing in our experience of the world" (Scott 2006, 61). This indicates that ontological emergence is not dependent on "ideas" that follow encounters, but instead on simultaneous encounters.

While the idea of simultaneous coming-into-being supports the concept of relationality, relationships with the Virgin of Alcalá can also indicate cases of deliberate coming-into-being where epistemologies are indeed present. Ideas and beliefs, as well as material "protocol" (such as what is the "norm" in terms of an offering), often accompany and inform performances of veneration. Relational engagement with statues is mostly intentional. Like enchantment, it is not a spontaneous inevitability, but instead a continual potentiality. Yet the volatile nature of relationality suggests that sometimes relationships do, in fact, emerge as a result of a simultaneous encounter, surprising those parties involved.

Over the years, I have observed many tourists visiting the shrine complex, the majority of whom have not appeared to be affected by being in the presence of the statue. Furthermore, I have also observed many relationships and devotions which can be considered "everyday." For example, it is the custom of many people in the village to visit the shrine at least once a week. They walk in, genuflect, sometimes leave flowers, and walk out again. Nevertheless, during the course of my fieldwork at the shrine of the Virgin of Alcalá, I have twice observed—on two separate occasions—what can be considered "episodes of enchantment": once on a September evening in 2007, the night before the Virgin's annual procession, and once during the day in June 2009, when English tourists were visiting the shrine for the first time. Both cases involved women, with their partners, who were not Catholic and had no prior relationship with the Virgin, the village, or the area. In both instances, the woman stopped suddenly in front of the statue, her eyes welled up with tears, and she began to cry. These were cases of spontaneous relational encounters where no "intentional" engagement had been planned and there was no prior knowledge of ritual etiquette or suggested ways to approach the Virgin.

In comparison to these spontaneous encounters, let us turn again to the accounts given by the *camaristas*. Not only do the *camaristas* fall into trance-like states during the ritual process, time takes on a different quality ("four hours felt like 20 minutes"), which is another indication that enchantment is happening. Thus, it may be suggested here that enchantment can be part of a modern response to being in the presence of a religious statue as much as it forms part of a more prescribed "religious," votive response. Enchantment can be either spontaneous or planned, a "state" that is brought about by prescribed gestures or ritual acts, as well by an unpredicted surprise.

Agency, Representation, and Enchanted Objects

A modernist understanding of "objects" (as opposed to subjects) is that only humans have the ability to attribute enchanting qualities to objects. Yet some objects succeed in causing some kind of commotion in the lives of humans. The endless polemics that have surrounded religious objects specifically, from the 8th-century Byzantine Empire to the Protestant Reformation and beyond, are testimony to this statement. As Margaret Miles says: "Iconoclasts and iconodules argued about images because they acknowledged their power, disagreeing only about the religious implications of that power" (1995, 167). This idea can be extended to objects in culture more generally. Yet through the use of modern language and discourse, the power of objects has been made safe; two prime examples of this are the concepts of "agency" and "representation."

Agency, as it is understood most commonly in the social sciences as "exclusively an attribute of [human] persons" (Pickering, 2010, 194), is unlikely to account for the ontological potentialities of religious statues such as the Virgin. In addressing how agency is utilized in the social sciences, Ingold says:

the material world can only be brought back to life in the dreams of
theorists by conjuring a magical mind-dust that, sprinkled among its
constituents, is supposed to set them physically in motion.

(Ingold 2011a, 28)

As mentioned above, in the classic Tylorean (1913 [1871]) understanding of animism, alien spirits take up residence in things of nature and matter. For modernists, the concept of "agency" serves a similar purpose. Enchantment as a category is administered in similar ways. It denotes a state of mystification and mysteriousness, and for this reason it is often applied categorically to situations where "the irrational" is inexplicable. This could, however, be part and parcel of its typical confusion with the concept of "magic." Furthermore, according to James Leach, Gell's approach to "social agency" emphasizes "representation." He writes:

> When all is said and done, we are left with the individual mind and its representations, and with the idea that non-humans can only be agents by proxy: There are real subjects, namely we ourselves, and then there are those second-class citizens of subject-dom (i.e., objects and the like).
>
> (Leach 2007, 183)

The relationship between agency and representation is made clear by Leach. Being two sides of the same metaphorical coin, both emphasize human intentionality over the ability of objects to "act," to have their own forms of agency, or to be able to "enchant" of their own accord—as can, according to fetishists, the fetish.

"Representation" on a similar note is also problematic when it comes to understanding the roles of religious (and other) objects. When objects (religious objects specifically) have "agency" or are "representational" of something else, they are rendered powerless, by default placing human "agents" at the helm. In a critique of representation, Viveiros de Castro says:

> The Cartesian break with medieval scholasticism produced a radical simplification of European ontology by positing only two principles or substances: unextended thought and extended matter. Modern thought began with that simplification; and its massive conversion of ontological into epistemological questions (questions of representation) is still with us, a conversion prompted by the fact that every mode of being not assimilable to obdurate 'matter' had to be swallowed up by 'mind'.
>
> (Viveiros de Castro 2004, 482)

While devotees in Alcalá know that they venerate a "statue," or that which is doctrinally at least meant to be a "representation" of the universal idea of Mary, this appears to be of little importance vis-à-vis the actual relationships that devotees have with it. It is within this tension between doctrinal and vernacular practices that the concept of "enchantment" can provide alternative angles from which to overcome the "ontological poverty" discussed by Viveiros de Castro with regard to categories such as "symbolism," "metaphor" and "representation." Keeping these issues in mind, let us look once again at the Virgin of Alcalá.

The *santero* told me that the Virgin of Alcalá has her own power (*ella tiene el poder*). She grants miracles, and if she does not want to grant a petition or request, she will not do it. I found that his belief reflects a common understanding of the statue. Although devotees know that the statue is a statue and a supposed representation of the universal Virgin Mary, her local, vernacular form is treated and addressed otherwise. This indicates that power is attributed to the actual statue rather than to the "universal Mary." If the Virgin has power of her own accord (independent of Jesus or God), then this exemplifies the case of Pels's fetishistic "spirit of matter" (1998, 91), where power is present and inherent in matter. Furthermore, the idea that the Virgin is more powerful than her devotees (they are at "her" will, so to speak) raises questions with regard to how enchantment might work in non-egalitarian relationships. As Holbraad said about the powder of Cuban diviners being power (2007), in this case the statue *is* power, and the powerful discourses surrounding the Virgin (e.g., stories, testimonies, *ex votos*) have the power to inspire or at least set the scene for enchantment to occur.

These component parts of the whole of the shrine experience can be considered in many different metaphorical ways. First, they can be considered "assemblages," whereby the conditions must be "correct" (as with "magic") for enchantment to take place (enchantment should never be taken as a given, as, like love, it can come and go). If we follow a line of animist reasoning, the "liveliness" of the Virgin emerges with the momentary nourishment of relationships and devotion. Reflecting Scott's idea of ontological emergence, Ingold writes:

> It has been conventional to describe animism as a system of belief that imputes life to inert objects. But [...] such imputation is more typical of people in western societies who dream of finding life on other planets than of indigenous peoples to whom the label of animism has been generally applied. These peoples are united not in their belief but in a way of being that is alive and open to a world in continuous birth. In this animic ontology, beings do not propel themselves across a ready-made world but rather issue forth through a world-in-formation, along the lines of their relationships. (Ingold 2011b, 66)

It is along these "lines" discussed by Ingold that both enchantment and the ontological emergence of the Virgin are possible. Enchantment is an organic, relationally co-inspired, conditional response to a variety of factors, all of which must be working in tune with one another for it to *take place*. Dualities such as "representation" or "agency," as they are typically understood, do not apply to Ingold's "world-in-formation" discussion. Thus, the potentiality of enchantment is dependent upon ontological emergence. If persons (statue-persons and human-persons) emerge in each other's presence, whereby each becomes a subject of devotion and of encounter, then the ground has been made fertile for enchantment to occur, happen, or come into being.

Conclusion

This chapter has established that enchantment is an unpredictable, wild occurrence that has the power to render those who experience it ("subject" or "object") surprised. Oftentimes, as evidenced by the fieldwork accounts in this chapter, it is an unexpected arrival between "human person" and "thing." Enchantment can be either spontaneous or planned, a "state" that is brought about by prescribed gestures or ritual acts, or by an unpredicted surprise. It can, however, also occur on a mass scale with crowds of devotees falling under the spell of a religious statue, like that of the Virgin of Alcalá. Accounts of enchantment, such as those told by the *camaristas*, inform us as to some of the uncanny ways in which so-called objects "act" and even enchant, where the familiar becomes unfamiliar, and where the boundaries that categorically separate the sacred from the profane dissolve. Furthermore, these accounts help scholars to re-think modern categories where conceptions of causality and agency effectively mute and pacify what is often experienced by devotees as vital and engaging. Enchantment, much like the fetish, exists in unstable spaces. Vernacular Spanish Catholics and their deep, intimate relationship with the Virgin of Alcalá de los Gazules further inspire new approaches to animism that challenge modern conceptions of agency and representation, making room for different ways in which enchantment can be understood. The Virgin is sung to, dressed, bathed, and treated as a powerful person, and this indicates that animist, relational encounters are taking place. To greater and lesser degrees, the ideas of Curry (2012, 2013), Harvey (2005), Latour (1993, 2010), Ingold (2011a, 2011b), and Scott (2006) have aided in exploring the dynamics of enchantment, and they have informed the assertion that enchantment is a relational discourse. It can be suggested here that enchantment also forms part of a modern response to being in the presence of religious statues as much as it forms part of a more prescribed "religious" votive response. After all, enchantment is relational, and it is this mixing of the sacred with the profane—as seen in the work of the *camaristas* among others—that facilitates religious experiences.

References

Buber, M. 1996. *I and Thou*. Translated by W. Kaufmann. New York: Touchstone.

Curry, P. 2013. "The Third Road: Faerie in Hypermodernity." In *The Handbook of Contemporary Animism*, edited by G. Harvey, 468-478. Durham: Acumen.

———. 2012. "Enchantment and Modernity." *PAN: Philosophy, Activism. Nature* 12: 76-89.

Durkheim, E. 1975 [1912]. *The Elementary Forms of Religious Life*. Translated by J. W. Swain. New York: Free Press.

Gell, A. 1998. *Art and Agency: An Anthropological Theory*. Oxford: Clarendon Press.

Graeber, D. 2005. "Fetishism as Social Creativity: or, Fetishes are Gods in the Process of Construction." *Anthropological Theory* 5(4): 407-438.

Hallowell, A. I. 1960. "Ojibwa Ontology, Behavior, and World View." In *Culture in History: Essays in Honor of Paul Radin*, edited by S. Diamond, 19-52. New York: Columbia University Press. (Reprinted in *Reading in Indigenous Religions*. Edited by G. Harvey, 18-49. London: Continuum. 2002.)

Harvey, G. 2005. *Animism: Respecting the Living World*. Kent Town: Wakefield Press.

Holbraad, M. 2007. "The Power of Powder: Multiplicity and Motion in the Divinatory Cosmology of Cuban Ifa (or *mana*, again)." In *Thinking through Things: Theorising Artefacts Ethnographically*, edited by A. Henare, M. Holbraad, M. and S. Wastell, 189-225. London: Routledge.

Ingold, T. 2011a. "Materials against Materiality." In *Being Alive: Essays on Movement, Knowledge and Description*, 19-32. London: Routledge.

———. 2011b. "When ANT meets SPIDER: Social theory for Anthropods." In *Being Alive: Essays on Movement, Knowledge and Description*, 89-94. London: Routledge.

———. 2007. *Lines: A Brief History*. Abingdon: Routledge.

Latour, B. 2010. *On the Modern Cult of the Factish Gods*. Translated by H. MacLean and C. Porter. Durham, NC: Duke University Press.

———. 1993. *We Have Never Been Modern*. Translated by C. Porter. Cambridge, MA: Harvard University Press.

Leach, J. 2007. "Differentiation and Encompassment: A Critique of Alfred Gell's Theory of the Abduction of Creativity." In *Thinking through Things: Theorising Artefacts Ethnographically*, edited by A. Henare, M. Holbraad, and S. Wastell, 167-188. London: Routledge.

Miles, M. 1995. "Image." In *Critical Terms for Religious Studies,* edited by M.C. Taylor, 160–172. Chicago: The University of Chicago Press.

Orsi, R. A. 2009. "Abundant History: Marian Apparitions as Alternative Modernity." In *Moved by Mary: The Power of Pilgrimage in the Modern World*, edited by A-K. Hermkens, W. Jansen and C. Notermans, 215–225. Farnham: Ashgate.

Pels, P. 2008. "The Modern Fear of Matter: Reflections on the Protestantism of Victorian Science." *Material Religion: The Journal of Objects, Art and Belief* 4(3): 264–283.

———. 1998. "The Spirit of Matter: On Fetish, Rarity, Fact, and Fancy." In *Border Fetishisms: Material Objects in Unstable Spaces*, edited by P. Spyer, 91–121. London: Routledge.

Pickering, A. 2010. "Material Culture and the Dance of Agency." In *The Oxford Handbook of Material Culture Studies*, edited by D. Hicks and M. Beaudry, 191–208. Oxford: Oxford University Press.

Primiano, L. N. 1995. "Vernacular Religion and the Search for Method in Religious Folklife." *Western Folklore* (54)1: 37–56.

Scott, C. 2006. "Spirit and Practical Knowledge in the Person of the Bear among Wemindji Cree Hunters." *Ethnos* [Online] 71(5): 51–66. <http://dx.doi.org/10.1080/00141840600603178> [Accessed 25 August 2009].

Tylor, E. 1913 [1871]. *Primitive Culture*, 2 vols. London: John Murray.

Viveiros de Castro, E. 2004. "Exchanging Perspectives: the Transformation of Objects into Subjects in Amerindian Cosmologies." *Common Knowledge* 10(3): 463–484.

Weber, M. 1991. "Science as a Vocation." In *Max Weber: Essays in* Sociology, edited and translated by H. H. Gerth and C. Wright Mills, 129–156. Oxford: Routledge.

About the Author

Amy Whitehead, PhD, is a tutor at the University of Wales Sofia Centre for the Study of Cosmology in Culture, and an associate lecturer in Religious Studies at Oxford Brookes University. Her research interests deal with religious materiality, animism, ritual studies and contemporary forms of paganism. She has published the monograph *Religious Statues and Personhood: Testing the Role of Materiality*, London: Bloomsbury (2013), among other publications.

— 4 —

Empowerment and the Articulation of Agency among Finnish Yoga Practitioners

MÅNS BROO AND CHRISTIANE KÖNIGSTEDT

Yoga structurally shares the reputation of empowering the individual with many other contemporary spiritual and esoteric practices. At the same time, these practitioners also share a tendency to externalize agency and attribute events and individual actions to higher powers or "fate," or "destiny." It is sometimes argued that engaging in such "spiritual" practices leads people to minimize their responsibility for their own lives. Thus, agency matters, and this chapter examines how enabled agency is attributed in narratives of Finnish yoga practitioners. How do practitioners view their relationship to their practice and what do they feel that they as individuals gain through it? These questions will be discussed using a notion of agency that emphasizes its socio-cultural intermediateness, focusing in this way on the reported influences behind agency insofar as it is presented as being co-composed of entangled human and non-human actors, on what life-reality is reflected and (re-)constructed, and on what the performing agent aims to construct in relation to others. Instead of the binary view of some critics, we found attributions of enabled agency to the individual to be interwoven with different externalizations thereof, which point towards new strategies that individuals choose to relate themselves to the world they live in.

Keywords: yoga, agency, rhetoric, fate, free will

Introduction

Like elsewhere in Finland, different types of yoga practices are popular in Turku/Åbo, the country's previous, mediaeval capital. Yoga is popularly seen as an empowering practice, and this perception is widely shared in the interviews that Måns Broo conducted with yoga teachers in Turku as part of the recently concluded "Post-Secular Culture and a Changing Religious Landscape" Centre of Excellence research project at Åbo Akademi University (2009–2014). This project was devoted to qualitative and ethnographic investigations of the contemporary religious field in Finland, of which Westernized yoga constitutes one significant element (see Broo *et al.*, 2015).

In this chapter, we will examine how empowerment, understood as an enabled form of agency, is constructed by yoga practitioners, using in-depth interviews with yoga teachers in Turku, Finland as our material. How do they view their introduction to yoga, and furthermore, what do they feel happens when they exercise it? How do practitioners view their relationship to their practice and what do they feel that they as individuals gain through it? We wish to discuss these questions by using a notion of agency that emphasizes its socio-cultural intermediateness, focusing in this way on the reported influences behind agency (insofar as it is presented as being co-composed of entangled human and non-human actors), on what life-reality is reflected and (re-)constructed, and on what the performing agent aims to construct in relation to others. Yoga structurally shares the reputation of empowering the individual with many other contemporary spiritual and esoteric practices, something that makes an analysis of the narratives of agency an exciting endeavour which is not necessarily limited to yoga practice alone.

Agency

"Agency" as such can be approached in various ways. Sociologists and anthropologists have pondered questions about the psychological, social, and ideological aspects of agency, but temporal and spatial aspects have also been considered. We will start with the linguistic anthropologist Laura Ahearn's (2001, 112–113) short, open, and practical definition of agency as referring to "the socio-culturally mediated capacity to act." This definition claims that at the core, social structures shape agency but are likewise shaped by agency. Agency here is neither to be equated with "free will" nor perfectly determined by structure, be it cultural or social. Ahearn (2001, 113) follows Ortner's understanding of "loose structure," which she understands as analogous to culture in terms of grammar and the speaking patterns of languages. Thus, languages change over time, and within the rules of grammar and speaking patterns there are virtually infinite opportunities to say the same thing in a grammatically correct manner while changing emphasis—and, accordingly, aspects of meaning. This approach implies that agency, including the very act of speech, contributes to shaping social structure. What people say thus not only reflects, but (re-)enforces and occasionally changes their social reality. Individual narratives, therefore, provide insight into what they and their reference group perceive as real or appropriate.

This point may be elucidated by a related approach. Karlyn Kohrs-Campbell (2005, 5) writes from a dialectical perspective on rhetorical agency that rhetors/authors, being linked to cultures and collectives and forced to negotiate between institutional powers, are important points of "articulation of agency" rather than its sources. Agency is here understood "as a participatory and complex composition, as a matrix of often semi-invisible factors in temporal (and sometimes transient and context-bound) interplay with one another" (Kohrs-Campbell 2005, 3). Although not every person may count as an author or rhetor in the strict sense of being a spokesperson of a group and being heard by a wider audience, the people interviewed here are teachers connected with schools and students. Therefore, they can be assumed to be constrained and enabled, analogous to Kohrs-Campbell's use of rhetor, as "points of articulation" in the way they talk about their experiences with yoga.

It has to be kept in mind, however, that Kohrs-Campbell's basic assumption, derived from her studies of the work of Sartre and illustrated by her case of Jimmy Carter (Kohrs-Campbell 2005, 1), as well as our extension of it to individuals practising yoga, are to be understood as analytical. Such an assumption reflects an increasingly common view of the present world as facing a democratization of authority, which allows the agency of individuals to be seen as a result of multiple actors and resources outside the agent, so that their multiplicity becomes somehow "semi-visible." Nevertheless, the large debate around free will and externally resourced agency is not decided, of course, and it will likely not be so within the foreseeable future. Rather, we approach the question here by following Ahearn's and Ortner's conceptualization of a "loose structure," as described above.

Against this backdrop, we believe that we are justified in researching agency by looking at the accounts of yoga practitioners as long as we accept that these accounts are not directly transferrable to wider society and understand them as legitimizations and explanations of agency (Königstedt 2008, 2012, 180–181). Drawing on these interviews, precisely on people's descriptions of their experiences of practising yoga and their yoga-related life courses, we can get deeper insights into conceptualizations and ascriptions of agency, conceptualizations of personhood, and causality among yoga practitioners in Turku. Furthermore, through these communicative patterns we are able to investigate how this community or milieu sees itself and wants to be seen. At the same time, these individual practitioners inform us about their socio-culturally intermediated capacity to act, that is, how they feel constrained and enabled.

Terhi Utriainen, Tuija Hovi and Måns Broo (2012, 201) wrote in a previous article that an approach to agency from this perspective should take into account detailed and often subtle life-historical, cultural, sociopolitical and imaginary aspects, such as the different kinds of "others" at work in religious worldviews and practices. We consider that these aspects are expressed in the material on which our analysis is grounded. Furthermore,

> [...] agency should be approached as a fragile and multifaceted potential in its various transitive moments of empowerment, but also in those of lack, suffering, and frailty. Detecting and describing such moments of strength or frailty is important in order to discern, first, how different boundaries are crossed, and by that, made visible, and, secondly, what kinds of actors can be seen at work at these borderlines, either as resources or as counter-resources. (Utriainen *et al.* 2012, 202)

Therefore, we will look for expressions of experiences of moments of frailty and strength in the narratives. This is not the only dyad of complementary meanings that we will encounter: the stories told literally twist and turn around choice and destiny as well. The findings will be interpreted step by step in terms of their significance for the attribution of agency and subsequently discussed in a broader framework of agency, responsibility and performative means.

Coming to Yoga

Let us begin with a moment of frailty by looking at two stories of being introduced to yoga. Similar to conversion narratives (see e.g., Rambo, 1993 or Stromberg 1993) "choice" and "destiny" are often interwoven in the stories that the informants shared with Måns Broo. The following two accounts of "John" and "Mary" (IF mgt 2010-033 and IF mgt 2011-109) are not necessarily typical, but nonetheless they serve as interesting examples that empirically exemplify the theoretical and methodological approach discussed above.

John is the main teacher at one of the largest yoga schools in Turku. He is a single man in his late thirties, who daily spends about one and a half hours on his own yoga practice, in addition to his teaching. John began his story of how he came to yoga by mentioning that he had had a somewhat troubled childhood, where he had been a witness to domestic violence. To this he attributed what he called "his restless mind and tendency to depression." But all of a sudden, in one of the moments when John felt troubled and without any obvious reason, his grandmother gave him a book on spiritual topics. Immediately following this fateful encounter (John would eventually meet the author of that particular book in connection with another important life change), he rather surprisingly asserted his own personal agency. Seemingly independently of his grandmother or any other identifiable external agent, he took up martial arts, became interested in Taoism and made a conscious study of the subject. At around thirty years of age, he says he entered into what he called a "searching phase."

> J: In a way I became a believer, not in any particular faith or religion, but I started believing in a higher power, even though I never joined any group; rather, I quit the [Evangelical Lutheran] Church.
>
> MB: How did this belief come about?
>
> J: Not all at once, but suddenly—not over a very long time—all these books that I had been reading on spirituality started to make even more sense. And somehow, over some time I just started to feel that I needed a faith in some higher power, one that I did not want to define by some particular name.
>
> MB: So there was no particular outer reason?
>
> J: No, not really. At that time I took up all kinds of practices in earnest; I tried out some "New Age" stuff and at some point this Ashtanga yoga as well. By then I had already tried all kinds of things and had no dramatic expectations. I ended up in my first yoga course because a friend of mine wanted to go, but he didn't want to go alone, so he asked me along. As it turned out, he never went, since he left to study somewhere else, but I went as I had already signed up.
>
> (IF mgt 2010-033)

What we find here is an interesting combination of choice and destiny, which alternate and sometimes even occur at the same time. John is first given a book by his grandmother, and then he reports to have continued his self-education by reading spiritual books as part of a "searching phase." This can be understood as a romantic, individualist quest for the truth, in which his own agentic independence was highlighted. Then, all of a sudden, an understanding came to him, and he became a believer "in a way." Note John's wording: *I started to feel that I needed a faith in some higher power*. John does not become a believer, or even start to become one—he merely *starts* to *feel* that he *needs* a very vaguely defined faith. John now questions and underemphasizes his own agency, but this is partly for rhetorical reasons—it is typical of the kind of language that he uses. John is the dedicated, hard-working leader of one of the largest yoga schools in Turku, but while acknowledging that the school is totally dependent on him, he makes it sound like he became its leader quite accidentally.

This interweaving of choice and destiny is a recurring thread in John's narrative. Consider the following example:

> Then, somehow, when I had been practicing three years, I became a teacher when I was asked to become one and that of course somehow changed the way I looked at yoga. It became a bigger, an even bigger part of my life, and at this point it was already more difficult, I mean, it was something that it wasn't so easy to escape from anymore! (Laughter.)
>
> (IF mgt 2010-033)

While John laughs at his statement that yoga "wasn't so easy to escape from anymore," he again considerably underplays his own agency. He became a teacher when other agents pushed him in that direction, and his view of yoga changed by simply being a teacher, that is, through the agency of teaching yoga itself. Investing yoga practice with independent agency is common in yoga circles, as Måns Broo has shown elsewhere (2012).

Another example involves Mary, a woman in her early thirties, who is engaged in higher academic studies while also pursuing a teacher's training course at one of the smaller yoga schools in Turku. Her own practice takes around an hour and a half daily, but unlike John, so far she only teaches a couple of groups a week. Much like John, Mary emphasizes destiny as a central aspect of her coming to yoga. She retells a chance meeting with a professor who sang the praises of a particular type of yoga at a conference dinner. She then researched that type of yoga on the internet and eventually took it up. Shortly afterwards, she found that her school sometimes offers intensive practices early on Sunday mornings. That practice sounded a bit scary, with its special rules and regulations, but she was intrigued. She talked with a teacher and asked about the following Sunday morning, but he said that there would be no practice then. But then:

> All of a sudden he called me. Yes, there would be sadhana [practice] that morning the next day. He called at about ten at night and said, "It will be held after all," and that he had remembered wrongly. "It will be held, so if you want to go, go there tomorrow morning." So I asked him, "How did you find my number?," since I knew my name is so ordinary, since there are so many with the same name in Turku. And he said that he called directory assistance and, yes, they gave him eighteen numbers,

but he intuitively just picked one, and it was the right one. I kind of felt, "Wow, that yoga teacher certainly has great intuition!"

(IF mgt 2011-109)

Mary indeed went there the next day, only to find herself alone with the school's main teacher. After practicing, they sat and spoke for many hours, and the teacher convinced her to join their teacher-training programme. "*So this is my little* Autobiography of a Yogi, *she said, "full of such funny coincidences."* These are coincidences, perhaps, but there was also a concerted effort by external agents for Mary to first engage (the professor) with this particular brand of yoga and then deepen (the teacher) her involvement, rather similar to the missionary activities of various faith groups. In fact, in common with many conversion narratives, Mary externalizes her own agency almost completely. In her narrative, she describes her first months of practice at the school rather briefly, but focuses on the more interesting and exciting events of entering a more committed level of practice. Of course, understating one's own effort is a typically feminine rhetoric in Finland as well, but Mary's account is nevertheless striking.

When asked whether she believed that her interest in yoga stemmed from a previous life, Mary said that she does not think of it like that, but that she can pinpoint her first connection to Eastern spirituality to her childhood.

> As a child and young girl, I had a very poor relationship with my mother. Instead I had kind of a surrogate mother, a family friend, with whom I was very close. And while it is true that she didn't practice yoga, she spoke about earlier lives and reincarnation, and she offered me a—what should I say—a completely new perspective, a spiritual perspective. I believe it came through her. And I remember her giving me—yes, she gave me a Bhagavad Gita or something once. [...] And when I chanced to get that yoga book in my hand, this is what happened!
>
> (IF mgt 2011-109)

Just as in John's case, Mary's initial interest in yoga is described as having been stimulated by a significant external party; thus, she minimizes her own agency again. While this person did not directly introduce Mary to yoga, she reports that her coming to yoga was a direct result of the "new perspective" that she received from her and the spiritual book she was given. While John intermingles choice, fate and destiny in his narrative by alternating between independent agentic action and the influence of external agents, Mary consistently remains silent about her own efforts. This may partially be explained by feminine habitus, but it also speaks to the particularity of her experience, that is, of being made the object of the concerted efforts of several external agents. In some sense, then, according to her, Mary's path to yoga was her fate.

But what are "fate" and "destiny" here? When another informant was asked whether he believed in destiny, he gave the following answer:

> We have gathered all kinds of experiences during this life, and when we then make different choices, bigger or smaller, our decision may be an outcome of these earlier experiences. We have gathered a kind of wisdom that we act according to. So, for example, I believe that if we were born again in the same family as now and at the same time, we would relive our lives in the same way. But were we to be born again in the same place with the wisdom we now have, we would of course live our lives differently. So one thing leads to the other, and I don't think there really are wrong choices. If someone makes a poor choice and it takes him a long time to reach his goal, it just means he didn't have the necessary experience needed for a faster path. But when he has once taken the round-about, the next time he can make the other choice. In a way, you choose according to your experience. So in this sense, I am inclined to believe in destiny.
>
> (IF mgt 2011-025)

This statement reflects a rather rigid view of fate or destiny. According to this informant, life is predestined or at least predictable, because, according to him, if we were to be born again in the same circumstances, and at the same time in history, we would relive our lives in just the same way. Since our choices are dependent on our experiences, against this background the term "wrong choice" is really an oxymoron.

Among most yoga practitioners, fate and destiny seem to play an important role alongside modernity's risk-calculating ethos and emphasis on personal responsibility. In one sense, this is not at all surprising. In all societies and throughout history, people have tried to negotiate a path between fate and their own potential for agency. And what is more human than looking around and realizing how utterly entangled we are in our bodies, our pasts and the expectations placed on us by society? In spite of this, we live our lives in the desperate hope that the choices we make will make a difference. In short, most people experience situations where they are in control and situations where they are out of control. However, it is particularly worth emphasizing in regard to our examples that in our late modern—or, if you will, post-secular society—the concept of "fate" remains or again becomes an important factor in negotiating agency. This can also be observed with other contemporary spiritual practices. If agency, as we have argued, is to be understood as a participatory and complex composition, that is, as a matrix of often semi-invisible factors in temporal interplay with one another, then "fate" or "destiny" is one possible articulation of those factors, which are not clearly understood or recognized in detail.

Furthermore, in life-history accounts, our examples show that fate fulfils two other, equally important functions. First, attributing an important part of one's major life events to fate can be seen as a rhetorical device that appears to modestly downplay one's own merits, but at the same time it often places greater emphasis on them, without seeming to involve any boasting. After all, John is quite aware that the interviewer knows him to be a successful and active man who carefully navigates different worlds, including academia, music and yoga. In addition to these, he is also able to arrange his life in such a way that he can spend two months in India every year. Speaking as if he has just been passively following fate's twists and turns all along his journey, he comes across as a humble, modest guy. On the one hand, this is very much in keeping with Finnish cultural norms; on the other, John's manner of talking about his own path to yoga and way of investing yoga with independent agency are an integral part of yogic discourse (see e.g., Horton and Harvey 2012).

Yoga Practice as an Independent Agent

All the interviewees in the study regard what they call "the philosophy of yoga" to be important to their ongoing yogic transformation. What this philosophy actually comprises was described in many various ways. Everyone reported having read or at least having tried to read Patañjali's classic *Yoga Sutra* (fourth century CE), but more important were modern texts, such as those by Ken Wilber (IF mgt 2010-033), Eckhart Tolle or Jon Kabat-Zinn (IF mgt 2011-025). However, much more central than the study of related literature, which seems in several cases to have been more or less incidental, was the physical practice itself. Sarah Strauss (2005, 10) articulates a viewpoint held by many of the informants when she calls yoga "a form of embodied knowledge," which no amount of reading can impart. It is no coincidence that the most common question when two yogis meet is "how has your practice been?," rather than "how do you do?" This emphasizes on the one hand the primacy of personal experience in yoga and, on the other hand, that yoga is not only seen as a means to achieve some specific end, but as important identity capital in itself, to use the term of the social psychologists James Côte and Charles Levine (2002).

While the corporeal, quotidian nature of this practice is evident in the interviews—many people spoke of injuries (IF mgt 2010-033) or becoming bored or uninspired at times (IF mgt 2011-025)—it was at the same time seen to be somehow sacred, as if transcending ordinary life. The informants deemed their practice to be a source of strength for body and mind (IF mgt 2011-024); a way to help deal with anxiety (IF mgt 2011-096), stress (IF mgt 2011-109) and sleeplessness (IF mgt 2011-108); giving new perspectives on life (IF mgt 2011-025, IF mgt 2011-107), increased courage (IF mgt 2011-108), and flexibility in dealing with all kinds of people (IF mgt 2011-046); and leading to a sense of unity with all of creation (IF mgt 2010-033) or "a higher whole" (IF mgt 2011-049).

Yoga practice was also perceived as strengthening and helping one to cope with life's eventualities. As Utriainen *et al.* (2012, 207) have written, Anthony Giddens maintains that "destiny"—or, rather, "fate"—has lost much of its hold in modernity. In traditional societies, fate, in the sense of *fortuna*, a preordained course of events, meant that in an important sense the future was not in the hands of humans but in the hands of the gods. Today people want to control their futures, not least because they are held accountable for their life decisions. Post-traditional societies are thus increasingly characterized by a growing awareness of many kinds of risks, and, accordingly, by elaborate risk calculations and risk-management efforts at both social and individual levels. Both groups and individuals aim at what Giddens calls a "colonization of the future" by various political, scientific, and technological means. Important examples of these means include economic calculation and medical technology. People today are invited to take advice and make assessments that help them rationally navigate a risk society and control—or at least minimize—known risks. It is through preparing themselves against eventualities that people provide themselves with futures that are seen as secure. It becomes abundantly clear from the above that yoga is part of such preparation.

Freedom and Control

Among the benefits reported to come from yoga, freedom is emphasized quite often. One informant felt that yoga gave her freedom from competitiveness, at least in the beginning:

> I felt that within dance there was just so much competitiveness, it was so hard and visible. Everybody was always speaking about who is better or worse than someone else, who is more interesting or more artistic. I thought that I would lose this competitiveness completely in yoga, and in the beginning it really was like that. But now there are more schools, and while there is no direct competition between them, everyone has their own style, and to me it is a pity that there is no cooperation. Everyone just does their own thing. Perhaps they don't even know what the others are doing. They are not even interested. Whenever a new school opens, I like to visit it and see what the place looks like, who the teachers are, what kind of students they have and all. But nobody ever visits me. (IF mgt 2011-024)

In other words, this practitioner reported appreciation for the freedom that yoga gave her from the restraints that she experienced in dancing class; that is, the joy she got out of dance was reduced by what she perceived as negative competition. Instead of reacting against this attitude, she (at least partially) turned away from dance. Later in the interview, she expressed disappointment at discovering some competition within yoga as well, between different yoga schools. She did take action, though with little success. Yoga thus first enabled this practitioner to avoid something perceived as negative (competitiveness) and, second, it prepared her to deal with it when it eventually reappeared. In that sense, yoga seems to have enhanced her personal freedom "negatively" and "positively" at the same time, allowing her to avoid a specific context by offering an alternative and also empowering her to deal with similar challenges within the new context, instead of letting them become restrictive for her again.

Furthermore, the changes brought about by yoga are sometimes explicitly claimed to help increase the independent agency of the individual. One of the interviewees explained that her husband very much dislikes her involvement in yoga. After skirting the issue a while, she said:

> – But yes, of course it is insulting to so very often be put down when this [yoga] is such a big thing for me, for my view on life. On the other hand, perhaps this is connected with something larger… I have changed so much during the last few years. I think he links these scary changes with yoga. "She doesn't follow the rules anymore."
>
> – I just have to ask: what kind of changes?
>
> – Well, that is kind of personal… All right, I have been rather kept down. No longer [laughter]! I have started recreating my life in some ways. It's connected, for example, with my leaving off alcohol. From there, these important changes in my life began.
>
> – Was it connected with yoga or a reaction to something else?
>
> – A reaction to something else. Yoga was also there, but it was an important part of my life already before this. But yes, it has been one big helping factor.
>
> (IF mgt 2011-096)

While the interviewee does not agree with her husband in placing yoga at the centre of the changes in her life and marital relations, it is nevertheless portrayed here as special in the sense of possessing agency of its own, as a "big helping factor" in furthering her own agency. Once again, personal and external agency are intertwined.

The Relational Dynamics of Enchantment and Sacralization

While it is not a major topic in the interviews, some reported their yoga practice as giving rise to various out-of-the-ordinary experiences, at least partially outside the control of the agentic personality. One person said:

> I have experienced this kind of spontaneous crying. All of a sudden these tears just came, and you don't know when you started crying or why. Something is happening in the body, but it is also very difficult to understand. It is a very good feeling, some kind of release in the body, but at the same time it is also a scary feeling: something happened in my head, in my emotions. It is scary but it also shows you that something is happening. (IF mgt 2011-024)

The tears here may be taken as an indicator of losing or giving up control, of letting go of self-restraint. We can again draw on Giddens to contrast the multi-skilled individual agent and yoga as leading to experiences which are—at some point—out of one's personal control. Another interviewee spoke at length about a wonderful experience that she had had in connection to yoga several years back, at a difficult time in her life, after a busy day:

> I did my yoga practice in the evening, and suddenly so many physical locks started opening up, and more so mental locks. I felt like crying — it was so powerful. I didn't know what it was. I had read a lot of yoga literature, but yoga was more like a hobby for me. But I guess I had just been searching so much. Now I got some answers, but so quickly and so much that I couldn't understand what it was all about. Even now I don't know what it really was, but my consciousness was flooded with answers to the questions that I had been thinking about for years, and with such power and force that I couldn't sleep for like four nights, but just wrote down everything. I was all kind of speeded up, but I don't feel that I was in any kind of psychosis or the like, for I was 100% present. I just saw and experienced everything in a really open way. When I saw people, I saw them all differently — I felt that I am you and you are me. The feeling was completely inconceivable and it lasted about a week.
> (IF mgt 2011-108)

While the experience itself faded, the informant claims that it relieved a depression that she had battled for years and that it was instrumental in her becoming a yoga teacher (IF mgt 2011-108). Again, actively doing yoga led to the practice having a dramatic effect on the practitioner.

Another person spoke about several so-called out-of-body experiences in connection with intensive yogic practice:

> Once I was awoken by the sensation of some kind of energy rising up from the root of the spine. It felt warm and I did nothing. I was all

> relaxed, and all by itself it started to straighten up my back, my back was straightened up. My body was all numb so that I could not do anything, like when leaving the body: first you have to start to move a little before you get back, back into the body. In the experience I was also a bit cautious, I wanted to get back into the body, and in five or ten seconds the experience was over. I didn't dare go along with it.
>
> (IF mgt 2011-025)

Contrary to the experience of the previous person, this informant explicitly called his experiences "scary":

> My first out-of-body experience was when I was dreaming about some kind of a snake. I was in the water and a poor swimmer, and the snake was gaining on me. And then from being frightened, I went into this kind of out-of-body experience. So these [experiences] were not always that positive! (IF mgt 2011-025)

Out-of-body experiences are thus perceived ambiguously, but in both cases they are linked to a loss of control, that is, to the practice itself taking over agentic control. Yoga is not simply something that the practitioner does; it is also unique in the sense of having agency of its own.

Discussion and Conclusion

We began this article by proposing that agency, including the very act of speech, helps to shape social structure. What can we then learn from the narratives shared above? The most obvious conclusion concerns the externalization of agency. Only rarely do the practitioners interviewed here articulate having made a conscious decision. Rather, both taking up yoga and having powerful experiences in yoga practice seem to depend on external actors, be they human (such as teachers or important others) or nonhuman (the practice itself). But what does that mean and what does it tell about the life reality of our informants?

If we take a closer look at the prevailing conceptualization of personhood in this material, we see that in places it differs from many common modern social norms. Usually the individual is considered to be the master of his own destiny, while external authority or supportive external agents are rarely taken into account. From the point of view of the individual subject, this may easily be a situation of over-complexity, which Niklas Luhmann (2000) has diagnosed as typical of modernity, where external authority may be present but often invisible.

There are problems, of course, with the latter ontological conceptualization of personhood (the presence of an invisible, external authority), which may well indicate need on the part of our interviewees. It places sole responsibility for the individual's success or failure on his or her own shoulders, and thus it may easily be perceived as overwhelming. It further ignores institutional or structural forces that restrain the potential to exercise agency, evoking the picture of an almost unrestrained capacity to act—and ascription of failure to the principal actor alone. Under the influence of ideas from the European Enlightenment, persons subscribing to such an understanding of personhood often further incorporate values like "rationality" and assumptions of free will, thus also creating an expectation for the individual to be a relatively autonomous source of agency, concomitant with full responsibility for their actions and life choices, as well as partly for things that happen to them.

We meet almost the opposite understanding of the human persona (and indeed agency) when we examine Latour's subject and the Latourian analytical—or, even better, ontological—perspective: here there is little, if anything, beyond the sum of external influences. Such conceptualizations of agency have been severely criticized by political groups (see Barth, 2006), while some research traditions on human agency have generally viewed them critically for similar reasons: they seem to underemphasize the need and the potential for humans to take responsibility for their actions (see Cerulo 2009, 532–533). Thus, discussing "agency" always has an ideological side, since the very basic assumptions of to whom and to what extent agency and its subsequent effects can be ascribed are seemingly axiomatic. They matter in terms of the evaluation and ascription of success and failure, or, on a broader level, even demands on political participation towards the individual or remuneration of damages. The way in which agency and influence are articulated by yoga practitioners—in many cases as forces from outside that have guided or even pushed them—resembles discourses within contemporary spirituality, but also the basic assumptions of Latour's ontology. While subject-centred views currently seem to be relatively dominant and do to some extent constitute the basic assumptions underlying social scientific research, they may easily leave other conceptualizations of "agency" invisible to the researcher. Latour's Actor Network Theory (ANT) may be criticized in many respects, but it offers a valuable tool to describe non-subject-centred ascriptions of agency, as it has largely anticipated a similar conceptualization of the subject (i.e., "agency" and external influences).

However, none of the interviewees went so far as to discount personal agency altogether. Instead they seemed to try to negotiate a middle way. John and the other interviewees did not consider themselves as devoid of any agentic capacity. Borrowing Ahearn's phrase, we could call their rhetoric negotiation of agency a participatory composition, where many kinds of actors are given their own place—or, phrased differently, where different modes and sources of agency are described as interwoven. This is something we may find in other forms of contemporary spirituality as well, within narratives that depict feelings of lacking something and being in need of spiritual growth in order to be a "more complete person," to be healthy and to cope with one's personal life. The informants of another study similarly tended to describe their spiritual practice as being open to exactly such kinds of influences—books, spiritual consultants or practices—that connected them to the "bigger whole" while they were experimenting with methods (practices) to reach their aims (Königstedt 2012, 185, 187, 189). Significant here is the recognition and use of an individual's own capacity to act, when practices are changed if they seem not to provide the effect aimed at. From this perspective, the participatory composition of agency we have found here can be considered as one relatively widespread aspect of contemporary spiritual worldviews.

Such a negotiation between different sources of agency is not unique for Finnish yoga practitioners. Downplaying one's own success may, however, be considered a common Finnish trope, especially among women, which makes it also descriptive of the form of Finnish cultural habits within the social structure. "Yes, be successful, but remain modest, since you were helped all along the way" seems to sum it up. What we have here, then, is also a core element of authenticity within Finnish life histories. That such a trope might be understood differently in a different cultural setting goes without saying, and it may, for example, explain differences in the extent to which it is articulated. In terms of contemporary spirituality and religiosity, however, what is essential is that the attribution of agency forms a combination of one's own decisions and external influences. External influence may be seen here as the ideal type for religio-spiritual narratives of action, while the active subject may remain predominant in secular narratives.

Following this, the next question would be: since we find composite agency as prevalent in this material, who and what are these external agents and what exactly are they doing when the subject reports being externally guided? First, as has been shown here, relevant actors may be relatives, books that mention yoga, or specific teachers, which are spontaneously and sometimes surprisingly encountered. In short, they may be incidents that have led the practitioner to the practice itself. These encounters are, as we have seen, often ascribed to "fate" or an inner inexplicable drive, but rarely to one's own conscious decisions.

Secondly, the yoga practice itself can be seen as a "mediator" (Latour, 2005, 46–47) between two different states of consciousness: between all yoga practitioners on a social level as well as between everyday experiences and experiences of a diffuse higher power, while the practitioner herself or himself is rarely emphasized. In the interviews, we found narratives of being healed, strengthened or "released," sometimes with regard to perfectly quotidian matters, but also in more dramatic contexts. Such experiences may be seen as joyful or scary, but even in the latter case they are not understood as being harmful but rather demanding a different type of processing. The emphasis here is on frailty and a loss of control.

This emphasis on loss of control is paradoxical, considering, thirdly, the attention to discipline and controlled practice that the informants also gave in the interviews. But it is also supported by "freedom" being a central theme in all the narratives, whether it be understood socially or as an experience during the practice itself. Perhaps ironically, this "freedom" is seldom described in positive terms—that is, as the freedom to do what one wants—but rather as a negative freedom of being released from the restraints of one's body, from visible or invisible links to the social world, and sometimes as being overwhelmed by a higher, unspecified but benevolent power. This freedom can also be extended in various directions. Being free from one's own body, for instance, can also be understood as being free from the responsibility-laden self, which is perceived as restraining one's "real self." Freedom, then, is not the capacity to do what one wants, but to be in the position of not having to do anything. Whether such a negative view of freedom should be linked to the metaphysics of traditional Indian yogic worldviews is beside the point here; what is important is its presence. Yoga may be a transnational cultural product (Strauss 2005, 9), but that does not mean that it lacks local flavour in its individual and localized forms. To the contrary, that may be one of the reasons for the popularity of yoga transnationally.

The notion of "freedom," described and understood as one aim of yoga practitioners to be reached through the practice, is also interestingly connected with the miraculous encounters that led to the practice, resulting in a description of a unique and individual way of salvation. It can therefore be understood as containing a critique of the conception of the responsibility-laden self, opposed to narratives that describe factual empirical experiences of other sources of agency—or, differently put, an alternative ontology. But instead of simply replacing the common view of individual agency by this other understanding, we find a construction of composite agency which combines both. While the existence of a consciously deciding individual is not at all denied, the responsibility—and accordingly also the burden—of this individual becomes limited through references to external agents. While it is not possible to evaluate here if this in fact alters the common conceptualization of agency in general, it should be recognized that those who hold this belief do not seclude themselves socially but communicate their views.

Having said this, we need to bring attention once more to the role of narrative performance. The reference to fate, often used as describing a factor that influenced "coming to yoga," must not solely be understood as an expression of an alternative ontology revealing the crucial needs of the interviewees. Instead, in the Finnish case, it should also be seen as a cultural practice, fulfilling an outside demand for individual modesty and authenticity on the one hand. On the other, it is also genuinely attractive in the sense of eliciting the listener's interest: fate simply makes for good storytelling as a plausible narrative pattern. How capturing and exciting can a story be that is told only chronologically? Rather, it is fortuitous encounters with strange books and even stranger professors, teachers appearing and disappearing from one's life at critical situations, and intuitively found phone numbers that bring life, myth and magic to stories. And without magic the storyteller might just as well remain silent.

References

Ahearn, L. M. 2001. "Language and Agency." *Annual Review of Anthropology* 30(9): 109–137.

Barth, C. 2006. *Über alles in der Welt – Esoterik und Leitkultur. Eine Einführung in die Kritik irrationaler Welterklärungen*. Aschaffenburg: Alibri Verlag.

Broo, M. 2012. "Yoga Practices as Identity Capital: Preliminary Notes from Turku, Finland." In *Post-secular Religious Practices*, edited by T. Ahlbäck and B. Dahla, 24–34. Scripta Instituti Donneriani Aboensis XXII. Åbo/Turku: The Donner Institute for Research in Religious and Cultural History.

Broo, M., M. Moberg, T. Ramstedt and T. Utriainen. 2015. "Diversification, Mainstreaming, Commercialization, and Domestication—New Religious Movements and Trends in Finland." In *Handbook of New Nordic Religions*, edited by J. R. Lewis and I. Bårdsen Tollefsen, 141–156. Leiden: Brill.

Cerulo, K. A. 2009. "Nonhumans in Social Interaction." *Annual Review of Sociology* 35: 531–552.

Côté, J. E. and C. G. Levine. 2002. *Identity Formation, Agency and Culture. A Social Psychological Synthesis*. London: Psychology Press.

Horton, C. and R. Harvey. 2012. *21st Century Yoga: Culture, Politics and Practice*. Chicago, IL: Cleio Books.

Kohrs-Campbell, K. 2005. "Agency: Promiscuous and Protean." *Communication and Critical/Cultural Studies* 2: 1–19.

Königstedt, C. 2012. "Religio-spiritual Strategies of Self-help and Empowerment in Everyday Life. Selected Cases of Spirituality in Germany." In *Post-Secular Religious Practices*, edited by T. Ahlbeck and B. Dahla. 178–200. Scripta

Instituti Donneriani Aboensis XXII. Åbo/Turku: The Donner Institute for Research in Religious and Cultural History.

———. 2008. *Individualisierte Religiosität und der Einfluss auf die praktische Lebensführung am Beispiel des "New Age"- Komplex.* Magisterarbeit: Universität Göttingen.

Latour, B. 2005. *Reassembling the Social: An Introduction to Actor-Network-Theory.* Oxford: Oxford University Press.

Luhmann, N. 2000 [1968]. *Vertrauen. Ein Mechanismus der Reduktion sozialer Komplexität.* 4th ed. Stuttgart: UTB, Lucius&Lucius.

Rambo, L. 1993. *Understanding Religious Conversion.* New Haven, CT: Yale University Press.

Strauss, S. 2005. *Positioning Yoga. Balancing Acts across Cultures.* Oxford: Berg.

Stromberg, P. S. 1993. *Language and Self-transformation. A Study of the Christian Conversion Narrative.* Cambridge: Cambridge University Press.

Utriainen, T., T. Hovi and M. Broo. 2012. "Combining Choice and Destiny: Identity and Agency within Post-Secular Well-Being Practices." In *Post-Secular Society,* edited by P. Nynäs, M. Lassander and T. Utriainen, 187–216. New Brunswick, NJ: Transaction Publishers.

Other sources

Måns Broo & Christiane Königstedt:

Interviews by Måns Broo, kept in the Cultura archive at Åbo Akademi University.

IF mgt 2010-033

IF mgt 2011-024

IF mgt 2011-025

IF mgt 2011-046

IF mgt 2011-049

IF mgt 2011-096

IF mgt 2011-107

IF mgt 2011-108

IF mgt 2011-109

About the Authors

Måns Broo Måns Broo works as University Researcher in Comparative Religion at Åbo Akademi University. His publications include critically acclaimed translations of Sanskrit texts into Swedish and Finnish. At present, his research interests focus on yoga, both in its classical and modern forms, as well as on modern Hinduism and ritual studies.

Christiane Königstedt has worked and taught as a research assistant at the University of Münster (Germany) and holds a Ph.D. from Leipzig University (Germany), which she was awarded for her thesis on possible reasons for the French secularists' activities against contemporary non-traditional forms of religion. Currently she is working on a new project on shifting boundaries between the religious and the secular and has published articles about contemporary spirituality, its influence on individual life conduct and New Religious Movements in relation to secular societies.

— 5 —

Mastery and Modernity: Control Issues in the Disenchantment Tale

LINDA ANNUNEN AND PEIK INGMAN

The general aim of this chapter is to distinguish between two ways of aligning oneself in relation to unpredictability. This distinction allows us to nuance the significance of modern stances on mastery and control for how we understand the disenchantment tale. One way represents the ("official") stance of disenchanted moderns (religious or not), while the other appreciates the potentially empowering effects of surrendering to enchantment without thereby necessarily denying the risks involved. We will argue the following: 1) reducing life to engaging only in predictable affairs and opting for reliance over trust is impoverishing and ignores the need to attend to concerns regarding the precariousness of individuals' capacity to trust; 2) one can engage in enchantment without denying that it may be risky; and 3) as long as enchantment is retrospectively translated into calculation (trust is retrospectively translated into reliance), the negative effects of unpredictable relational dynamics *seemingly* remain the effects of "letting go" (as opposed to the more complex effects of what happened afterwards, that is, the unpredictable but productive effects of compositions). We conclude by noting that another form of mastery is conceivable. It is not a mastery of "letting go," but a mastery of engaging *well* with those things one co-composes, having let go (of certainty).

Keywords: control, trust, reliance, composition, guilt, blame

This chapter is the outcome of a speculative collaboration between the authors. It began through a mutual fascination with issues concerning control and trance states. As we developed the arguments, however, the central issue we found ourselves debating and at times disagreeing on concerned Bruno Latour's conception of mastery. We agreed that it is a central issue in making sense of modernity and elaborating what is at stake in enchantment (and disenchantment). However, Annunen expressed concerns over a simplistic generalization, whereby the issues would be polarised in terms of, on the one hand, either "having control" and "being controlled," and on the other hand, "letting go." Hence, what follows is to a large extent an effort to elaborate on the distinction between control as mastery, in the sense that Latour uses the term, and other forms of control, specifically in terms of what the implications might be for our understanding of the notion of enchantment and its relevance for modernity.

We began by exploring instances where enchantment, in the sense of "being enchanted," appears to involve actively allowing oneself to be affected. We wanted to argue that this allowing should be understood as resisting an impulse to control the course of events, so as to allow for surprising developments. Such restraint can be understood as resisting the urge to try to master something. However, Annunen challenged this description by noting that restraint could be called another *form* of mastery, not least because it can be cultivated. As we entertained this notion, two theoretically distinct issues emerged that seem crucial for making sense of the concerns involved. These two issues were: 1) enchantment understood in terms of liberation ("letting go") from calculation and the need to predict, and 2) enchantment understood in terms of engaging in a productive but unpredictable relational process of composition.[1]

We did not begin by thinking in terms of there being two forms of mastery (for instance, "the mastery of the West" and "the mastery of the East"). Indeed, we tried to avoid both Orientalism and Occidentalism. The reason for sometimes using somewhat simplistic frames here is to facilitate comparison and contrast. Yet the aim of the chapter is not in itself to compare and contrast, as much as to nuance what such contrasting brings to light. By contrasting the two forms, we endeavour to clarify the centrality of these distinctions for understanding the significance of the disenchantment tale for modernity.

The Enlightenment involved a liberation narrative that gave enchantment a bad name. This is because the issue was simplistically framed as a zero-sum game. Either you *have* control or something controls you.

---

1. The particular significance and implications of "productive" will be clarified as we go on.

In more recent times, we have witnessed other liberation narratives, such as those entertained within the hippie counter-culture movement beginning in the 1960s. Liberation was again largely framed in terms of negative freedom: freedom *from* conformity. For many and for various reasons, Charles Manson came to represent a "warning example" of the dangers of "letting go," which was thus apparently confirmed as a kind of slippery slope to chaos. Our point is that this discussion, whether one should "let go" or not, tends to ignore—to put it somewhat crudely—what happens *after* one "lets go." Once this neglect is understood and appreciated, however, the concerns appear in a different light. The "issue" of enchantment actually seems to revolve around the trustworthiness and manageability of that which one surrenders to when "letting go." Thus, the crucial questions are: 1) what is it that one is letting go *to*, and 2) what can be done if surrendering leads to a negative end? The answers to these questions point to at least two quite different conceptions of mastery.

The general aim of this chapter is to distinguish between two ways of aligning oneself in relation to unpredictability. One represents the ("official") stance of disenchanted moderns (religious or not), while the other appreciates the potentially empowering effects of surrendering to enchantment without thereby necessarily denying the risks involved. In order to facilitate a meaningful comparison, we first need to establish the symmetry between these two forms. Establishing symmetry allows us to be as curious about modernist "inanimism" (Latour 2010a, 483) as we are about non-modern animism. We will employ Latour's term "composition" (2010a) to afford ourselves a non-modern perspective on modernity.

Actor-Network Theory: The Sociology of Translation

In 1986, the sociologist Michel Callon published a highly influential, ground-breaking article on the domestication of scallops. It was ground-breaking not because of widespread interdisciplinary interest in the domestication of scallops, but because the article managed to succinctly demonstrate the practical implications and benefits of combining three central principles which would become the hallmarks of what Callon called a sociology of translation, also known as actor-network theory (ANT): "agnosticism (impartiality between actors engaged in controversy), generalised symmetry (the commitment to explain conflicting viewpoints in the same terms) and free association (the abandonment of all a priori distinctions between the natural and the social)"(Callon 1986, 196). In 2005, Bruno Latour provided a more systematic textbook definition (2005), where above all he emphasized the point that "the social" is not a distinct thing that we can differentiate from the non-social, but that it should be understood only as an adjective or an adverb pertaining to circulation. When we want to look closer at something "social," we would then look at *how* something (goods, values, affects, concepts, skills, and so forth) circulates among relevant participants, rather than attending to a particular domain that is conceived of as distinct from other domains, such as nature, culture or science.

The reason why this was referred to as the sociology of translation is that the focus was shifted onto the formative effects of circulation. As "something" circulates from one point to another in a network, it more or less subtly changes along the way. ANT calls this change "translation," which, although at times rather subtle, refers to the tension between sameness and difference. As this "something" (referred to here in vague terms not in order to mystify it, but in order not to predefine what domain it belongs in and what it can do) travels in networks—as it circulates—it both changes yet retains some of its earlier attributes. This is one aspect of it. The other aspect is that this "something" also acts as an affordance to those between and through whom it circulates. Such a focus on circulation allows us to recognize individuals—actors—as situated participants in an ongoing process of composing a social that circulates. It allows us to understand an actor as (at least potentially) concerned about her relational ability to translate *well* this heterogeneous social which circulates through her. In turn, this challenges us as researchers to find out what "well" means in particular circumstances and to ask what kinds of concerns are involved in people's assessments of how "well" they manage[2] their relations. As we will see, what differentiates the two forms of mastery is precisely their stance on and reasoning around what is at stake in translating *well*.

Not a Zero-Sum Game

Throughout the chapter, we deliberately shift the focus away from a distinction between religion and secularity, as well as religion and science, onto situated concerns about relative control. This is in line with the principle of generalized symmetry, in the spirit of which Latour has undertaken what he refers to as the anthropology of the Moderns. Moderns, as Latour describes them, largely manage their anxiety over having limited control by believing in mastery. This belief in mastery involves

---

2. Here "manage" includes strategies such as delegating or surrendering control to others. It may therefore include stances such as "accepting one's fate," as well as eschewing dependent relationships. Our aim is not to presume how people are concerned about their relationships, only to better understand different ways of assessing what is at stake in being in relation.

a tendency to understand agency in terms of a zero-sum game. Latour describes it as a kind of "double-entry accounting" where

> whatever came from the outside was *deducted* from the total sum of action allotted to the agents "inside." With that type of balance sheet, the more threads you added in order to *make you act* from the outside, the *less you yourself* acted: the conclusion of this accounting procedure was inescapable. And if you wished, for some moral or political reason, to save the actor's intention, initiative, and creativity, the only way left was to increase the total sum of action coming from the inside by *cutting some of the threads*, thus denying the role of what is now seen as so many "bondages," "external constraints," "limits to freedom," etc. Either you were a free subject or you lived in abject subjection.
>
> (Latour 2005, 215)

In *On the Modern Cult of the Factish Gods* (2010b), Latour provides a caricature of Moderns in the form of a comic strip. A man goes from imagining himself as self-assuredly smoking a cigarette to considering if the cigarette is not in fact smoking him. His point is that this is how Moderns (mis)understand fetishism. Gods are either our making (we "smoke" them) or they are allowed to become our masters (they "smoke" us), which is why they must be destroyed if we are to be "free." Latour has argued that ANT allows us to explore an individual's agency by paying attention to the character and quality of her attachments. As opposed to mastering or being mastered, attachments allow for other perspectives, ones where "to be attached is to hold and to be held" (2005a, 217) simultaneously. This entails an ontological ambiguity concerning causality. Smoking a cigarette allows it to make us smoke it, but we are not thereby reduced to an effect of the cigarette.

However, let us stay with the analogy a bit longer. Smoking a cigarette is argued by many to serve as a "gateway" to circumstances whereby we give up control and become enslaved. Others would argue that such claims are absurdly exaggerated. Be that as it may, we suggest that such a concern translates enchantment into what could more appropriately be termed "possession" by default. The example helps make the point that attachments are risky, acknowledging that enchantment *might* lead to possession (e.g., addiction, an unwanted constriction of agency), but not necessarily. This point then allows us to articulate what we take to be the central concern: *whether or not we feel we can afford to allow ourselves to co-compose compositions whose effects we cannot predict.* What "afford" means depends on how we understand the risks involved. Attitudes or stances towards enchantment can then be differentiated based on their view of unpredictability: specifically, whether or not unpredictability is at all seen in terms of having positive potential. On the one hand, we find (modern) stances that attempt to resolve vulnerability through predictability (e.g., knowledge, calculability), understood as mastery. On the other hand, we find stances that consider an ability to endure unpredictability as a prerequisite for gaining access to emergent agentic capacities. These emergent capacities emerge neither from mastery nor from rendering oneself a conduit of an external force—another master—but out of forms of relational engagement.

The Fruit of a Kind of Active Abandonment

In an intriguing chapter entitled "A sociology of attachment: Music amateurs, drug users," Emilie Gomart and Antoine Hennion focus on objects of study "which cannot easily be treated as actions. Objects which insist on that which 'arrives', not on that which is 'performed'"(1999). That which "arrives" pertains to "the course of the world" in a way that involves an actor, but does not render her the master of action.

> To "abandon yourself to a tune" is a phrase in which "yourself" denies the possibility of "pure" abandonment. It is not exclusively passive; it involves the participation of both the person and the object. Ignoring the mutual exclusion of "passion" and "passivity" imposed by the theory of action, the human "actor" might pass through a series of peculiar states (being open, patient, receptive, sensitive). These models of being/acting weave together what seemed to be polar opposites—passivity and activity, determining and determined, collective and individual, and intention as against causality. (Gomart and Hennion 1999, 226–227)

While we agree with the above, we think that it might be useful to consider two theoretically distinct "moments" involved. The effect of letting go may be euphoric, intense relief, and so on. Is the engagement in such release what constitutes passion? Our question pertains to William Burroughs's famous remark in *Junkie: Confessions of an Unredeemed Drug Addict* (1953): "Perhaps all pleasure is relief." Or, again, is passion what is facilitated by (what we gain access to through) such release? This distinction may seem laboured, but we think that it may help us to distinguish between two different concerns regarding enchantment.

The first "moment" pertains to a transition from control to surrender and to negative freedom, to liberation *from*. The second "moment" involves going beyond this transition and inhabiting the "space" of enchantment. We think that this distinction allows us to differentiate between a "leap of faith," itself a crucial moment, and the "what" that one leaps *to*. What we are here calling "leaping" or "letting go" is an "act" that can still be conceived of in a characteristically Modern way. Indeed, modern conceptions based on mastery have no problem conceiving the possibility of surrendering control. Such surrender simply tends to be understood as shifting control from one actor to another. "Having" control, whereby nothing comes as a surprise, is hence contrasted with "letting go." We argue that intellectualization and rationalization—the processes of disenchantment—tend to understand letting go in terms of an irresponsible move, but that, in order to make sense of this, we cannot remain in the binary question of letting go or not letting go. The crucial contrast between the mastery of enchantment-seekers and the mastery of disenchantment is not to be found here, but rather by entertaining the question what happens after we "let go." What is it that the former appear to have faith in that the latter views with distrust?

The Paranoia of Retrospective "Knowing"

The philosopher Adam S. Miller has translated Latour's principle of irreduction into the concept of "resistant availability." He writes, quoting Latour: "Each object comes to be what it is 'through the difference it creates in resisting others' (Latour 1988, 159) and these differences follow the contours of an object's stubborn opposition to reduction" (Miller 2013, 51). In Latour's ontology, we do not have access to the extremes of complete availability and complete resistance. All availability involves resistance for the simple reason that no object is reducible to another. I may consider myself as rendering myself "fully" available to something, but due to my ontological irreducibility, there will always be an inescapable resistance involved. It is important to note that this resistance may *or may not* involve my attitude. Similarly, it is not possible to fully resist either, because in a relational ontology, resistance is actually a form of availability—a form of alignment. Our starting point in entering into relation with something therefore always involves a tension between resistance and availability. "An object's stubborn opposition to reduction" renders the notion of mastery confused, insofar as mastery is understood as fully resisting something that renders itself fully available to us or vice versa. Let us consider this further in terms of modern Christian religiosity and modern faith in "an in principle calculable world."

Modern conceptions of the relationship between an adherent and God often describe religiosity in terms of a transaction between distinct parties. You do "your part" and "God will do His." Consider, for instance, the following two quotes by Russell M. Nelson, an authority (an Apostle) in the Church of Jesus Christ of Latter Day Saints (LDS):

> For each of you to receive revelation unique to your own needs and responsibilities, certain guidelines prevail. The Lord asks you to develop "faith, hope, charity and love, with an eye single to the glory of God."

> Then with your firm "faith, virtue, knowledge, temperance, patience, brotherly kindness, godliness, charity, humility, [and] diligence," you may ask, and you will receive; you may knock, and it will be opened unto you.³ (Nelson 2009)

> Obedience allows God's blessings to flow without constraint. He will bless His obedient children with freedom from bondage and misery. And He will bless them with more light. (Nelson 2011)

Notice the characteristic division of labour. A certain kind of alignment that is centred on "worthiness" is considered to render an adherent available to receive the blessings of God. But it is not only about blessings and rewards; it is also about becoming a "vessel" through which God can work. This involves a cultivated practice of surrendering control, of *allowing* something more or less unpredictable to happen and endeavouring to remain a mediator of this desired force by remaining worthy.

What interests us here are the terms under which one enters into this agreement. In the quotes above, the terms are such that worthiness is presumed to lead to blessings and becoming used as a vehicle of God's work. However, we want to note three things: first, that the terms differ from a business transaction in that, if it appears that God is not doing His part, such circumstances tend to be interpreted in ways that avoid holding God accountable. Second, "obey God and you will be free from bondage" seems irredeemably irrational from the perspective of a zero-sum game. These two issues are often used to criticize religious people. The critique, on both counts, is characteristically Modern. The first critique leads to entanglement in the infamous problem of theodicy, while the latter tends towards understanding obedience as more or less synonymous with bondage. From a Latourian perspective, however,

> freedom becomes the right not to be deprived of ties that render existence possible, ties emptied of all ideals of determination, of a false theology of creation ex nihilo. If it is correct that we must replace the ancient opposition between the attached and the detached with the substitution of good and bad attachments, this replacement would leave us only feeling stifled if it were not supplemented and completed by a second idea, i.e., the deliverance from mastery altogether: at all points of the network of attachments, the node is that of a make-make, not of a make nor of a made. That at least is a different project of emancipation, which is as vigorous as the former but much more credible because it obliges *us not to confuse living without control with living without attachments.*
> (Latour 2010b, 59, italics in the original)

---

3. Here Nelson is quoting from one of the holy scriptures of the LDS church, *The Doctrine and Covenants*. Hence the citation marks.

In a perspective that does not understand obedience in terms of a division of labour between a master and subject, whether an attachment is good or bad is evaluated in terms of its effects. Were we to remain within a regime of mastery, good attachments are those in which you are a master and bad attachments are those in which someone or something else is "the master." However, in a compositionist ontology, freedom is not attained simply by cutting ties.

The implication, we argue, is that the question shifts from whether or not God is doing His part (and whether or not God is held accountable) to the question of whether or not *attaching to/with God* is acknowledged to involve any potentially negative effects and what the prospects are of attending to such negative effects, were such to emerge. The issue is no longer God's in/fallibility; nor is it the adherent's moral dilemma about whether it is, in general, "good" to obey or not to obey. The issue is what adherents make of their productive relationship *with* God. One may note the conspicuous absence of a type of assessment found quite commonly in regard to other relationships, particularly romantic ones: "we were simply not good for one another" or "we just had bad chemistry." This pertains to the third thing that we want to note. Entering into a relationship with God is also widely understood in terms of becoming a co-composer of "God's work." This involves surrendering control, not necessarily *to* God, but rather to the unpredictable effects of the relationship. Our point is that such surrender need not prove problematic; indeed, the act of individuals attaching to (their) God(/gods) often has effects that in most interpretations would be called "good." Insofar as an adherent surrenders control to something that is by definition unpredictable (if indeed it is genuine surrender), yet categorically refuses to consider problems in any other way than in terms of his own worthiness in the eyes of God, the problem is not that he surrenders control but that he may be doing it in an irresponsible or flawed way.

Again, we are not saying that the responsibility should fall on God. We are arguing that it is important to consider the way in which the question a) of whether or not an attachment to/with God involves the potential of being or becoming bad is typically translated into the question b) of whether or not an adherent is worthy enough. This explanation deflects attention from questions concerning the quality of the attachment itself, ascertained through entertaining its relational effects: what becomes of God and the adherent, as well as other actors influenced by the relationship, through their encounters?

Max Weber began his famous talk "The Disenchantment of Modern Life" by noting a similar idea of counting on some other agency/agencies to afford us with various abilities to act.

The Relational Dynamics of Enchantment and Sacralization

> Unless he is a physicist, one who rides on the streetcar has no idea how the car happened to get into motion. And he does not need to know. He is satisfied that he may "count" on the behavior of the streetcar, and he orients his conduct according to this expectation; but he knows nothing about what it takes to produce such a car so that it can move. [...] The increasing intellectualization and rationalization do not, therefore, indicate an increased and general knowledge of the conditions under which one lives. It means something else, namely, the knowledge or belief that if one but wished one *could* learn it at any time. Hence, it means that principally there are no mysterious incalculable forces that come into play, but rather that one can, in principle, master all things by calculation. This means that the world is disenchanted. One need no longer have recourse to magical means in order to master or implore the spirits, as did the savage, for whom such mysterious powers existed. Technical means and calculations perform the service. This above all is what intellectualization means. (Weber 1946, 155)

What we find similar here to our discussion above is the affordance of a retrospective explanation. While the Modern religious adherent "counts on" God while seemingly neglecting to consider the quality of her attachment as productive of, in some cases, rather widespread effects—effects not only on others, but on herself and God as well—we find here the notion of "an in principle calculable world" that allows those who hold it to similarly ignore the effects of relational dynamics.

How is this done? The manoeuvre is related to a form of hindsight, which more or less strategically ignores the circumstance that an "act, once actualized, is different from the indeterminacy of its performance" (Grosz 2010, 147). Any potential anxiety about this indeterminacy is kept in check by the Weberian streetcar passenger by believing in an "in principle calculable world." Interestingly, the manoeuvre we want to investigate also characterizes paranoia as a mode of relating. As Eve Sedgwick has noted, "the first imperative of paranoia is *There must be no bad surprises,* and indeed, the aversion to surprise seems to be what cements the intimacy between paranoia and knowledge per se..."(Sedgwick 2003, 130). The inappropriateness of the notion of a calculable world as a solution to the problem of managing indeterminacy may elude us insofar as it enters the picture as an afterthought aimed at refuting surprise itself.

Intellectualization pertains to the belief in an in principle calculable world in that the latter functions as a response to bad surprises. It allows us to respond to surprises by refuting that they actually were or had to be surprises. The incident was simply a "mistake"—someone's mistake (if not ours, then someone else's)—where "mistake" signals that we can go on believing in mastery through calculation without asking ourselves whether or not that was the appropriate question. This is because conceptualizing a problem as a mistake entails conceptualizing it in terms of a "right response to a radically exterior/ized other" (Barad 2007, 393). Instead of trying to understand what happened in terms of mediation—in terms of how a problem "arrived"—we "solve" the problem by translating the problem into a problem of mastery. Had we (or someone else) only *known*, this would not have happened. Sedgwick explains:

> The unidirectionally future-oriented vigilance of paranoia generates, paradoxically, a complex relation to temporality that burrows both backward and forward: because there must be no bad surprises, and because learning of the possibility of a bad surprise would itself constitute a bad surprise, paranoia requires that bad news always already be known. (Sedgwick 2003, 130)

When we come up against bad surprises, blame serves to reify the notion that the problem was the *absence* of the mastery of predictive calculation. Yet mistakes are not necessarily thereby responded to through increased efforts to render the world all the more calculable, all the more predictable, in order to prevent bad surprises. Instead, the response may involve a conviction that has no connection whatsoever with actual calculation, only with the notion of "an in principle calculable world." The belief in mastery facilitates responding to a recurring incident involving bad surprises over and over again by deriding ourselves or others with the notion that "someone should (and could) have known" without ever actually doing anything about it or reflecting on the matter further. This "should have" is entirely predicated on the "in principle" efficacy of calculation and prediction, as opposed to their actual efficacy in eliminating problems or improving our ability to manage affairs.

Trust and Reliance

If we again consider the distinction between 1) "letting go" as liberation from and 2) "letting go" as surrendering to becoming a co-composer of an unpredictable composition, we can consider the above in terms of another relevant distinction, increasingly made in moral philosophy, between reliance and trust. One of the first philosophers to discuss this distinction is Lars Hertzberg, who argued: "Reliance has a more or less specific content: one relies on a person *for particular purposes*" (Hertzberg 1994, 119). Olli Lagerspetz explains that Hertzberg's distinction is "a way to demarcate trust from other cases where the other is treated as a means to an end only" (Lagerspetz 2015, 16). An interesting difference between trust and reliance, then, is that "trust is, as it were, open-ended in a way that reliance is not. [...] When we turn to a trusted friend for help and advice, we often hope for the unpredictable, the second opinion, the creative thinking that helps us forward" (Lagerspetz 2015, 16–17). Lagerspetz contrasts trust with rational betting, where what is at stake is known and decided beforehand. While reliance in these descriptions does not pose any problems for a person who believes in mastery, because relying on something can always be evaluated in terms of whether or not it was instrumental to do so, trust could be understood as involving us in an unpredictable composition. Thus, what is at stake is not only the reliability of the object, but the participant's capacity to trust—a capacity that is vulnerable to becoming diminished through experiences of betrayal. Lagerspetz notes that:

> Hertzberg uses the contrast between trust and reliance as a way to open up a perspective on trust, *not* from the point of view of an agent who decides to "place" certain expectations on someone or something, but from that of the person who *receives* trust. Once we recognize that someone else trusts us, we implicitly *agree* that deliberately letting her down would amount to betrayal and expose us to blame. (Lagerspetz 2015, 18)

The crucial distinction, as we see it, is that trust acknowledges relationships that "test" not the utility of the participants for one another, but their trustworthiness for one another. It differs from reliance in that *what* one trusts is afforded "a say" in "where" the relationship takes them. Insofar as we stress "becoming a vehicle of God's work," it is evident that said relationship is not merely one of reliance.

Bad surprises may be responded to in terms of "well, it's all part of God's plan" or "I have not been worthy enough," or they may be responded to with "in principle, this could have been avoided." Either way, what these translations afford is that we can *retain* our worldview because the response does not actually even try to understand what was at stake in the indeterminacy of the occurrence that emerged as a (bad) surprise. Belief in 1) an in principle calculable world and/or 2) an infallible God (or an infallible Science, for that matter) affords a retrospective assessment, whereby what may actually have been trust is translated into reliance. It is not necessarily the case that Moderns refuse to trust in a relational enchantment and refuse to co-compose unpredictable compositions. Rather, as Weber notes, we do this quite routinely. Something interesting occurs when our engagements turn out to have negative effects: we revert to blaming ourselves for having foolishly relied on something else. Hence, we no longer feel the need to ask whether there might have been a better answer to what the problem was than one based on a "right response" through calculation or prescriptions concerning worthiness.

Modern attachment to an in principle calculable world and/or to an infallible God can be understood as examples of what Lauren Berlant has called "cruel optimism":

> Whatever the *experience* of optimism is in particular, then, the *affective structure* of an optimistic attachment involves a sustaining inclination to return to the scene of fantasy that enables you to expect that *this* time, nearness to *this* thing will help you or a world to become different in just the right way. But, again, optimism is cruel when the object/scene that ignites a sense of possibility actually makes it impossible to attain the expansive transformation for which a person or a people risks striving; and, doubly, it is cruel insofar as the very pleasures of being inside a relation have become sustaining regardless of the content of the relation, such that a person or a world finds itself bound to a situation of profound threat that is, at the same time, profoundly confirming.
> (Berlant 2011, 2)

By translating relationships of trust into relationships of reliance, we protect ourselves from attending to concerns that cannot be remedied through mastery. Mastery thus remains seemingly plausible as a solution to life's challenges. We remain optimistic—and, arguably, cruelly so. We simply have to be more careful about *what* we rely on (without ever allowing ourselves to feel betrayed by the notion of an in principle calculable world or an infallible God). With trust, on the other hand, the issue is more complex. It can include worries about how our general capacity for trust may become injured—namely, our capacity to *endure* engagement in compositions that we acknowledge and allow to be unpredictable. We may also entertain concerns regarding whether or not *we* are trustworthy to engage with, particularly in relationships where unpredictability is not understood as a categorically bad thing.

Guilt and Self-blame

Worries over trustworthiness are effectively deflected by translating the negative effects of encounters (that may have involved trust) into occasions for self-blame (for having relied on the "wrong" things). As the sociologist and psychoanalyst Donald Carveth describes it, "we evade *feeling* guilty by going directly to self-punishment. Unfortunately, evading feeling guilt in this way precludes the rational evaluation of such guilt that would enable us to decide whether to accept and make reparation for it, or reject it as irrational and ungrounded" (2006, 188). Such deliberation involves precisely attending to concerns over the sustainability of trust (understood as involving unpredictability) as a relational "resource." It involves attending to concerns such as "if something unfortunate occurs, will I be able to make reparation?" and "will you be available for this reparative work?" As Carveth notes, it was Melanie Klein who provided us with the crucial distinction between persecutory guilt and reparative guilt (Klein 1948), a distinction that allows us to recognize the folly of simply equating guilt with self-blame:

> If I injure someone and while he bleeds I self-flagellate, that is useless persecutory guilt; but if I put down my cat-o'-nine-tails and get busy bandaging, that is *reparative* guilt. It is commonly heard today that guilt is a useless and harmful emotion that we should get rid of. But that applies only to persecutory guilt which is utterly narcissistic, self-involved, and irrelevant to the needs of the injured party. In reparative guilt we manage to get our minds off ourselves long enough to take note of the needs of the injured other and to make reparation. (Carveth 2016)

Hence, attending to trust issues is more complex than assessing who or what is reliable for different purposes. In part, this is because reparation of injuries involves repairing or navigating a precarious ability to trust. It is this relational concern that is poorly captured by the modern deprecation (and glorification) of "letting go." Discussing the relevance of Emmanuel Levinas's philosophy for a relational ontology, Karen Barad notes:

> We [...] are always already responsible to the others with whom we are entangled, not through conscious intent but through the various ontological entanglements that materiality entails. [...] Ethics is therefore not about right response to a radically exterior/ized other, but about responsibility and accountability for the lively relationalities of becoming of which we are a part. (Barad 2007, 393)

The implication, we would like to suggest, is that assessing whether or not enchantment is a good thing or a bad thing is poorly done by translating it into a *choice* between the caricatures of a Modern control freak and a non-modern escapist. What is at stake is rather the trustworthiness of co-composers of compositions for one another when co-composing those compositions and questions concerning our ability to attend to emergent issues without reducing them to the question of who/what is to blame. We will not develop this further, but we would like to draw attention to the relevance these concerns have for discourses on enchantment and disenchantment. Disenchantment effectively disqualified a staggering number of relational apparatuses, not only human-supernatural hybrids, but more or less all human-nonhuman hybrids, through the persuasive power attained by pointing out that some of them appeared to have negative effects. This development could be translated into an assessment whereby enchantment was something we simply could not "afford"; it was deemed too risky. In the name of symmetry, one can of course also ask, can we afford to live without enchantment? The above discussion allows us to nuance this question as follows: can we afford to live with the consequences of retrospectively translating enchantment into the effects of a zero-sum game?

We have now argued the following: 1) reducing life to engaging only in (in principle) predictable affairs and opting for reliance over trust is impoverishing and ignores the need to attend to concerns regarding the precariousness of individuals' capacity to trust; 2) one can engage in enchantment without denying that it may be risky; and 3) as long as enchantment is retrospectively translated into calculation (trust is retrospectively translated into reliance), the negative effects of unpredictable relational dynamics remain *seemingly* the effects of "letting go" (as opposed to the more complex effects of what happened after, that is, the unpredictable but productive effects of compositions).

Resisting Resisting

Let us now focus on how resisting availability for engagement in co-acting might entail denying ourselves access to certain affordances. Achieving a stance that takes things for granted has obvious benefits. Consider the following quotes of West African drumming practices in Finland, from interviews conducted by Linda Annunen:

> Then when the hand technique improves and then when you're playing for instance one rhythm for a really long time, like half an hour straight or two hours straight, now then all kinds of new dimensions and perspectives that were previously unknown suddenly really start surfacing. So somehow, the things that I hear, I notice that my eyes aren't looking anywhere anymore, the hands are hitting just the right spots and I don't need to worry about that either. And that, that then I can just like ... that I'm truly present in my body. (IF mgt 2013/031)

The challenge is to allow oneself to not resist—in a sense, to resist one's inclination to try to control something. Another way of putting it is that trust often develops by overcoming an initial inclination to doubt (in this case, the unpredictable effects of the encounter between "body" and "rhythm"). A participant in Peik Ingman's research on the relational challenges of queer members of Christian families told him that her first experience of hearing Christian hymns was rather negative. She thought they sounded "silly." At the time, they were not able to inspire a sense of belonging, let alone passion. Within a few years, however, through the experience of singing along—singing together—these same hymns developed into what she emphasized as one of the most rewarding elements of her Christian practice. Initial resistance had given way to an availability that was deeply satisfying and (positively) enchanting in ways that she had not been able to conceive of before (IF mgt 2012/013). Having overcome her initial resistance, she *achieved* a welcome availability. In the beginning, the songs gave rise to an experience with which she sceptically aligned herself. We can imagine her, with time, standing among the other singers, allowing the hymn to flow through her, allowing a positive, productive encounter and partaking, seemingly effortlessly, simultaneously in its reception and its production. Although we might call it "effortless," it was clearly also an "achievement," a kind of "comportment" that she had cultivated, a capacity to translate well.

Let us examine two more quotes by drummers on the tension between availability and resistance:

> Then when you reach that level where you don't need to think about how your hands are whisking [...] and then when you've realized that by thinking you're only making it worse. (IF mgt 2012/014)

> I can detach from my body, like seriously so it feels really funny, that I'm looking: that hand is whisking and I'm in no way responsible for what the hand is doing! And if I think about this thing—if, as has happened the first times, that I'm spooked by it, I'm so amazed by it that I start thinking that "how is this [possible]?," "what's going on here and is this like normal?"—[...] then it goes away. But then later on I've understood that you just gotta let it lead, that you shouldn't at all resist, at all think about what it is and sacrifice a single thought and feeling to what, just be happy about it, that "yes! Now, now it's going again!"
>
> (IF mgt 2013/031)

Through this quote we can recognize how the word 'responsible' haunts our discussion in general. The drummer is "in no way responsible for what the hand is doing," yet she could very understandably be *held* responsible for what her hand is doing. In terms of responsibility, the implication is that one should allow oneself to act in ways where one is not responsible—in the sense of understanding oneself as the causal agent—for what one is doing. This does not mean that one could/would not subsequently *take* responsibility for this, if what is happening seems to demand it. It appears, then, that what is needed is really the ability/capacity to resist a kind of intellectual control, to then and there resist trying to make sense of it, which only seems to interfere with alignment. Not only is it a question of initially allowing something, it is an ongoing achievement. Yet it is *not* an achievement that in any way precludes that we take responsibility for it by later considering the diffractive effects of our engagement.

What happens then when we do not render ourselves available, if we resist by thinking too much?

> You can sort of get stuck there, like stuck in your thoughts, waiting, 'cause then, then when the call came, there it went already—if you weren't "with it," the whole song possibly topples because of it. [...] the demands on the playing, already that like connects really strongly the group's members, 'cause you have to constantly try to find the relationship between your own rhythm and what the others are doing.
>
> (IF mgt 2012/014)

"The whole song possibly topples because of it." Because of what? The whole song topples if someone is not "in the game," if someone is preoccupied and therefore unavailable. The problem is, arguably, not a lack of mastery but a lack of availability or the wrong kind of resistance. What we are saying is that when the whole song does *not* "topple," it is basically because the drummers allow themselves to be recruited into a collective doing—an "apparatus" or a "composition."

What the drummers are doing is not substantially different from what Moderns in general do, except for the explicit appreciation of not being in charge. The belief that "in principle" everything is calculable serves as a *means* to allow us to render ourselves available and not enact incompatibility (by constantly questioning conventions). Yet, we would argue, it does not mean that we are not enchanted. Rather, this describes something about *how* we are enchanted. If you like, it describes being enchanted by believing in disenchantment. In actuality, in actual practice, our actions are possible because we render ourselves available to being moved by things we can never—and often do not even try to—master. What is at stake is not mastery, but how we deal with our inescapable lack of it. How do we cope given our limited control as mediators among mediators?

Enchantment, Privilege and Risk

What needs to be pointed out is that most of us have co-composed countless compositions in the course of our lives; such limited control has not only seemed non-problematic, but it has been empowering and reassuring. Consider how a drummer evocatively describes rhythm as akin to a mother's embrace:

> I mean it's like something, you know like when you hear the rhythm, it's that same wonderful mother's embrace in which you can cradle no matter how difficult times you're going through, you can still... It always

tells you something, it's not in words but it tells you always that [...] either something joyful or then that everything's gonna work out.

(IF mgt 2013/031)

Associations often allow us to remain enchanted in ways that afford us the precious luxury of respite from a world that appears to demand that we know beforehand what will happen. The trouble is that the character and effects of associations (that reassure us) are never quite stable; they may change. Associating without questioning can be or become something that we no longer feel we can afford to do. Another queer research participant described a longing for something, a kind of taken-for-grantedness that we could very well call trust, which she no longer considered safe to engage in after disclosing her homosexuality to her conservative Christian family:

> I can sometimes feel that if people start talking about spirituality or meditation and stuff like that, that warning bells start ringing in the back of my mind. One is still like needing to inspect everything really like in detail. But at the same time, since I have so much experience with prayer, with hymns [...] if one would take out God from it [...] after all, those experiences have been really positive. And I can miss that. I can feel that it would be amazing to, you know, have a prayer meeting with people one likes. And just that togetherness in it... but I'm so terrified of the conditionality that's there. [...] like songs one used to listen to as a kid, like religious songs that are incredibly beautiful and the melodies that one used to listen to so much. My mom used to sing them to us in the evenings; there's such a sense of security connected to them, it's really hard to deal with. Sometimes I can... 'cause I do have those hymnbooks. I was given them and I've kept them, and I can sing them if I'm by myself, 'cause then I have control over it. But if I for instance go to church or to like a wedding or something, then I don't do it; then I don't sing along because there's other people who interpret things into it and I don't have control over religion then. (IF mgt 2012/004)

This should not be taken as the participant previously *having had* control, but rather bemoaning the loss of a situatedness where she could allow herself to participate in ways that could tolerate surprises. She seems to mourn the absence of terms through which she could again allow herself to engage in what could be called enchantment. A participant in Annunen's research project noted: "In some groups kids have started going into trance. I don't have a clue as to how you get someone out of a trance. And like, I've seen a man with some kind of developmental disability going into some weird state and like totally lost it from the drumming" (IF mgt 2013/001). The significance of both of these quotes, in light of the discussion above, is that concerns around enchantment seem to revolve around *affording* to "let go" and, particularly, whether or not realistic means of dealing with potential negative effects are sufficiently entertained. In both cases, letting go is acknowledged to potentially lead to "possession," to becoming "badly connected," but not in the automatic way that a zero-sum game presumes.

What, then, is at stake in the other form of mastery? The romantic poet John Keats referred in the 19th century to what he called "negative capability": "[...] it struck me what quality went to form a Man of Achievement, especially in Literature, and which Shakespeare possessed so enormously—I mean Negative Capability, that is, when a man is capable of being in uncertainties, mysteries, doubts, without any irritable reaching after fact and reason" (Keats 1899, 277). Being in uncertainty is a prerequisite for overcoming mastery, because allowing other actants to influence the course of events (or recognizing that they do so) entails uncertainty. Entering into relations where we accept the inevitability of surprises does not, however, need to involve the reification of mysteries. Such reification can be interpreted as a side effect of the disenchantment story. We may very well manage to make sense of uncertainties. In order to do that, however, we first need to acknowledge that they are uncertainties. Another form of mastery is conceivable, then. It is not a mastery of "letting go," but a mastery of engaging well with those things one co-composes with, having let go (of certainty).

Acknowledgments

Peik Ingman would like to express his gratitude to Mari Lindman for encouragement, intriguing conversations and insightful commentary, which contributed considerably to the development of the arguments in this chapter, whose eventual articulations the authors nonetheless accept full responsibility for.

References

Barad, K. 2007. *Meeting the Universe Halfway: Quantum Physics and the Entanglement of Matter and Meaning*. Durham, NC: Duke University Press.

Berlant, L. 2011. *Cruel Optimism*. Durham, NC: Duke University Press.

Burroughs, W. 1953. *Junkie: Confessions of an Unredeemed Drug Addict*. New York: Ace Books.

Callon, M. 1986. "Some Elements of a Sociology of Translation: Domestication of the Scallops and the Fishermen of St Brieuc Bay." In *Power, Action and Belief: A New Sociology of Knowledge?*, edited by J. Law, 196–223. London: Routledge.

Carveth, D. L. 2016. "'Guilt." In *Vocabulary for the Study of Religion,"* edited by R. A. Segal and K. von Stuckrad. Brill Online. Reference. <http://reference-works.brillonline.com/entries/vocabulary-for-the-study-of-religion/guilt-COM_00000322> [Accessed 03 January 2016].

———. 2006. "Self-Punishment as Guilt Evasion: Theoretical Issues." *Canadian Journal of Psychoanalysis* 14: 176–198.

Gomart, E. and A. Hennion. 1999. "A Sociology of Attachment: Music Amateurs, Drug Users." In *Actor Network Theory and After*, edited by J. Law and J. Hassard, 220–247. Oxford: Blackwell Publishers.

Grosz, E. 2010. "Feminism, Materialism, and Freedom." In *New Materialisms: Ontology, Agency, and Politics*, edited by D. Coole and S. Frost, 139–157. Durham, NC: Duke University Press.

Hertzberg, L. 1994. *The Limits of Experience*. Acta Philosophica Fennica 56. Helsinki: Societas Philosophica Fennica.

Keats, J. 2001. "Lamia." *John Keats: Major Works*, edited by Elizabeth Cook, 305–322. Oxford: Oxford University Press.

Lagerspetz, O. 2015. *Trust, Ethics and Human Reason*. London: Bloomsbury Academic.

Latour, B. 2010a. "An Attempt at a 'Compositionist Manifesto.'" *New Literary History* 4(3): 471–490.

———. 2010b. *On the Modern Cult of the Factish Gods*. Translated by H. MacLean and C. Porter. Durham, NC: Duke University Press.

———. 2005. *Reassembling the Social: An Introduction to Actor-Network-Theory*. Oxford: Oxford University Press.

———. 1988. *The Pasteurization of France*. Translated by A. Sheridan and J. Law. Cambridge, MA: Harvard University Press.

Miller, D. 2013. *Speculative Grace: Bruno Latour and Object-Oriented Theology*. New York: Fordham University Press.

Nelson, R.M. 2011. "Face the Future with Faith." <https://www.lds.org/general-conference/2011/04/face-the-future-with-faith?lang=eng> [Accessed 4 November 2015].

———. 2009. "Ask, Seek, Knock." <https://www.lds.org/general-conference/2009/10/ask-seek-knock?lang=eng> [Accessed 4 November 2015].

Sedgwick, E. Kosofsky. 2003. *Touching Feeling: Affect, Pedagogy, Performativity*. Durham, NC: Duke University Press.

Weber, M. 1991 [1946]. *From Max Weber: Essays in Sociology*. Translated and edited by H. H. Gerth and C. Wright Mills. Oxford: Oxford University Press.

Other sources

Linda Annunen and Peik Ingman:

Interviews by Linda Annunen and Peik Ingman, kept in the Cultura archive at Åbo Akademi University.

IF mgt 2013/031

IF mgt 2012/013

IF mgt 2012/014

About the Authors

Linda Annunen is a PhD candidate in Comparative Religion at Åbo Akademi University. She is currently writing her doctoral thesis on West African and shamanistic drumming in contemporary Finnish cities in terms of ritual theories. Her research interests include ritual studies, theorizations of space and place, urban anthropology, and religion and entertainment.

Peik Ingman is a PhD candidate in Comparative Religion at Åbo Akademi University. He is currently working on a doctoral thesis with the working title "Sacralization and the Gift: Queer Family Members in Christian Families." His research combines actor-network theory, philosophy of science and object relations theory.

PART II

Political Concerns

— 6 —

Recomposing Religion:
Radical Agnosticism and Transformative Speech

Michael Barnes Norton

Bruno Latour argues that modern thought drastically misunderstands the religious in at least two ways: by assuming that religions are constituted by "beliefs" and by assuming that religious language is meant to transmit information (the content of "beliefs"). These characterizations are based on what Latour calls the "modernist settlement," the result of which is a view of the world as strictly bifurcated between nature and culture. This chapter develops an understanding of religious practice that follows Latour's departure from this modernist position and can instead let religions speak for themselves. It explores the implications of the rejection of "belief in belief"—the idea that so-called primitive or superstitious religious ideas are held by their adherents in ways that modern social sciences take to be unreflective or simply backward. It also examines Latour's claim that religious speech is not primarily about transmitting informational content, but instead aims at the transformation of its audience as well as its speakers. Lastly, it argues that in order to take these claims seriously it is imperative that we understand the religious in terms of its immanent, material constituents—nonhuman as well as human. This not only involves reconceiving religion on its own; it also entails resituating religious speech and practice within a more broadly democratic political sphere in which critical, secular perspectives are not strictly opposed to religious ones. Rethinking

Keywords: Bruno Latour, religion, religious belief, secularism, agnosticism

religions along these lines allows us to compose a prospective future for the philosophy of religion in which religious life may be accounted for in all its multiform reality.

Introduction

Across the approaches to religion offered by contemporary anthropology, sociology, philosophy, and of course the contentiously polymorphous discipline named religious studies, it has become something of a cliché to say that no single definition adequately applies to all of the phenomena we conventionally label religious. Furthermore, the extent to which modern Western concepts of religion fail to grasp even the most important aspects of Western religious traditions—not to mention those residing outside the increasingly hazy boundaries of the West—is becoming more and more clear. For his part, Bruno Latour argues that modern Western thought misunderstands the religious in at least two ways: 1) by assuming that religions are primarily constituted as such by adherence to sets of beliefs and that the function of religious language is to articulate and communicate the propositional content of such beliefs, and 2) by understanding religions as primarily concerned with that which is far removed from the world of the everyday. Instead, Latour claims that in order for an adequate understanding of religious life, and especially religious language, to be achieved, we must abandon the modernist belief in "beliefs" and recognize the ways in which religions work to direct their adherents' attention to what is closest to them. In this chapter, my aim is to synthesize—to "compose"—a Latourian philosophy of religious language, drawing from a variety of his works from the past two decades. This can then serve as a starting point for an understanding of religious practice that bypasses the terms set up by the modern project of disenchantment. First, I will examine the notion of "composition" as an alternative to the critique championed in the wake of what Latour calls the "modernist settlement," an arrangement that depends on a continuous purification of the supposedly mutually exclusive categories of nature and culture. It is in the context of this settlement, Latour argues, that the belief in the centrality and efficacy of beliefs has emerged, yet this belief obscures a more important distinction at work in religious language: one between talk that informs and talk that transforms. After exploring Latour's argument that religious language aims to be the latter rather than the former, I will show how religious attitudes and behaviours may be best understood (however counterintuitive this may be) as radically agnostic. It is through an understanding and appreciation of radical agnosticism that the specifically religious mode of existence can be best brought to light.

What Does It Mean to (Re)Compose?

Latour offers composition as a methodological (or perhaps more accurately, an attitudinal) alternative to critique. The power—and, according to Latour, the weakness—of critique is that it depends at least implicitly on the presupposition of a reality or truth lying behind the object of critique. Whether or not this is a wholly accurate characterization of any and every critical perspective, it is a helpful picture against which to contrast composition, for which the central question is not "is X real or illusory?" but rather "is X composed well or badly?" Composing involves making connections and establishing ties, creating harmonies between entities or processes (like in a musical composition), and putting phenomena in order (such as when one "composes oneself"). Importantly, composition also always involves the possibility of decomposition insofar as connections may be broken, harmonies may dissolve, and order may collapse into chaos. Compositions are contingent and inherently mutable; whether and to what extent they are able to persist for a significant length of time and interact meaningfully with other composed entities depends on and determines how well they are composed. A composition that succeeds in persisting, for the time being, is composed relatively well, whereas one that fails to persist is composed badly. The terms 'well' and 'badly' used here, we should note, are not in themselves value-laden; to say that something is composed well does not imply that it or its effects are good or beneficial. A particular composition's success or failure, however, depends entirely on its interactions with other compositions (not on any correspondence to a reality supposedly underlying the arrangement of compositions), so compositions that tend toward destructive interactions with other compositions would also tend toward their own failure. As a philosophical perspective, compositionism "takes up the task of building a common world" precisely because it recognizes the inescapably relational nature of the beings it addresses (Latour 2010a, 474).

Latour explains that the compositionist attitude emphasizes immanence to a degree that the modern critical perspective cannot, because the latter relies implicitly on the idea of a true world beyond the apparent one. This is the case even (and perhaps especially) in cases of secular critiques that aim to desacralize and demythologize: the thoroughly disenchanted, often mechanistic, material world remains the *terra firma* in relation to which critique consistently sets its course amid the often challenging seas of appearance and superstition. What critique remains unable to do, however, is the positive work of building connections and repairing relationships. Having once accepted the idea of a gap between appearance and reality, critique is well-equipped to expose this gap but ill-equipped to bridge it. Compositionism, on the other hand, not only sets out to bridge such gaps. It is unwilling to concede their existence in the first place. Latour argues that distinctions such as those between nature and culture, science and politics (or religion), and ultimately the "facts" of the world and human "constructions" are in large part the result of what he calls the "modernist settlement"—a strategy for thinking about the world and ourselves that has the unfortunate consequence of separating "into incommensurable problems questions that cannot be solved separately and have to be tackled all at once" (Latour 1999, 310). Tackling questions that simultaneously involve science, politics, economics—and, yes, religion—is precisely the task that compositionism sets for itself, insofar as it is concerned with articulating strongly constructed assemblages and brokering firm negotiations between them.

Compositionism as a methodology is meant not to introduce ways of assembling new ideas or products, but rather as a way of recognizing the compositional nature of reality itself. Latour argues that since the advent of the modern era, the work of composition that is constantly underway within and between beings has been swept under the rug. In *We Have Never Been Modern*, Latour calls "translation" the set of practices that generates connections between mixtures of different types of beings, arguing that modern thought opposes this against a second set of practices called "purification." This opposition, he writes, "creates two entirely distinct ontological zones: that of human beings on the one hand; that of nonhumans on the other"—in other words, the social and the natural. Practices of translation and purification rely on each other in order to make sense and be efficacious, but it has increasingly been the task of modernization to focus on purification and obscure the work of translation. Yet, Latour maintains that, paradoxically, the more modernity has emphasized purification at the expense of translation, the more fecund translation has in practice actually become. An immense proliferation of composed, hybrid beings has thus erupted at the expense of our ability (or willingness) to properly accept their existence as such (Latour 1993, 10–12).

Religion comes into play vis-à-vis the work of purification in at least two ways. First, the beings that make up the content of religious belief and practice—gods, relics, buildings, clothing, and so forth—are subjected like any other beings to the modernist division between nature and culture. Either something belongs in the human ontological sphere, as a human being or as the product of human activity, or it belongs in the natural sphere and is subject to the rule of natural forces. The contents of both of these separate spheres, however, remain subject to the same modernist critique that gives rise to the division between nature and culture in the first place. The strictly critical approaches to monotheism in the West, for instance, put forward by Feuerbach, Marx, Durkheim, or Freud, for example, aim to conquer it by dividing its contents between the tightly controlled spheres of nature and culture. Thus arises what Latour calls "a very strange type of pluralism," in which the whole world is divided between a single natural world and a variety of cultural worlds—religion being counted among the latter (Latour 2001, 217). Religious belief may be retained alongside the operation of this bifurcation, but only if God is kept at a distance; religious beliefs and practices must be relegated to a specially designated private sphere posited over and against the public sphere of modern politics on the one hand and the impersonal world of nature on the other. God remains available as a final authority in cases that elude easy explanation, according to the work of purification, but otherwise He withdraws from view—except in the privacy of one's own home and one's own heart, which is still allowed to have its own reasons (Latour 1993, 33).

A second way in which religious beliefs and practices are connected to the modernist work of purification is perhaps less readily apparent: this is the way in which certain religious traditions have from the outset provided motivating forces in the process of modernization. Thus, modernity has never been a phenomenon wholly separated from religious impulses. The anthropologist Webb Keane argues that the desire for religious reform found in Protestant Christianity may account for at least part of the moral impetus that lies behind the modern project, envisioning the work of purification as part of the salvific mission of European Christianity. As Keane observes, Latour tends to organize his discussions of purification around scientific practice or political philosophy, but he "does not give a strong explanation of what drives the purification or of what organizes the various different domains of action such that they fall into an overarching tendency with a single direction and lend it the sense of moral progress" (Keane 2007, 77). Part of the force behind this progressive tendency, which enables modernity to create the sense of an absolute break with its past, is the drive toward reform found in a wide variety of religious traditions and Protestant Christianity in particular. For our purposes, Keane's argument on this issue can be taken in three parts: first, that the progressive character of modernity is at least partially constituted by a moral impetus toward reform; second, that this drive to reform is characteristic of Christianity generally, and *a fortiori* of Protestant Christianity; and third, that this Christian drive to reform and its connection to the modernist work of purification can be seen most clearly in the work of missionaries outside the West. Christian missionaries often took it as their purpose to cure the attachments to superstitions and fetishes that they found among the peoples with whom they came into contact. Thus, the missionary denunciation of fetishism levelled against (currently or recently) non-Christian peoples can be seen as part of the work of purification, as it finds in what it takes to be fetishistic beliefs and practices unacceptable admixtures of the natural and the cultural, inert matter and free will, or the immanent and the transcendent (Keane 2007, 54). Yet, the idea of fetishism depends on what Latour calls the naïve belief in naïve belief—that is, the belief that the purified standpoint of modernity, in which natural facts are cleanly separated from human constructs, reveals an objectively verifiable reality against which the ostensibly pre-modern reality of the fetishist can easily be shown to be mere illusion (Latour 1999, 274).

Latour characterizes the modernist critique of the fetish as a kind of iconoclasm. The modern iconoclast sees in the fetish an object that holds no meaning or potency in itself; it is only something "onto which we have projected, erroneously, our fancies, our labor, our hopes and passions" (Latour 1999, 270). It is thus the iconoclast's mission to shed light on the facts in order to show those who believe in the fetish that it is nothing more than a powerless artifact. Yet, this iconoclastic critique does not fundamentally contend with superstition or credulity concerning mere objects, natural forces, or social structures; instead, Latour maintains, the anti-fetishism of modernity aims to destroy certain modes of discourse and activity that hamper the work of purification. The iconoclasm of the modernist critique tends to attempt to reduce all discourse to the exchange of information, thus not recognizing that the aim of the "belief" that it attributes to the fetishist is not to articulate and communicate irrational dogma but rather to enact a particular form of life. In charging persons (i.e., others) with having fetishistic attitudes and "naïve belief," the modernist critique misses the real, existential import of the discourse it claims to understand better than those who routinely participate in it.

Fetishism, as it is understood by the iconoclast, is always an accusation. It is attributed to others who are taken to be, at best, mistaken in their beliefs, and it always carries with it moral overtones. Latour explains:

> Some person, or some people, are accused of being taken in—or worse, of cynically manipulating credulous believers—by someone who is sure of escaping from this illusion and wants to free others as well [the modern iconoclast]: either from naïve belief or from being manipulative. But if anti-fetishism is clearly an *accusation*, it is not a *description* of what happens with those who believe or are manipulated. (Latour 1999, 270)

Rather than describing the discourse and action of believers in ways that remain faithful to the contours of these phenomena, the iconoclast projects naïve belief onto those who thus stand accused. It is only under the shadow of this accusation that the accused *become* naïve, credulous, or irrational; such categories are imposed by the modernist critique on that which resists the work of purification. It is thus the iconoclast, rather than those accused of fetishism or naïve belief, who holds onto a belief against the testimony of the world. The iconoclast believes in something called "belief." However, this conception of naïve belief itself testifies to the struggle between the work of purification and that which resists it (Latour 1999, 271–2). Ultimately, what iconoclasm fails to recognize is that the objective truth it champions is no less constructed than that which it critiques. Regardless of the work of purification that places them on opposite sides of a deep divide, "facts" and "fetishes" are both fabricated (Latour 1999, 272).

As Latour explains in the brochure for the 2002 *Iconoclash* exhibit, it is often held that "the more the human hand can be seen as having worked on an image, the weaker is the image's claim to truth." The work of the modern iconoclast has fundamentally been to reveal the human hand at work in the construction of religious beliefs and practices. However, the halo surrounding that which is not constructed has been both retained and defended with regard to the facts that form the basis for scientific inquiry. "If you show the hand at work in the human fabric of science, you are accused of sullying the sanctity of objectivity, of ruining its transcendence, of forbidding any claim to truth, of putting to the torch the only source of enlightenment we may have" (Latour 2010b, 71). Latour's aim is not to show that in fact we have no access to truth, or that all truth is merely relative or subjective, but just the opposite: to show that we have many kinds of access to truth, and that to say that something is constructed or fabricated is not to say that it is not real. In the modernist settlement, facts are taken to be objectively certain precisely because they are supposedly not constructed (despite the etymology of the word 'fact'); fetishes, on the other hand, are just those things which are not real (or whose meaning or power is not real) because they have been revealed to be products of human construction. If we concede, however, that both the fact and the fetish are fabricated in some way or other by interactions between humans and objects, then we open up the possibility of recombining these categories across the divide established by the work of purification. What we are left with is what Latour calls the "factish," in which the practice of construction and the reality of the world are not simply connected, but indeed are never divided (Latour 2010b, 22). Factishes exist on both sides of the line set up by the work of purification, because they need not be conceived as inert matter subject to objective physical laws nor as supernatural beings possessing agency in a modern sense. The more a factish is connected to a complex network of fabrications, the stronger its claim to truth; likewise, the more efficacious a factish is in transforming those who interact with it, the stronger its moral demand. The autonomy and power of a factish comes because of, not despite, its being constructed (Latour 1999, 275). The reality of a factish is to be determined only as part of a chain of references that also involves the behaviours and commitments of other beings who relate to and interact with it. Furthermore, as Isabelle Stengers points out, no element of such a networked chain would retain absolute causal or ontological priority over another element, since the reality of each element reciprocally depends on that of the others with which it is connected. In Stengers' view, this opens up space for a new understanding of sacredness as something which calls forth an obligation precisely out of the interdependency of factishes—an obligation, however, that would only pertain to those already engaged in practical relationships with the factishes among which it emerges (Stengers 2010, 80). Such an understanding of sacredness would blur the modernist line between religion and non-religion, insofar as it undermines any rigorous distinction between the transcendent and the immanent. Yet, it is precisely the modernist division between religion and non-religion that has both defined religion as such and subsequently made it so difficult to grasp.

Transformation and the Politics of Agnosticism

As mentioned previously, the modern work of purification constructs religion as a private matter, setting up in relation to it a public sphere that is "secular" to the extent that it has been purified of those "beliefs" which do not stand up to critical scrutiny. Insofar as the project of secularization accepts and reinforces the modern distinction between "facts" and "beliefs" while attempting to purge or silence discourses concerning the latter, it adopts a position that we may initially be inclined to call agnosticism. This variety of agnosticism, in Latour's words, "consists of a selective refusal to believe *in* the content of belief—usually God, more generally fetishisms ...; more recently popular culture; and eventually scientific facts themselves," with the last case being the point at which the spectre of postmodern relativism slips across the university campus from humanities seminar rooms and begins to haunt the laboratories (Latour 1999, 275). Ultimately, in all these examples, the point is not to be fooled and that we always be on our guard against conceptual illusions. In other words, here we are clearly dealing with the critical agnosticism of the modern iconoclast.

There is, however, a more radical form of agnosticism, which Latour argues more properly deserves the name: the abandonment of the belief in belief. In his words:

> I will define *agnosticism*, not as the doubting of values, powers, ideas, truths, distinctions, or constructions, but as the doubt exerted *against this doubt* itself, against the notion that *belief* could in any way be what holds any of these forms of life together. If we do away with belief (in beliefs) then we can explore the other models of action and mastery. (Latour 1999, 276)

The adoption of such a position would have wide-ranging and diverse consequences for our understanding of the place of religious commitments and public discourse—not the least of which is that it would promote a radical democratization of political discourse. No privileged position could be assumed for any "critical" or "enlightened" perspective, as each position would be faced with the same task of demonstrating (and never once and for all) its own consistency, soundness, and sustainability. Latour's argument compels us to understand religion in a different way than it has traditionally been understood by the mainstream of modern and contemporary philosophy. As long as we understand religious traditions as primarily having to do with beliefs, we will necessarily be led toward the idea that there will arise intractable disagreements over such beliefs, disagreements that can by themselves lead to ruinous consequences for the supposedly otherwise well-ordered public sphere. On the contrary, Latour's account suggests that, if people do in fact have these types of beliefs, they are not in themselves a necessary part of religious life. Rather, they become such only as the product of the modern project of secularization, which has demanded that religion play according to a set of rules that it had no say in writing.

In his discussion of the oft-misunderstood relationship between religious and scientific discourse, Latour distinguishes between what he calls "in-formation talk" and "trans-formation talk" (Latour 2010b, 102). Information talk is the mode of discourse within which we are used to operating in public, in areas such as politics and science, where the goal is to communicate from one point to another with the smoothest possible transportation of content. This mode of discourse functions very well in those areas to which it belongs; however, modernity has done it at least two serious injustices. The first is that it has distorted the model itself, so that its ideal is no longer understood to be a successful translation of content from one environment to another due to the effort of a chain of intermediaries.[1] Instead, the discursive ideal of modern reason is the unimpeded conveyance of parcels of information without any

---

1. On the translation of information and the role of intermediaries, see Latour 1999, 24–79.

translation, so that the intermediaries involved become invisible to the greatest degree possible. Latour euphemistically calls this model "double-click communication" (Latour 2010b, 106). The second injustice levied by modernity, though, is that this flattened-out discursive ideal gets extended beyond its scope and applied not only to science and politics but also to areas such as religion, which are not properly constituted by information talk at all but rather by transformation talk.

The difference between information talk and transformation talk does not primarily have to do with what is said; still less does it map evenly onto the modern distinction between public reason and private feeling. Transformation talk, as its name implies, is concerned chiefly with change: specifically, with the transformation of the speaker. It is not focused on communicating particular content so much as on successfully effecting a particular attunement. Latour's example is that of one person saying "I love you" to another: in most if not all cases, this utterance is not meant to convey information but instead to make the speaker present to the addressee in a certain way. Religious discourse, Latour argues, functions in this way as well, and to impose on it not only the idea that it consists primarily of "beliefs" but also that such beliefs are articulated according to the model of double-click communication is entirely to misunderstand it (Latour 2010b, 108). In religious discourse, just as in the endearments exchanged between lovers, the aim is the transformation of the speakers rather than the communication of a message; thus, elements like tone and bearing are sometimes more important than the particular words used. Modernist critique cannot help but overlook this emphasis on transformation when it understands religion solely in terms of beliefs.

This mischaracterization of religious discourse is part and parcel of the secularizing drive to purify the public sphere of irrational influences. For if religious discourse is understood simply as a type of double-click communication concerned with beliefs about supernatural beings or other sorts of mysteries, then it quickly appears at odds with "scientific" reason. As far as religion and science are both understood as offering descriptions of the world, their descriptions seem to compete against each other; as far as religion and politics are understood as offering different prescriptions for the proper organization and conduct of human lives, their prescriptions seem to be ill-suited to each other. Thus, as long as such an understanding of the constitution and operation of religious discourse holds sway, it remains a reasonable conclusion to consign religion to its own private sphere away from political discourse and power—that is, religion belongs in mosques, synagogues, churches, and temples (and mostly on weekends); in families' living rooms; or simply and quietly within the heart of the individual.

However, it is obvious that religious discourse has never been content to resign itself to these places, and this is largely because the distinctions on which the modern project of secularization rests have not actually obtained and cannot do so. Both information talk and transformation talk cut across divisions between public and private spheres, because, again, it is their function and not their content that differentiates them. What the work of purification—including the project of secularization—asks us to do is to divide our commitments, associations, arrangements, or ideas (all of which Latour calls "propositions") into two halves, even before we have the chance to understand them properly (Latour 2004, 215). It puts the cart before the horse, insofar as it demands that we know what kind of talk we will engage in—and that we position ourselves accordingly— before we begin to speak.

It may rightly be said that the project of secularization—indeed, the modernist settlement in general—is itself composed of a particular set of discourses that work to transform its speakers and hearers into modern subjects and to enact in the world the very distinctions that Latour finds untenable. However, it is characteristic of the transformative discourses of modernization that they do not recognize themselves as transformative. In addition, the bifurcation of the world that is part and parcel of modernization aims, however subtly or implicitly, not only at ignoring transformative discourse but at making it impossible. This is an unrealizable goal, not only because the work of modernization itself relies on the very discursive strategies that it claims to reject, but also because transformative discourse (in the broadest possible sense) is at work to some extent in every process of composition. We cannot make our way through the world without it. For this reason, simply focusing on transformation talk and breaking down modernity's conceptual barriers are not by themselves enough to guarantee positive ethical or political effects ("I hate you" can be just as transformative a phrase as "I love you"). Yet, recognizing the extent to which our familiar categories are built on a lack of acknowledgement of transformation talk can at least open new opportunities for future compositions.

In this vein, Latour advocates leaving behind the sharp distinction between the natural and political spheres so that we may, among other things, better integrate the demands of nonhuman beings into our common world. A similar (re-)integration of religious discourse into public discourse can be achieved through the application of Latour's radical agnosticism to our understanding of not only of religion but also politics. To be clear, this would not be a simple inclusion of religious speech in the political arena as these both now stand; without a drastic change in how we understand both political and religious discourse, we would only be confirming the very fears in response to which secularization operates. If, however, we are finally able to abandon the belief in belief, to deploy information talk effectively (and without reducing it to double-click communication), and to give closer attention to the operation and effects of religions' transformation talk, then the sharp divisions between public and private spheres would no longer be necessary. Not that there would no longer be contention, but the agonistics of post-secular politics would necessarily include religious commitments and discourses alongside non-religious ones (insofar as this distinction would remain viable). Without recourse to or contention over the veracity or falsity of beliefs, though, such discourse would be able to more adequately reflect the multiplicity of relationships always at work in the world.

If beliefs are no longer what is in question when we consider the place or function of religious discourse, then certainly such discourse can more easily find a place within a broader discursive sphere. It would, at the same time, have to be the case that what we have come to think of as strictly public values are no longer determined according to positions on an ideological map whose topology is laid out in advance. In much the same way as the metaphysics that Latour advocates is "experimental" (Latour 2004, 57)—that is, open to new ways of forming connections, and subject to constant revision—the composition of a common discursive space in which religious, political, and even scientific talk can operate would also have to be experimental. Experimentalism concerning the conditions and forms of discourse and radical agnosticism concerning the content of discourse mutually facilitate one another in the project of building an ever more viable and democratic common world, and it is within such a common world that the new understanding of sacredness as obligation grounded in practical interdependent relationships may be manifest in response to those beings that emerge according to the divine mode of existence.

Religion as Redirection, and the Divine Mode of Existence

In addition to the reduction of transformation talk to double-click-style information talk, Latour holds that one of the most pernicious misconceptions of religion is that it is chiefly concerned with what is far removed from the everyday (i.e., with the transcendent). This is, in a sense, a product of the belief in belief, insofar as such a notion produces a picture of religion whose main function is to propagate ideas about that which is either poorly understood or beyond the reach of human knowledge. On the contrary, it is modern science that concerns itself with what is farthest away from our ordinary experience: from distant galaxies to microscopic organisms and subatomic particles. Religion, on the other hand, is concerned with the practice of everyday life; the transformation at issue in religious discourse aims to direct our attention back toward that which is nearest to us (Latour 2010b, 110). This is what Latour means when he says that religion "does not even try to *grasp* anything" and that it "leads nowhere": religious discourse is never (or at least never primarily) informational in the way that scientific discourse is; it does not lead us along chains of references toward the world, but rather works at reorienting our ways of being in the world (Latour 2010b, 110; 2013b, 33).

This modern misunderstanding of religious discourse has additionally given rise to the idea that "religion" exists simply as an institutional bulwark against the advances of knowledge and reason. Latour distinguishes this concept of "religion"—"what passes for religion today"—from the religion about which he wants to speak by noting the ways in which the former has come to be associated with an ideal of stability and certainty, something that he wishes to associate with "fundamentalism" rather than religion proper (Latour 2013a, 300). Instead, we ought to understand both religious discourse and the objects of such discourse as characterized by hesitation, risk, and fragility (Latour 2013b, 121). This is because, on the one hand, religious discourse calls for constant repetition and renewal in order for it to remain efficacious and, on the other hand, because the existence of religious beings depends on this constant renewal of religious discourse.

On the first point, Latour claims that "religion is reprise par excellence, the ceaseless renewal of speech by speech itself," in which speech does not, again, attempt to grasp or refer to anything beyond itself but rather only leads back to itself (Latour 2013a, 306). Instead of producing empty metaphysics without grounding in the world—a charge commonly made against religious discourse by its modern critics—religious speech is subject to a set of felicity conditions wholly distinct from those that produce information talk. These felicity conditions, oriented toward the transformation of the speaker, involve comprehensibility, direction toward the present situation, and (perhaps most importantly) efficacy (Latour 2013b, 55). That is, religious discourse must *make a difference* or else it fails. This why it must both remain hesitant and continually renew itself; it cannot ever conclusively avoid the risk of failure to transform.

If religious speech does not refer beyond itself, though, what are we to make of the objects of such speech—that is, the beings evoked in and by religious discourse? As noted above, Latour claims that such beings' very existence depends precisely on the successful renewal of religious discourse. Following Étienne Souriau, Latour distinguishes between several different "modes of existence," arguing that the modern privileging of double-click communication has resulted in an ontological hegemony that not only ignores but actively suppresses such difference. As part and parcel of the work of purification, facts (which are supposedly simply given rather than constructed) are accorded full existence. Everything else is granted, at most, existence in a dependent and qualified sense. From this perspective, to say that religious beings are dependent on religious discourse is to say they are dependent on human practice and thus not real. According to Latour, of course, reality is always the result of the interrelationships between existents, so that everything from gods to garbage cans to blades of grass are simultaneously real and fabricated. What distinguishes different types of beings, then, is not whether or not they are "real" (or their degree of reality), but the ways in which they become real. The religious (or divine) mode of existence, then, depends on the fabrication of immanently transformative relationships brought about through successful religious speech. Whether it is the "seating" of an Orisha by a Candomblé practitioner (Latour 2010b, 6), the reverence shown by Dalits for their local *saligram* in a modern Indian novel (Latour 1999, 268), or the prayers of medieval French peasants reflected in the architecture of a church in Montcombroux (Latour 2013b, 12), what is at stake is the establishment of relationships through practices like rites, reverences, and prayers, such that the beings to whom these practices are addressed can come into and continue in existence. Furthermore, the type of existence proper to religious beings is such that it can never be assured. This is the source of the demand for continual renewal of religious discourse, for "one must go through the process again and again to be quite confident that one has seen them, sensed them, prayed to them" (Latour 2013a, 309). Thus the hesitation that Latour claims is inherent to religious speech: not even discourse that satisfies all its felicity conditions carries with it certainty about its success.

Ultimately, this way of understanding the mode of existence of religious beings shows us that such beings, in Latour's words, "have the peculiar feature of being *ways of speaking*" (Latour 2013a, 310). Since they are so inextricably bound up with religious discourse, their very existence cannot be distinguished from the discourse in which they appear. The felicity conditions of this discourse are thus the conditions of the possibility of their being at all. Yet, this does not make them less real. Religious discourses, together with all the non-discursive practices that also make up the contexts of religious life, constitute real communities and traditions that are either renewed by way of inheritance and translation or are slowly forgotten—or else petrify into the kind of institutions that Latour associates with "fundamentalism," which is ultimately a by-product of the work of purification and the belief in belief. It is the real, living tradition that is able to relate itself to real divinities, for these divinities simply are the ways of speaking and being by which the religious tradition is constituted as such. "There is no G[od]," says Latour, "that is not this very labour of revival and evaluation, reform and straying, the very passing of the word through this great virtual and indistinct people" (Latour 2013b, 161)—that is, the people whose hesitant speech conveys not belief but the radical agnosticism of transformative faith.

Conclusion

To be religious, according to Latour's understanding of the concept, is always to be in the process of recomposing. Religion, we might then say, is nothing other than recomposition, and the sense of the sacred or the divine most appropriate to it would be one that reflects an interdependent relationship between the subjects and objects of religious discourse. Such discourse is not primarily—or, according to Latour, not at all—about propositional "belief" or the conveyance of information; in this way, both religious speech itself and the attitude of the religious speaker are radically agnostic. Adequately heeding the radical agnosticism of religious discourse has significant implications not only for our understanding of religion. Furthermore, it is important to note that "religion" is not one thing, that the different traditions or modes of life that we call "religious" will (re)compose themselves in sometimes drastically different ways. It also impacts our understanding of the structure and function of the political, understood as the broader discursive space in which instances of both religious and other kinds of speech emerge and experimentally engage each other and the world.

References

Keane, W. 2007. *Christian Moderns: Freedom and Fetish in the Mission Encounter*, Berkeley: University of California Press.

Latour, B. 2013a. *An Inquiry into Modes of Existence: An Anthropology of the Moderns*. Translated by C. Porter. Cambridge, MA: Harvard University Press.

———. 2013b. *Rejoicing: Or the Torments of Religious Speech*. Translated by J. Rose, Cambridge: Polity.

———. 2010a. "An Attempt at a 'Compositionist Manifesto.'" *New Literary History* 4(3): 471–490.

———. 2010b. *On the Modern Cult of the Factish Gods*. Translated by H. MacLean and C. Porter. Durham, NC: Duke University Press.

———. 2004. *Politics of Nature: How to Bring the Sciences into Democracy*. Translated by C. Porter. Cambridge, MA: Harvard University Press.

———. 2002. "What Is Iconoclash?" In *Iconoclash: Beyond the Image Wars in Science, Religion and Art*, edited by B. Latour and P. Weibel, 16–40. Cambridge, MA: MIT Press.

———. 2001. "'Thou Shalt Not Take the Lord's Name in Vain'—Being a Sort of Sermon on the Hesitations of Religious Speech." *Res* 39: 215–234.

———. 1999. *Pandora's Hope. Essays on the reality of Science Studies.* Cambridge, MA: Harvard University Press.

———. 1993. *We Have Never Been Modern.* Translated by C. Porter. Cambridge, MA: Harvard University Press.

Stengers, I. 2010. *Cosmopolitics I.* Translated by R. Bononno. Minneapolis: University of Minnesota Press.

About the Author

Michael Barnes Norton is Assistant Professor in the Department of Philosophy and Interdisciplinary Studies at the University of Arkansas at Little Rock. He received a PhD in Philosophy from Villanova University in 2011, and he specializes in philosophy of religion, deconstruction, and phenomenology. He has published work on Derrida, post-colonialism, and religious pluralism, and his current research focuses on the work of Bruno Latour and new materialist approaches to religion.

— 7 —

Re-enchanting Body and Religion in a Secular Society: Touch of an Angel

Terhi Utriainen

Many modern Finnish women recount that angels can touch and enchant their minds, bodies and quotidian lives. Most of these women are members of the Evangelical Lutheran Church of Finland, but find the discourses and practices offered by the church increasingly secular and outdated and, most importantly, emotionally disengaging. Some of them also claim that they are not welcome in church with their newly found enchantment with angels, and instead they are told that their spirituality is too childish, sentimental or magical. Drawing on ethnographic material, this chapter argues that what is often depicted as "the touch of an angel" has become an intimate and both spiritually and bodily enchanting alterity for those engaged. Through such operations as ritual, metaphor and use of the subjunctive, angel enchantments articulate important relational matters of concern. These enchantments reveal intriguing, often transitory and sometimes unsettling dynamics of presence and absence of religious difference in a complex and precarious modern world.

Embodied Relations

Once the angels start to work with you, there will come a time when you get to "know" or "feel" them around you. It is just a matter of experimenting. I know they can create miracles and bring great peace of mind and strength to the suffering and the weak. Never think you are too

---

Keywords: enchantment, embodiment, magic, metaphor, subjunctive, women

> small or insignificant for them to attend you. They love to be of service in any way they can. (Beleta Greenaway 2009, xi)

Besides often being sources or fields of "enchantment," in common with other things and institutions which human beings engage and attach themselves to, religion can in many ways also become disenchanted as well as re-enchanted. My ethnography with Finnish women who have started to entertain active, intimate and animated relations with angels provides an example of one religious form or mode losing its enchanting potential, while another form—a particular symbol or metaphor that carries and articulates that new form—gains in enchanting power. One key issue in my material seems to be how women feel that angels can touch and enchant their quotidian and spiritual lives. If we follow Jane Bennett, enchantment is above all about making a difference. To be enchanted by something is "to be struck and shaken by the extraordinary that lives amid the familiar and the everyday," and, furthermore, "to participate in a momentary immobilizing encounter; it is to be transfixed, spellbound" (Bennett 2001, 4–5). Most importantly for the present chapter, *enchantment is dynamic*: it can be a momentary (sensory) event, something that flares and soon fades, but brings in a sensible difference; it can be either actively created and enacted or spontaneously encountered, but it is difficult to hold on to and it resists control in the end.

It can be argued that our human *enchantability* is anchored in our bodies: that human bodies need and desire to be enchanted. This need and desire is perhaps rooted in the fundamentally relational way in which our human materiality exists in the world: our embodied subjectivity is not isolated, fixed and bounded, but instead open, moving, vibrating and volatile, as for instance Elisabeth Grosz (1994) writes when refiguring (sexed) bodies. Phenomenologists such as Maurice Merleau-Ponty and Gail Weiss (1999), as well as the anthropologist of religion Thomas Csordas (2004), maintain that we are bodily open to various kinds of alterities—or, we also could say, to dynamics of difference—with which we relate and communicate and, furthermore, become. It is very much our bodily permeability and enchantability that binds us together with things in the world; it is tied with old affections, and it engenders new things and gives pleasure (to the limit of healing and ecstasy), but it also makes us vulnerable and mortal in the end. Living human bodies are open to things, ranging from air, nourishment and the touch of others to historically sedimented meanings—such as (images and narratives of) gods, spirits, ancestors or other otherworldly powers, be that for better or for worse (e.g., Orsi 2005). Morny Joy (2011, 221–222) reminds us also that otherness, including religious otherness, can take many either positive or negative forms in human life. Yet it is important to emphasize that it is only sometimes, and under some circumstances, that the more extraordinary forms of difference, and new assemblages that come into being with them, come to be called "religious" (Taves 2009). At other times, in other contexts, for some particular reason or from another person's perspective, they might be taken to belong to the realm of magic, aesthetics, entertainment, dream, eroticism or sheer imagination (e.g., Elkins and Morgan 2009; Partridge 2004).

Moreover, language may engage in enchanted relations in complicating ways: enchantments are described and justified as something, such as "religious" or "non-religious," "transcendent" or "magical" (to the interviewer or other interlocutor, or the self) or in different ways touched upon with often metaphoric words and narratives which then become semi-independent co-composers in what happens. As literary and communication studies have demonstrated, when an experience is reported it takes on a new form and often also a life of its own in which agency, in the sense of "authorship," may become quite uncertain and in many ways transferred (e.g., Campbell 2005). The sociologist of religion Courtney Bender (2008) reflects on the important issue of how religious experience and language complement and often also complicate one another. Language that describes experience, or ritual, to someone also contributes to the experience and its effects, and thus becomes involved in how credible the experience becomes. This often happens through subtle notions and images that language carries, as well as by linguistic operations such as negation and comparison. One important operation is the *subjunctive*, that is, the grammatical mode which communicates potentialities instead of facts.[1] Language can thus become part of agency in most complex ways.

The Weberian story of disenchantment entails that while "religion" can undoubtedly become one sphere of potentially enchanting relations, it can also in many ways become a closed space and dead letter in which allure and miracles seem to be ruled out, in order that control and regulation of experience and interaction—as well as normative judgement of what may or may not be included in making things happen—can take place. Rationalization, bureaucratization and secularization are oft-mentioned examples of this process of taming and dampening openly emotional and bodily engaging religion. Some forms of relating to religious difference can also turn mute, uninspiring and disenchanted, or simply untimely and irrelevant to some people, while other forms become appealing, enlivening and even urgent. Let's explore how angels, *relating to them and speaking about them*, are involved in these kinds of dynamics today.

---

1. On the subjunctive mood in the operation of ritual, see Seligman 2010.

Women and Angels

Even though the majority of the women whom I met during a two-year course of research were members of the Evangelical Lutheran Church of Finland, they maintained that they were no longer affected or touched by the discourses and practices offered by the Church, finding them increasingly secular yet normative, word-oriented, passivating and outdated. Some of them also said that they felt that they were not welcome in church with their newly found enchantment with angels, instead being told that their spirituality was too childish, emotional or magical. These particular women were not attracted by such available "alternative" forms of religion as Neopaganism or Charismatic Christianity, however. They were instead drawn to the new forms of the traditional Christian figures of angels, as promoted by contemporary culture and introduced to them by friends and media.

I argue that what is often depicted by my research participants and the many materials they circulate in their networks as "the touch of an angel" had become an intimate and, for some, also an exciting difference. It came to represent a difference with which they were able to relate to as well as experience, create and imagine—often not only individually, but also together—something important in their often complex modern lives. The touch of an angel provides something that, for them, a relatively disenchanted Lutheran religion is unable to give. In this way angels articulate a timely and transforming difference and relation, a veritable matter of concern (Latour 2004), in a precarious society and secular time.

Since becoming enchanted with angels seems to appeal particularly to women, we can also see that this practice in an interesting way (even if this was not often explicitly communicated) circulates and reinterprets the traditional motive of the *annunciation of Mary* in a disenchanted Lutheran world. There are hundreds of versions by artists from different times depicting the archangel Gabriel sent by God to deliver the message of incarnation to Mary, which is the core miracle of Christianity. It is possible to see this image as a half-hidden yet agentive subtext of the stories and setting told to me. Namely, in the centre of angel practices we can see an angel appearing to an "ordinary" woman, bringing a message that will change life.

The observations made in this chapter draw on my fieldwork, including individual and group interviews with over twenty interviewees, observations in various kinds of events such as angel healing, books, media material, and miscellaneous artefacts that circulate in the global and local angel culture, and a questionnaire.[2] According to the questionnaire

---

2. The research was part of a larger project "Post-secular culture and a changing religious landscape in Finland" based in Åbo Akademi University (Turku, Finland), 2010–2014.

(N263) given by me and my students to an audience of over one thousand Finns who came to listen to Lorna Byrne,[3] a well-known Irish-born angel writer and healer in Helsinki in 2011, 94 percent of those interested in angels were women—an even larger proportion than most studies have revealed for alternative spirituality.[4] Most of these women (73.8 percent) are members of the Evangelical Lutheran Church of Finland;[5] in terms of ethnicity and class, these white women come from working-class and middle-class backgrounds with educational and professional expertise in such fields as commerce and administration, education, and social and health services; they range in age from 20 to 70, with most being around 40 to 50 years old.

Angel practices, which are also popular in other countries besides Finland, can be described as present-day lived vernacular religion in the sense that they are not organized or even encouraged by religious institutions. Instead they are relatively democratic and cross-religious, being easy to participate in and integrate into modern lives.[6] My research participants (both those who answered the questionnaire and those interviewed and observed)—being mostly Lutherans or ex-Lutherans but also in their own way between religions—can to some extent be compared to the "Fusers" studied by Giselle Vincett (2008), who combine Christianity and Goddess religion; however, one important difference is that they do not identify themselves as pagan or feminist. They come closer to the formerly Christian women studied by Janet Eccles (2012), the "Holistic Switchers," who in many idiosyncratic ways are involved in alternative spiritualities. The "angel women" are not a homogenous group, but rather women who occupy a fluctuating continuum which is generally closer to Christianity than New Age spirituality, while being deeply involved with and integrated into secular Nordic society. When asked, my research participants responded that their favourite identity was "spiritual person."

There is a rich commercial side to popular angel culture, in particular in North America, an important exporter of the present phenomenon (Gardella 2007). It is thus possible to look critically at angel practices as something whereby the women participants have been lured into (commercial or childish) magic and led into wishful thinking. Alternatively,

---

3. On Lorna Byrne, see http://www.lornabyrne.com/.
4. See also Draper and Baker (2011); Uibu (2013) and Walter (2011) point out the preponderance of women in angel spirituality.
5. Of the whole population of Finland, 73.7 percent belonged to the Evangelical Lutheran Church in 2014.
6. Draper and Baker (2011), as well as Gilhus (2012), approach angel spirituality as a form of present-day folk religion.

they can be perceived as participants in a liberal, democratic, women-friendly religion that provides and articulates for them an important sense of personal agency as well as companionship; in various ways, this can be genuinely therapeutic, for instance, offering welcome means and instruments for dealing with emotions or a life-crisis (see Utriainen 2014). The first perspective, which might be said to belong to a hermeneutic of suspicion, is often dominant in secular sociology as well as, interestingly enough, in comments by male Lutheran theologians.[7] It goes without saying that the participants themselves favour the second perspective. It is also possible to see these women as reformative religious agents who are updating Christianity to better suit the modern world. Furthermore, angels may be seen as partners and co-actors with which it is possible to re-enchant a disenchanted Christianity.

Affective Bodily Enchantments

Much has been written on the process of reformation and modernization and the ways in which these processes have disenchanted Western experience and enactment of the body. For instance, still relevant is Philip Mellor and Chris Shilling's (1997) basically Weberian narrative of gradual secularization of bodies from the time of Reformation through such modernizing and rationalizing trends as industrialization and medicalization. Robert Orsi (2005, 12) suggests that this process has gone so far that modern bodies and senses are actively taught *not to* experience the presence of sacred powers. Interestingly, many of my interviewees discussed the secularity of the Lutheran church in Finland, meaning that the types of practices that they find attractive and helpful in their lives are easily dismissed as too unorthodox, childish or emotive. They recounted not finding transcendent partners, who would recognize their bodies and desires, in the present-day churchly space or realm.

The women I encountered did not elaborate on their bodies in ways that would be noticeable to outsiders: they do not dress or use their bodies in visually discernible ways, nor do most of them engage in demanding disciplines that would mould their bodies and minds (such as serious practice of yoga might do, for instance). These two manners of religious embodiment (dress as well as ritual types of discipline) can bring the religious/spiritual body visibly into the secular world. Instead, those who engage in angel practices are quite "ordinary" Finnish women whose

---

7. For secular writers, see Nevanlinna and Relander (2011); for Christian commentators, see e.g., Juntunen (2009) and Miettinen (2012). All of these Finnish male writers, both secular and religious, take up the issue of angel practices as a misunderstanding, produced very much by commercial and popular culture, of the Lutheran way of conceiving of the figure of an angel.

bodily practices and rituals are mostly unnoticeable to outsiders. Yet, what I find in my interview tapes and field notes is women and their bodies and senses, who are open to subtle imaginary and ritual practices of enchantment at the fringe of their secular everyday lives (See also Utriainen 2011).

In the following discussion, I will focus on select moments and instances in my field notes and interviews that emphasize and elaborate on intimate and bodily practice and experience in order to see what kinds of delicately spellbound ways transformed and different bodily experiences these women desire and live through with angels, as well as what kinds of matters of concern emerged from such engagement. I can see in this picture two slightly different, even if often complementary, meanings of touch: first, the *feminine bodily culture of caring* (mostly for others, but also the self), which has often been emphasized in research on female religiosity (e.g., Woodhead and Sointu 2008; Tzrebiatowska and Bruce 2012; Utriainen 2010); and second, the fragments of *subtle embodied relations with alterity* which make an enchanted difference—moreover, a difference which they claim can be very effective and productive in their lives. My analysis can be seen as one possible ethnographic trajectory in searching for "religious" enchantment and its entanglement with gendered, everyday lives in a secular society and, interestingly also, secularized religion.

In the long history of Christian art and theology, angels have been imagined and depicted as enactments of divine power, which can be either benign or violent (Jones 2011; Gardella 2007). However, the angels that I was told about were, without exception, regarded as tender and caring: they were said to be there to help, support, and inspire humans and to make sure that individuals were never totally alone, but instead connected in a network of care, power and agency. The touch of an angel would be taken as a message that there is an (imaginable but also in some ways tangible) benevolent difference besides the human subject. Present-day angels are most importantly guardians and intermediaries; I was told by many women that they may appear in material and even human-like form, but their angelic materiality is a fluid and attractive combination of presence and absence. They are vibrant and volatile bodies that constantly come and go between God and humans, or, as expressed with less Christian language by some women in my research, between humans and cosmic light. Angels can appear in human shape or, for instance, as pillars of light. They can have wings or be without them in these accounts and experiences.

In many respects, angels seem like perfect companions and spirits for people in this precarious time, who often have to change their locations, professions, social belongings and other attachments, even worldviews and identities.[8] One of my interviewees, a woman artist in her thirties, expresses this modern condition of flow and uncertainty, and the place it provides for angels, in the following words:

> And because nothing is permanent, the only permanent thing is change, that's for sure ... we can't lean on anything, because everything changes all the time and there are new tasks waiting all the time ... and they [the angels] send me to some unbelievable spots, and that's the best thing here that life becomes so extremely exciting. (IF mgt 2011-033)[9]

Many interviewees not only told that they experience angels, but also *actively imagine and seek contact* with them. Indeed, this activity, which is also often in some ways a collective activity on the part of humans, is something that differs from traditional and more spontaneous encounters, where angels are generally said to appear to passive humans. Some claimed that they had seen or heard angels, but by no means did everybody say the same thing. Lorna Byrne, the Irish angel writer and mystic who paid several visits to Finland during my fieldwork, is famous for seeing angels everywhere and with everyone. When she gave her lectures in Helsinki, she told the audience that the place was packed with angels who came to be with the audience of one thousand Finnish women and a handful of men. By being attractive, funny and compassionate, the multitude of angels cause Byrne to smile repeatedly, and she describes these heavenly beings in detail: their appearance, their size, and their wings, which according to her are beautiful in myriad ways. When the audience posed questions about their own personal angels, wanting to know what they looked like, they actively engaged in together summoning, creating and making space for the angels by talking about them.

One of my interviewees, a middle-aged woman who took an avid interest not only in angels but in "everything spiritual," as she said, told me that Lorna Byrne's books[10] were important to her precisely because they describe angelic appearances in abundant detail. These books have thus become for her a proxy way of seeing angels; otherwise she merely "knows" their presence. For her, knowing was a matter of mind and cognition more than the senses—and she felt that the different epistemologies or ways of assuring presence—imagination included—were

---

8. It does not surprise me that Michel Serres (1993) has chosen the figure of an angel in his book *La Légende des Anges* to express the spirit and character of the turn of the Millennium in many respects: we can witness movement and transition in every possible walk of life.
9. The interviews are kept at the Cultura archive at Åbo Akademi University.
10. *Angels in my Hair* (2008), *Stairway to Heaven* (2010), *Message of Hope from Angels* (2012).

complementary. In group discussions such as "angel evenings," the women shared ideas and talked about this topic with enthusiasm, and it is my impression that those who claim to see angels with their eyes are bombarded by others with the request: tell me what my angel looks like! Sometimes angels are seen in flashes or balls of light ("orbs") that can appear in digital photographs; two of my interviewees presented me with their impressive angel photograph collections, which they displayed and circulated for others to see, too. This was a creative material and technological way of making angels present and visible—and mediating them to oneself as well as others—when it is not possible to see them with the naked eye.[11]

On the whole, angels can be contacted by means of any of the human senses, that is, by hearing, touching, smelling and even tasting, as well as by intuition and imagination—and these experiences were shared and circulated in the social networks. Learning to feel with one's skin was taught in the angel healing course in which I participated. The touch of an angel can, for instance, protect oneself and one's children. In one account, this touch took the form of the Archangel Michael's (imagined) protective overalls in which the mother dressed her small children every time she sent them out into the world. In this example, angelic touch in the form of overalls acted like a visualized bodily prayer for the children; in this way a familiar Christian ritual, prayer, becomes re-enchanted and relational in a way that was not encouraged in the standard version of Lutheranism.

I was often told about male angels, the women's favourite and most often mentioned archangel being Michael. One of my elderly interviewees recounted her intimate friendship with two male angels, a mighty archangel and her personal and more quotidian guardian angel, who has a very ordinary Finnish name. In her account, these angel relations became so intense that it made her husband jealous. Here we can see a quite concrete example of the social and transcendent spheres clashing. Other women, however, told me that angels are basically emanations of energy, and energy has no sex or gender. One recurring idea was that angels often take the form that the person needs them to take—and this makes them into very amenable, therapeutic companions.[12] Thus, it is possible to acknowledge that angels may be (therapeutic) human imaginations and projections, but admitting this does not deprive them of the quite real power they emanate: angels can be human-made and real gods simultaneously (Latour 2011).

---

11. Photographing spirits has a history as long as the history of photography itself; see e.g., Wojcik 2009.
12. Stephen Murken's (2009) psychological research interprets contemporary angels as projections, that is, as figures of wish-fulfilment.

Enjoyable and Healing Differences

The intimate bodily relations with angels are learned and cultivated in and through a variety of enchanting practices and rituals, such as healings and meditations, and many of these practices form a very portable relationship. One of the simplest techniques is to have an angel card with a message in one's purse or to wear an angel ornament or talisman around one's neck, where it can be touched, looked at and related to at any time. It is possible, for instance, to invite angels for a visit to one's home for a few days. Furthermore, "angel visitations"—echoing the traditional motif of the Annunciation to Mary (even if the women didn't explicitly identify the Annunciation as the model)—circulate on the Internet in the form of chain letters. The fact that one can easily take this relationship to many places and in different contexts may well be part of both the efficacy and pleasurable aspect of angel practices.

Such pleasure can be intense, in particular during angel healings that women provide both to others and to themselves. The technique that was taught at the course where I did my participant observation was based on learning the special healing energies embodied by different angels and then working to "channel" this energy to the person being healed. An important ritual gesture in healing was the enactment (or imitation) of the angels' wings by the healer rhythmically opening and closing her arms over the body of the person being healed (see also Utriainen, forthcoming); by being slowly repeated, this relatively simple gesture becomes quite suggestive and even slightly hypnotic, as I also experienced myself. According to the unpublished guidebook for the angel-healing course, self-healing can happen in the following way:

> Concentrate on sensing Your Own Angel's presence as clearly as possible and ask him/her[13] to blend in with your aura. Feel as if wings are growing from your backbone. Try to carefully move these wings. Let your wings turn forward and surround you and feel how you and your angel are one. After this, open your wings carefully and let them shrink back again. Thank your angel for this experience and let him/her leave your aura.

In this example, the angel is brought so close to the woman (into her "aura," that is, her energy body) that their difference nearly fades away, and the woman imagines that she grows wings with which she touches herself. Angel healing may be seen as one method of self-help often used by the women for clearing their confused or complex emotional states, for instance, or for comforting or empowering themselves (see more in Utriainen 2014).

---

13. In Finnish, there is only one pronoun for the third-person singular (*hän*), which does not distinguish gender. This allows the individual the freedom to fill in any—or no—gender. Angels can also be referred to as "it" (*se*).

Nevertheless, even in this momentary attempt at merging there is a difference: the angel is depicted as an other, not merely as part of the woman's self. The two small words "as if" mark the important difference created by metaphor, the subjunctive and poetic imagination: it is "as if" the wings would be growing from the woman's backbone, in such a way that the "as if" can be forgotten for a moment. It may well be that these small words, which quite subtly juxtapose this and another world, as well as their possible forms of agency, are very important actors on the stage; "as if" is not a straightforward comparison but instead a dynamic and also fragile potential coming together and entanglement of a woman and an angel.

Closeness to intimate alterity appears in a different way during "channelling" (that is, spirit possession), whereby an angel speaks and acts through a human subject. Channelling (which can be part of healing, but is also present in creating art, such as music or images, with angels) places the angel and the woman bodily inside one another; it does not in any simple sense make them one, but rather a *layered composition* of two beings in intense and intimate relation to one another.[14] Material "evidence" of angels can be found everywhere. It might be a light breeze on the skin or hair (Lorna Byrne's first book is entitled *Angels in my Hair*, and one woman said that angels always touch her on the nose). It might also be that a person is irresistibly drawn to particular colours, which seem to talk to her (all archangels have their respective colours and energies; for instance, Michael's colour is blue and Gabriel's is white).

A feather provides a frequently mentioned material proof of the appearance of an angel. During Lorna Byrne's lecture event, white feathers were scattered on the floor of the conference hall. Once when I was leaving the "angel evening" with one of the participants, she saw a small grey feather on the ground in front of the house, as we had heard many times that we might if we kept our eyes open. "Definitely," she said, "a message from an angel." Feathers are iconic of angels, but also indexical; they are understood to fall from angels' wings, and wings refer to the way in which angels move, that is, they fly. Wings can also be felt as a protective and caring embrace around humans (e.g., the angel overalls, during angel healing); a tickling and slightly exciting sensation on the skin feels like a touch of a feather, which can open the moment to surprise and difference, that is, to small miracles. Feathers are a manifestation of the very light, almost subliminal, touch and materiality of angels, a good example of something which combines presence and absence.[15]

---

14. See Adam Klin-Oron (2014) on the various aspects of involvement and commitment in the ethnographer's own experience for understanding the complexity of the iconic New Age ritual of channelling.
15. This might be compared to how the Portuguese women studied by Lena Gemzöe

Female Enchantments?

According to Meredith McGuire (2008, 157–183), religions construct and help to create gendered identities, lives and bodies. What kind of modern female identity, life and body might become expressed and enacted within the angel enchantments that I have sketched out here? Women who relate to angels are self-reflexive and responsible modern women who are told (by multiple aspects of the present society) to take care of their lives and well-being, as well as to learn new things as effectively and creatively as they can. They engage in social, cultural, personal and embodied imagination to sustain and change their lives. It is possible to discuss, but not easy to judge, to what degree enchantments like angel practices should be seen as a means for creative agency or, alternatively, a way of engaging in escapist fantasy.[16] As Gordon Lynch (2007, 7) says: "Writing about the new spirituality functions as a kind of religious and cultural Rorschach test, where what the researcher sees is often a projection of their own values, hopes and concerns."

Even though practitioners (writers, healers, speakers and the audience) are almost exclusively women, angel enchantments do not explicitly celebrate or even describe the female body and its difference, something that is otherwise relatively common in the field of alternative spirituality, particularly within neo-paganism (e.g., Salomonsen 2002; Trullsson 2010). There was no direct mention in my material, for instance, of pregnancy, giving birth, menstruation, menopause, or other aspects of the female body in relation to spirituality, as if these were not very meaningful issues—or else they were not disclosed for some other reason. The interviewees did talk about concrete male and female beings and some differences between them (for example, discussion about how men in general are not as interested in angels as women, since their "energies" are different), but they did not use gender or sex much in explanatory or metaphysically meaningful ways; this may partly be related to the Nordic ethos of gender equality. Thus, femininity itself was not explicitly enchanted. As I mentioned earlier, angels are often male; this is an interesting point, which I will briefly return to later. What I do find embedded in my interviews and field notes is how some women in a modern secular society desire the touch of this particular kind of sensuously enchanting other, which comes at least partly from the Christian cultural heritage.

(2000, 141–166) value and display flowers as momentary and fading material, which for them was very powerful in mediating the sacred.

16. Janice Radway (1984) touches on the same question when writing on how women engage romantic fiction. Her choice is to describe the practice in its complexity.

Angel enchantments create and make liveable female bodies that are not (and/or would not want to be) solitary and isolated modern (religious) agents, but embodied subjects in dynamic relations, that is, accompanied, supported, touched, and also empowered by something extraordinary that is taken as not quite of this world but nevertheless relatively easy to reach and relate to. Angel enchantments include difference, or alterity, which is not completely and wholly other—like a remote god might be, but instead subtly and *intimately other* (see Csordas 2004; Utriainen 2013a).[17] The intimate alterity or difference belonging to angel practices produces, through various material, pictorial, verbal and other mediations, diverse aspects of bodily sensation and pleasure that make quotidian life more enjoyable, exciting, and aesthetic.[18] That is, they help transcending of the everyday, to fly above it at least for a short moment. It is *as if* the women are growing gentle yet powerful wings with which they can take some distance from the sufferings—and sometimes sheer banalities—of life.

Hence, are angel enchantments with their bodily support and comfort a good or bad allure or charm for these women? I find it extremely difficult to answer either yes or no to this living paradox of religion (as well as many other attachments, of course): it makes people into both subjects of power and, at least potentially and momentarily, agents who, through their complex relatedness, can connect to power. For instance, the research of Saba Mahmood (2005) and Rebecca Lester (2005) reminds us that religion can create (personal or social) agency for women, but often in extremely complex and controversial ways. One may be the enchanter and become enchanted by something simultaneously. It is impossible not to see how angel culture is part and parcel of the Christian tradition, present-day neoliberal logic, and self-help culture, which easily turns both well-being and religion into market objects and seduces people into becoming gendered and embodied consumers (e.g., Gardella 2007; Moberg and Granqvist 2012; Gautier and Martikainen 2013). Angel enchantments and the near-magical pleasures they sometimes promise are promoted and made increasingly mainstream by such media as the book market, women's magazines, the Internet, and films that depict a woman with a male angel, such as *The City of Angels* or, in a more poetic way, *Wings of Desire* (e.g., Utriainen 2013b). Yet the picture is complicated

---

17. Interestingly, among some American evangelicals Tanya Luhrman (2004) finds very similar types of detailed intimacy with God, to the point of painting fingernails with Him.
18. Gemzöe (2000) writes on the combination of aesthetic material and religious experience being vital to the women she studied in Portugal; this combination is expressed most vividly in the culture of flowers.

and intriguing: even if something like angel enchantment is promoted and mediated by art as well as popular and consumer culture, it does not mean that its magic could not, in some magical or social way, also work—or that today it would not also be necessary to engage with or need magic in many "religious" and other ways, too (see e.g., Bennett 2001; Meyer and Pals 2003).

Enchanting with Others

My ethnography was an endeavour aimed at opening exploratory trajectories composed of many kinds of both "theoretical" and "empirical" bits and pieces about enchantment as something that matters in the lives of my research partners as well as around them. It depicts enchantment as an openness and desire to be touched, supported and surprised by difference. It also creates a picture in which the possibility to animate a metaphor is a potential example of enchantment in modern life. By means of angels (or some other disparity being awakened), life can become at least a little different.

There are definite rewards and outcomes from relating to angels as intimate others. One important reward is that with angels, the women did not feel alone, but in many ways connected, accompanied and supported.[19] There are also the (more or less momentary and transitory) aspects of joy, play, and pleasure, as well as the creativity involved and generated in the process of this multi-layered embodied imagination. These experiences are not much elaborated upon by Trzebiatowska and Bruce (2012), for instance, who in the course of (appropriately) placing emphasis on aspects of female traditions and the culture of caregiving seek sociological reasons for women's predominance in so-called holistic religiosity. However, bodily pleasure, as well as gendered bodily pleasure and its implications, often appears in studies of neo-paganism (e.g., Fedele 2013; Vincett 2008; Salomonsen 2002; Trulsson 2010). When the women relate to male angels, the ensuing pleasure can entail what I would call a *heterosensual* aspect, even if it is not openly erotic or sexual. In other words, through the difference of (often male) angels, these women felt good (or, in any case, better) in their (female) lives and bodies. Thus, in these encounters we may sometimes see the fascination of gender difference without sexual difference?

In many ways, an angel is clearly an important other in the accounts of the women studied. It is an other that can take many forms and aspects, and it relates to the women's minds and bodies from varying distances and through several kinds of verbal or other mediations. Care, support,

---

19. The support aspect was very important for women in the Estonian The Nest of Angels online forum (Uibu 2013).

pleasure, and surprise may all be present in these relationships. Even when the angel is "inside" the woman, either as a voice of intuition or insight or when it comes to act in the world very concretely through the woman's body in "channelling," it seems to be articulated as at least somewhat distinct from the woman herself—as if it was her double, shadow or mirror. In many ways, angels also connected (or disconnected) women with others. I suggest that this subtle difference of angels—understood at times as more or less metaphorical—is an important aspect that we must not lose sight of; very secularist studies of religion risk doing this, which is why we need more of a post-secular approach to gender and religion. The implication of practices like angel spirituality may be in how they depict and make use of the open, volatile, and enchantable body as a potentiality for displacing and transforming agency. It reminds of the evident—and perhaps in some ways indispensable—place and role of alterity and extraordinary others, in their various forms, even in modern experience (Braidotti 2008; see also Day 2012; Joy 2011).

We live in an age of an abundance of forms and ways of enchantment, which can either put us to sleep or make us act. Even if from a critical perspective the aforementioned practices might be regarded as mere fiction and imagination, this would evoke the issue of the potential value of imagination and (in this case religious) metaphor being animated and coming alive as important or even indispensable vehicles of becoming and transformation. The appreciation of imagination is one of the most important characteristics of Western esotericism, as pointed out, for example, by Antoine Faivre (2010). As Ann Taves (2010) emphasizes, however, imagination is always an active and inevitable part of religion. In particular, the more "religious" forms of enchantment may seem difficult for some secularist positions, including secularist feminist perspectives and positions of understanding and acceptance, perhaps because feminists are often the least religious group among women (see Aune 2011).[20] Be that as it may, the women I met (and the few men, too, but that is another story) actively engage in "religious" enchantment in their daily lives and through their bodies. This reveals that religion is one possible and quite active source of enchantment today.

Some of the women described in this chapter also take the risk of coming out of the closet of secularized and privatized religion to claim their lives with invisible others—with the sometimes controversial support and encouragement of media and popular culture, as well as friends. They themselves mention this being a risk in contemporary society, both in their personal and work life and in the Church. This risk-taking, I sug-

---

20. Jane Bennett (2001) is also critical of religious enchantment, even if she finds enchantment in general utterly important.

gest, is worthy of note in a society such as relatively secularized Lutheran Finland, where religion has become very much *only metaphorical* and where any kind of *animation is seldom encouraged:*[21] the kind of embodied and emotional religiosity present in angel spirituality is easily (and perhaps in many ways also understandably) disputed and confusing to many people and institutions.[22] By engaging in enchanted practices and talking about them, the angel women may be seen as at least calling into question—if not seriously subverting—the modern idea(l) of the individual, autonomous bounded and disenchanted subject and agent, either secular or conventionally religious. Thus, in subtle yet intriguing ways they re-enchant both the "secular" and to some degree also the "religious." This may be slightly unsettling to the present-day secular-religious balance, whether we like it or not.

References

Aune, K. 2011. "Much Less Religious, a Little More Spiritual: The Religious and Spiritual Views of Third-wave Feminists in the UK." *Feminist Review* 97: 32–55.

Bender, C. 2007. "Touching the Transcendent: Rethinking Religious Experience in the Sociological Study of Religion". In *Everyday Religion: Observing Modern Religious Lives*, edited by N. Ammerman, 201–218. Oxford: Oxford University Press.

Bennett, J. 2001. *The Enchantment of Modern Life: Attachments, Crossings, and Ethics.* Princeton, NJ: Princeton University Press.

Braidotti, R. 2008. "In Spite of the Times: The Postsecular Turn in Feminism." *Theory, Culture and Society* 25: 1–24.

Byrne, L. 2012. *A Message of Hope from the Angels.* London: Hodder & Stoughton.

———. 2010. *Stairways to Heaven.* London: Hodder & Stoughton.

———. 2008. *Angels in my Hair.* London: Century.

Campbell, K. Kohrs. 2005. "Agency: Promiscuous and Protean." *Communication and Critical/Cultural Studies* 2: 1–19.

Csordas, T. 2004. "Asymptote of the Ineffable. Embodiment, Alterity, and the Theory of Religion." *Current Anthropology* 45(2): 163–185.

Day, A. 2012. "Extraordinary Relationality: Ancestor Veneration in Late Euro-American Society". *Nordic Journal of Religion and Society* 25(2): 169–181.

---

21. That is, devoid of the supernatural. Angels as effective spirits increasingly came to be eliminated from subsequent catechisms of the twentieth century.
22. This can be compared with Norway, where angel religion has also become a troublesome case for the folk church; see Gilhus 2012.

Draper, S. and J. O. Baker. 2011. "Angelic Belief as American Folk Religion." *Sociological Forum* 26(3): 623–643.

Eccles, J. 2012. "Holistic Switchers: The Spiritual and Value Commitments of a Group of Older Women Church Leavers." *Journal of the Scientific Study of Religion* 1(2): 187–202.

Elkins, J. and D. Morgan, eds. 2009. *Re-enchantment*. London: Routledge.

Faivre, A. 2010. *Western Esotericism: A Concise History*. New York: State University of New York Press.

Fedele, A. 2013. *Looking for Mary Magdalene: Alternative Pilgrimage and Ritual Creativity at Catholic Shrines in France*. Oxford: Oxford University Press.

Gardella, P. 2007. *American Angels: Useful Spirits in the Material World*. Lawrence: University Press of Kansas.

Gautier, F. and T. Martikainen, eds. 2013. *Religion in Consumer Society: Brands, Consumers, and Markets*. Hampshire: Ashgate.

Gemzöe, L. 2000. *Feminine Matters: Women's Religious Practices in a Portuguese Town*. Stockholm Studies in Social Anthropology 47. Stockholm: Stockholm University.

Gilhus, I. S. 2012. "Angels in Norway: Religious Border-crossers and Border-markers." In *Vernacular Religion in Everyday Life: Expressions of Belief*, edited by M. Bowman and Ü. Valk, 230–245. Sheffield: Equinox.

Greenaway, B. 2009. *Simply Angels*. New York: Sterling/Zambezi.

Grosz, E. 1994. *Volatile Bodies: Toward a Corporeal Feminism*. Bloomington: Indiana University Press.

Jones, D.A. 2011. *Angels: A Very Short Introduction*. Oxford: Oxford University Press.

Joy, M. 2011. "Encountering Otherness." In *Continental Philosophy and Philosophy of Religion*, edited by M. Joy, 221–246. Dortrecht: Springer.

Juntunen, S. 2009. "Hyvistä enkeleistä". <sammelijuntunen.kotisivukone.com/59> [Accessed 25 August 2013].

Klin-Oron, A. 2014. "How I learned to Channel: Epistemology, Phenomenology and Practice in a New Age Course." *American Ethnologist* 41(4): 635–647.

Latour, B. 2011. "Fetish-Factish." *Material Religion* 7(1): 42-49.

———. 2004. "Why Has Critique Run out of Steam: From Matters of Fact to Matters of Concern." *Critical Inquiry* 30: 225–248.

Lester, R. 2005. *Jesus in Our Wombs. Embodying Modernity in a Mexican Convent*. Berkeley: University of California Press.

Luhrmann, T. 2004. "Metakinesis: How God Becomes Intimate in Contemporary U.S. Christianity." *American Anthropologist* 106(3): 518–528.

Lynch, G. 2007. *The New Spirituality: An Introduction to Progressive Belief in the Twenty-first Century.* London: I.B.Tauris.

Mahmood, S. 2005. *Politics of Piety: The Islamic Revival and the Feminist Subject.* Princeton, NJ: Princeton University Press.

McGuire, M.B. 2008. *Lived Religion: Faith and Practice in Everyday Life.* Oxford: Oxford University Press.

Mellor P. and C. Shilling. 1997. *Re-forming the Body: Religion, Community and Modernity.* London: Sage Publications.

Meyer, B. and P. Pals. 2003. *Magic and Modernity: Interfaces of Revelation and Concealment.* Stanford, CA: Stanford University Press.

Miettinen, E. 2012. *Enkelit – taivaalliset auttajat.* Helsinki: Kirjapaja.

Murken, S. 2009. "Mein Wille geschehe... Religionpsychologische Überlegungen zum Verhältnis von Religion und Wuncherfüllung." *Zeitscrift für Religions Wissenschaft* 17: 165–187.

Nevanlinna, T. and J. Relander. 2011. *Uskon sanat.* Helsinki: Teos.

Orsi, R. A. 2005. *Between Heaven and Earth: The Religious Worlds People Make and the Scholars who Study Them.* Princeton, NJ: Princeton University Press.

Partridge, C. 2004. *The Re-Enchantment of the West.* Vol.1. London: Continuum.

Radway, J. 1984. *Reading the Romance: Women, Patriarchy and Popular Literature.* Chapel Hill: The University of North Carolina Press.

Salomonsen, J. 2002. *Enchanted Feminism. Ritual, Gender and Divinity among the Reclaiming Witches of San Francisco.* London: Routledge.

Seligman, A.B. 2010. "Ritual and Sincerity: Certitude and the Other." *Philosophy and Social Criticism* 36(1): 9–39.

Serres, M. 1993. *La Légende des Anges.* Paris: Flammarion.

Taves, A. 2009. *Religious Experience Reconsidered: A Building-Block Approach to the Study of Religion and Other Special Things.* Princeton, NJ: Princeton University Press.

Trulsson, Å. 2010. *Cultivating the Sacred: Ritual Creativity and Practice among Women in Contemporary Europe.* Lund Studies in History of Religions 28. Lund: Lund University, Department of History and Anthropology of Religions.

Trzebiatowska, M. and S. Bruce. 2012. *Why are Women More Religious than Men?* Oxford: Oxford University Press.

Uibu, M. 2013. "Creating Meanings and Supportive Networks on the Spiritual Internet Forum "The Nest of Angels." *Journal of Ethnology and Folkloristics* 6(2): 69–86.

Utriainen, T. Forthcoming 2016. "Healing Enchantment: How does Angel Healing Work?" In *Spirit and Mind: Mental Health at the Intersection of Religion and Psychiatry*, edited by H. Basu, R. Littlewood, and A. S. Steinforth. London: LIT Verlag.

———. 2014. "Angels, Agency and Emotions: Global Religion for Women in Finland?" In *Finnish Women Making Religion: Between Ancestors and Angels*, edited by T. Utriainen and P. Salmesvuori, 237–254. New York: Palgrave Macmillan.

———. 2013a. "Doing Things with Angels: Agency, Alterity and Practices of Enchantment." In *New Age Spirituality: Rethinking Religion*, edited by S. Sutcliffe and I. Gilhus, 242–255. Durham: Acumen.

———. 2013b. "Uskontotaidetta ja enkelinsiipiä: kaksi tapausta suomalaisissa naistenlehdissä." *Media & Viestintä* 2: 40–52.

———. 2011. "The Post-Secular Position and Enchanted Bodies." In *Religion and The Body*, edited by T. Ahlbäck, 417–432. Åbo: The Donner Institute for Research in Religious and Cultural History.

———. 2010. "Agents of De-differentiation: Women Care-givers for the Dying in Finland." *Journal of Contemporary Religion* 25(3): 437–451.

Vincett, G. 2008. "The Fusers: New Forms of Spiritualized Christianity." In *Women and Religion in the West: Challenging Secularization*, edited by K. Aune, S. Sharma, and G. Vincett, 133–145. Hampshire: Ashgate.

Weiss, G. 1999. *Body Images: Embodiment as Intercorporeality*. London: Routledge.

Wojcik, D. 2009. "Spirits, Apparitions, and Traditions of Supernatural Photography." *Visual Resources* 25(1–2): 109–136.

Woodhead, L. and E. Sointu. 2008. "Spirituality, Gender, and Expressive Selfhood." *Journal for the Scientific Study of Religion* 47: 259–276.

About the Author

Terhi Utriainen is Docent and Acting Professor in the Study of Religions at the University of Helsinki. Her research and teaching interests include ethnography of lived religion, gender and embodiment, ritual studies, death, dying and suffering. She is co-editor of *Post-Secular Society* (2012) and *Between Ancestors and Angels: Finnish Women Making Religion* (2014).

— 8 —

Marian Apparitions: The Construction of Authenticity and Governance of Sacralization in the Shrine of Our Lady of the Rosary in Portugal

NORA MACHADO

Sacred visions, supernatural visitations and revelations appearing to chosen visionaries have for millennia been an important, if relatively marginal, form of Christian religiosity. One of the key concerns regarding these supernatural phenomena is their authenticity and their particular forms of sacrality. This chapter focuses on the ways in which the shrine of Fátima in Portugal grew into a sacred configuration that coalesced in the form of Marian sacrality, combining specific social, iconic and political elements involving different agents and agencies (e.g., charismatic virtuosos and their followers, as well as religious, political, and administrative institutions), but also objects and temporal/spatial patterns "charged" with spiritual power and significance (e.g., consecrated places, sacred statues and relics, holy dates, and sacred and powerful rites such as certain prayers and rituals). Specifically, this chapter concerns the social definition and governance of Marian sacrality in Fátima, Portugal.

Introduction: The Governance of the Sacred

To analyse the governance of sacrality in Portugal in a few pages would be a daunting task, not just because the literature on the shrine of Our Lady in Fátima alone can fill several library rooms, but also because this shrine, one of the largest in the world, evolved through a range of different identities as it played an important role in the history of Portugal and

Keywords: Fátima apparitions, sacred, externalization, purification, legitimation, governance

Europe during the Cold War: first as an expression of popular religiosity with syncretic roots in a poor, rural region of Portugal and indirectly as an anti-republican message from Heaven; then becoming a national shrine and symbol of Portugal as a unified Christian nation under the dictatorship of Salazar; and later as the "altar of the world" blessed by several popes, a symbolic religious centre in the war against communism in Europe.

However, the focus of this work is not to present a historical study, but to analyse the different key mechanisms that made possible Fátima's emergence and preservation as a sacred place, the multiple agents at local and national levels, the agency of potent sacred objects (e.g., sacred statues and relics, consecrated rosaries, holy water, and figurines, as well as sacred and powerful rites such as holy prayers and formulations), and holy rituals defining not just a holy space but also a holy time. In the case of Fátima, the configuration of all these elements as a form of meta-power framework (Burns and Hall 2012) conjured a place and time where the sacred could emerge and be maintained under the aegis of the Catholic church as a collective arena of spiritual communion between the divinity, the spiritual virtuosos as charismatic mediators, and pilgrims and followers in devout communing in the rituals. However, the impact of the configuration of places, rituals, actors and other agents that gave rise to the Fátima shrine also resulted from particular sociocultural and political conditions that provided the religious-organizational frame that made it possible.[1]

The Emblematic Apparitions of Our Lady of the Rosary in Fátima

The apparitions of Our Lady of Fátima in the Cova de Iria (i.e., Fátima) would become one of the most celebrated apparitions of the Virgin Mary in the 20th Century, one of the eleven officially approved apparitions of the Virgin, and a major devotional centre of contemporary Catholicism. Fátima is also a major site of Marian pilgrimage, receiving millions of pilgrims every year. It is the hub of a major tourist attraction and the main source of revenue for the town that grew up around it.[2]

---

1. When examining the sacred configurations of the Fátima shrine in this article, I build on such ideas and concepts as Burns and Hall's structuration, Latour's transformative speech, and more generally Goffman's analysis of frameworks and their logic and transformations.
2. The Shrine of Fátima attracts a large number of visitors: in 2011 these numbered around seven million (http://es.arautos.org/view/show/33856-santuario-de-fatima-registra-aumento-en-el-numero-de-visitantes-durante-el-2011), and up to 37,000 pilgrims arrived at the site on foot.

The Sociocultural Environment of Portugal at the Beginning of the 20th Century: A War Between Religious and Secular Forces

Until the beginning of the 20th century, Portugal was, like Spain, a Catholic monarchy. Already from the time of the Council of Trento in the 1500s, the Catholic Church was the moral and religious authority of the kingdom, being central to much of the mentality and identity of the country and controlling vast economic power. Providing counsellors to the court and educating the political elite, it fulfilled several functions of the state (such as hospitals, all social work and education in general) and played an important role in the Portuguese colonies. However, the influence of the Church in the centres of power started to wane by the mid-1700s with the emergence of liberalism. In 1750, the Marquis of Pombal, a powerful counsellor to the king, barred the Jesuits from public life in order to limit their strategic influence in the affairs of the Crown and the state. After some years of peaceful coexistence, around 1820 a new confrontation between the state and the Church took place in the form of new liberal reforms, which spelled the final abolishment of the Inquisition, the banning of several religious orders, and the expropriation of several properties of the church (Dix 2010).

By 1860, the influence of the Church had declined further and it was relatively weak. In 1910, the First Republic was established and the Monarchy was abolished. This also was a time of radical anticlerical measures.[3] The new government declared itself secular, cutting the Church off from the state in 1911 with the Law of Separation. It outlawed the teaching of Catholic religion at schools and universities, instituted civil marriage as the only valid form of marriage and legalized divorce, confiscated all church properties and expelled many religious orders. This new, openly hostile regime obviously threatened the very existence of the Catholic Church in Portugal. A political but also symbolic war then ensued between the Republic and the Church. New laws forbade the ring-

---

3. There are similarities here with the post-revolutionary situation of the Catholic Church in France, whose power after 1789 was minimal. For example, births, marriages and deaths (previously a religious responsibility of priests) were placed in the charge of secular authorities, not the priesthood. In spite of the re-established Concordat of 1810, the role of the Church in France had been greatly weakened. For example, in 1830, during the constitutional crisis that overthrew Charles X, "the archbishop's palace would be sacked, the sacristies of Notre Dame desecrated, Jesuit headquarters at Montrouge attacked. Churches had to close for a few days till passions abated." This was the social environment of the apparition of Our Lady of the Miraculous Medal to Saint Catherine Labouré in Paris in 1930, the apparitions of Our Lady of La Salette to the two peasant children in 1846, and the apparition of Our Lady of Lourdes to Saint Bernadette Soubirous, a shepherd girl, in 1858 (Weber 1988, 406).

ing of church bells and the public use of priestly robes; religious holidays were suspended and priests were required to seek approval from municipalities before carrying out public religious activities, such as the processions of saints or funeral parades. But the anticlerical regulations of the Republic, instead of defeating the Church, evoked a new spirit of resistance, revitalizing Catholic groups (Dix 2010).[4]

The First Republic was already confronted by several problems. These not only included the economic problems of inflation and a lack of resources, which were aggravated by Portugal entering into World War I and sending troops to the colonies, but also the instability of government coalitions and only marginal support from the unions. Strikes and demonstrations led to a climate of instability. A military coup in December 1917 ended the revolutionary government and the persecution of the Church. By 1932, the country would have 39 governments.

Fátima Configurations:
A Local Sacrality, a National Sacrality and World Sacrality[5]

The Apparitions of the Cova de Iria: A Charismatic Governance of Sacrality

By 1917, in the midst of great social instability, popular religiosity remained vital in Portugal. The culture was rooted in a traditional religiosity where saints answered prayers, healed and performed miracles, and where Heaven could send messengers to the chosen people in times of great distress in the form of prophetic visions and apparitions.[6] Popular religiosity flourished almost everywhere in the celebration of *festas* and *romarias* with processions of the patron saints of the various villages or

---

4. Both sides stood for sacred transcendent values. On one side these were marked by progress, enlightenment ideals and a world centred on secular humanism; on the other side were a world centred on salvation, the sacred truths revealed by God, and traditional familial and gender structures. In the countryside, where the social and political environment of the villages revolved around the regularities of everyday work and the rituals of the Church, many villagers sided with their local priest and parish (Dias Coelho 1987).

5. Historians tend to characterize the history of the shrine of Fátima in terms of Fatima I and Fatima II, where the former (I) is prior to the official recognition of the Church and the second (Fatima II) represents the official institutionalization of the shrine. That said, from the perspective of configurations of sacrality, the incipient Fátima of Cova de Iria can be treated as a separate phase, however short, due to the popular religiosity of the first period rapidly merging with the institutionalization process of the second period.

6. In a speech made to the Senate in 1917, Tomás da Fonseca denounced as "ridiculous and absurdly miraculous" apparitions such as those of Lindoso (on 10 May 1917) and Vila Nova de Ourem, calling them nothing more than manoeuvres of the church mobilizing against the liberal policies of the new republic.

cities, where people gathered for days to celebrate the saints, to pray for their help or to give thanks for a request that had been granted, and to fulfil *promessas* (prayers, penance or *ex-votos* promised to the saint or the Virgin as symbolic payment for an indulgence, healing or rescue from a desperate situation). However, these religious celebrations were also social encounters for eating and drinking together, as well as exchanging local products. In general, these meetings were a mixture of sacred and profane activities (Dias Coelho 1987).

As intercessor for humanity, the messages of the Virgin Mary were particularly well known to the population, and the imagery of the apparitions was familiar due to previous apparitions, like the apparition of the Virgin of Aparecida to simple fishermen in Brazil in 1700, the Virgin of Ortiga in the 17th century near Fátima appearing to a mute shepherdess, and the Virgin of La Salette to two young sheepherders (1846), not to mention the Marian apparitions in Lourdes, France to a meek shepherdess (1858) and thousands of others.[7]

On 13 May 1917 in Leiria (a poor, rural area 300 km north of Lisbon and outside Fátima), three illiterate children—ten-year-old Lúcia and her younger cousins, Jacinta and Francisco—experienced visions, first of an angel and later of a lady floating above the branches of an oak tree in the field of the Cova de Iria. In the visions the numinous lady told the children that she had come from Heaven and that her name was the Lady of the Rosary. She promised to return on the 13th day of each month for the following six months. In subsequent apparitions, the Lady communicated through Lúcia—the only one of the children who was able to hear and talk with her—the importance of doing penance, carrying out acts of reparation to save sinners, reciting the Rosary in her name, and praying for the end of the war. The Lady announced that Jesus and St. Joseph would appear next to the children and bring peace to the world. She also told them that they should build there a chapel to the Lady of the Rosary.[8]

Already after the second visitation, local crowds gathered at the site of the apparitions, alerted by word of mouth and local newspapers reporting on the story of the Virgin Mary miraculously appearing in the Cova

---

7. Of 174 shrines in Portugal, 131 (75%) are Marian (Lima 1997). In the nineteenth and twentieth centuries, the apparitions of the Virgin Mary in Europe were not infrequent, particularly between 1830 and 1933. In this period, the Church recognized approximately 15 major apparitions, including those of Lourdes (1858) and Fátima (1917), but also those of Cerreto, Porzus (Italy), Philipsdorf (Bohemia), Giertrzwalde (Poland), Knock (Ireland), and Beauraing and Banneux (Belgium).

8. Recollections from the first interview with the children by the local vicar, which was sent to the bishop in 1917. *Documentacao Critica de Fátima. Vol 1. Interrogatorios aos videntes* 1917, edited by Santuario de Fátima in 1992.

da Iria.⁹ On the announced last visitation of 17 October, a large crowd (believed to number more than 30,000), including several newspaper reporters, had gathered in the Cova da Iria, waiting for the Virgin to appear to the children.

That day the children had visions of the Holy Family, of Our Lady of Sorrows with Jesus Christ, of Our Lady of Mount Carmel, and of Saint Joseph and Jesus blessing the people. At the same time, many of those present witnessed the sun change colour and rotate like a wheel, as if it were "dancing"; this became known as the "miracle of the sun" (Torgal 1995, 2011).

The apparitions of the Virgin in Fátima were veritable performances, announced through Lúcia as proposed by the Virgin, taking place on the 13th of each consecutive month for six months (Torgal 1995, 2011). In this way, the visitations were momentous and timed. The children arrived at the site of the apparitions in a ritual procession that always took place at midday. The sign that a visitation had commenced was the children falling to their knees under the sacred tree, apparently in a trance, while Lúcia addressed a divine presence—invisible to all but her. This demonstrated that the apparition was happening, being evidence that the Virgin was truly there in contact with Lúcia, and that the people congregated could experience the emotional intensity of her presence.

Many of those present at the apparitions wrote letters and gave interviews to newspapers. They reported feeling healed and energized, and that these experiences felt real. This was for them the most relevant proof of the authenticity and the sacrality of the event at Fátima, and proof of their contact with the Virgin (Torgal 1995, 212-215). The fact that thousands of other devout visitors and pilgrims were gathered at the site was also seen as evidence to the assembly that they were participating in something extraordinary and important. The number of journalists and photographers sent by newspapers to record the event of the apparitions at the Cova de Iria gave yet more compelling evidence of the significance of the event. Something momentous was taking place there.

Many newspapers published news about the apparitions; the first was the Catholic press, but others followed, and soon even the national press covered the event, describing the apparitions as miraculous and extraordinary, thereby intensifying the expectation that something unusual and relevant was about to happen (Teixeira Fernandez 1999). Even in the republican newspapers, although they explicitly rejected the holi-

---

9. The apparitions and prophecies of Fátima are defined by the Catholic Church as "private revelations" (i.e., they are not articles of faith of the Church, and it is in theory up to the individual believer to accept or reject them). However, several popes have visited and openly prayed to Fátima, affirming their faith in the revelations.

ness of the visions, the phenomena of the apparitions of Fátima were very intensely discussed. While their explicit intention was to reject and ridicule the visions as superstition and popular mystification, the apparitions received considerable mass-media coverage (Teixeira Fernandez 1999), turning the apparition into a widely known event.

By the third apparition, practically all of the Portuguese newspapers were covering the news of the arrival of the Virgin at Fátima (Teixeira Fernandez 1999).[10] As noted above, what happened on the date of the visitation of October 13 became known as the "Miracle of the Sun." Not everyone saw the same thing, and witnesses provided widely varying descriptions of the "sun's dance." The movements of the sun appear to have been witnessed by people many kilometres away. By the time of the last apparition in October 1917, there had arisen in Portugal a full-fledged debate on the phenomenon of Fátima!

Starting from the time of the Reconquista,[11] there was a long tradition of Marian apparitions in the Iberian Peninsula. Devotion to saints, but especially to the Holy Mother under different appellations, would spur the construction of hundreds of sanctuaries and chapels in her name, and such devotion has been at the heart of Iberian popular religiosity. Villages had their own protector saints that they customarily asked for help. The most powerful images of protector saints were venerated in shrines, but they could often also be found near holy springs, deserted sites, and sacred trees. New saints emerged through apparitions as well as through the resurgence of devotion to old saints. Saints gained and lost popularity depending on their alleged efficacy and renown, which could be communicated to their devotees by signs (such as reported miracles on the saint's day, for example). But villagers also searched for other signs, including abnormal events, which corresponded with the saint's apparition or a particular day (Christian 1989, 1999).

Many mythical themes of older Marian apparitions reappeared in the sacred drama of Fátima, like the Virgin appearing to the faithful, meek and dispossessed (i.e., three illiterate children praying the Rosary on a hill while tending sheep). A form of light or an angel, the beautiful figure of the young Virgin Mary in white luminous robes, and miraculous healing by a holy place at an oak tree were all well-established elements of the local grammar of the sacred in the Iberian Peninsula (Christian 1989,

---

10. Leopoldo Nunes, a Catholic journalist and Fátima supporter, described Fátima as a refuge for believers in those difficult times when Catholicism was threatened in Portugal.

11. When "Christian" armies start regaining control of the peninsula from the "Moors," the Virgin appeared to pious believers on the frontier lines, supporting the advance of Christian armies toward the south (Pereira 2007).

1999). The recitation of the Rosary, the prayers to save sinners and the world from sin, the apocalyptic messages, the strange natural events following the apparition that had many of the signs of older and well-known Marian visitations—they had all happened before. So when these "signs" appeared, they carried the mark of divinity as the people knew it.[12]

A Sacred Catholic Place of Prayer and Devotion: Institutional Religious Governance of Sacrality

The Portuguese Catholic Church was not receptive to the Fátima apparition at first, and only in 1930 would it officially accept the apparitions as authentic (even if the matter was seriously debated since the Church started plans for the shrine in 1920 (Barreto 2002; Torgal 2011)). It can be said that the Church was initially ambivalent to the apparitions, while the local authorities tried to stop the pilgrims from arriving (following the legislation in force that banned unauthorized gatherings) (Cardoso Reis 2001). Furthermore, many liberals questioned the authenticity of the apparitions, believing that they were a clerical manipulation of popular beliefs, aimed at turning people away from "the freemasons in the government." For example, the senator Tomás da Fonseca in the Senate denounced the miraculous apparitions of Fátima as ridiculous and absurd as the apparitions of Lindoso or Vila Nova de Ourem—also tactics of the clerical reaction against the new liberal politics (da Fonseca 1958).

In spite of the official opposition and the condemnation of the liberals, Fátima grew into a well-known holy place throughout the country, and the number of pilgrims and visitors grew. With the initial help of the religious/conservative media and later promotion of the debate by liberal newspapers, the fame of the miraculous apparition spread far and wide, becoming a national issue (Cardoso Reis 2001).

The sacrality of Fátima step by step became a proven "miraculous fact" governed by the Church.[13] Local priests and prelates knew that the effervescence and sacrality surrounding the apparitions had a destabilizing potential, and that it was important to manage and govern this energy in order to stabilize and preserve it. They would attempt to do it for several

---

12. Apparitions were not an uncommon phenomenon in the region. There were approximately ten apparitions in 1916–1918 with similar characteristics as the Lady of the Rosary (Torgal 1995). For example, the apparition of the Lady of Peace, the vision of a woman in bright white, appeared to a shepherd boy in the region of Barral on the 10th and 11th of May 1917, that is two days before the Fátima apparition (the Lady of Peace also requested Rosary prayers for peace and promised to help the world).

13. In his analysis of Fátima, the historian Felipe Torgal claims that the preparatory measures for the construction of the shrine and the legitimation of the apparition started well before 1930, rather around 1920, when the deacon Formigão, a Lourdes devotee, started promoting Fátima.

years through processes of 1) externalization and stabilization, 2) purification and 3) legitimation.[14]

Externalization and Stabilization

After the apparitions it was not long before a statue of Our Lady of Fátima was carved (1920) and placed in a small sanctuary at the site. By 1921, the "Chapel of the Apparitions" was erected with a shrine for the Virgin on the site of the apparitions.[15]

The statue, the chapel and the shrine (as well as the devotional rules at the site) were essential material constructs that made possible the externalization (i.e., materialization and objectification) of the miracle of Fátima. This "material configuration" acted at the embodiment of subjective internal spiritual experiences of the presence of the Virgin, now imprinted into the statue, the chapel and the shrine as external and objective carriers of the divinity, sacred symbols full of power themselves.

In this way, the image of the Lady of the Rosary at Fátima is more than just any representation of the Virgin Mary. It became a sacred vessel, an object of veneration that pilgrims could approach, and which can produce miracles just by being touched, just by being near it. But the Chapel of the Apparitions at the Shrine are also external signs and materializations of something sacred and significant that happened there and left its mark.

The creation of this sacred object/place makes it possible for all those pilgrims to re-live the contact with the sacred and have access to spiritual experience through the sacred object, thus bridging the relationship between the believer and the divine (Kenna 1985). In this way the shrine is made not into a historical site but into a sacred living place, retaining the ability to evoke the presence of the sacred in the believer.[16]

The externalization of the apparition—here also a form of stabilization –was achieved through the ritual placing of the sacred statue at the chapel—with the characteristic demeanour, form and colours attributed to the Virgin of Fátima; by building the Chapel, thus demarcating the most sacred site, and by the consecrating of the Shrine by the Church. A more secular form of stabilization consisted in demarcating the land where the apparitions had taken place, and buying it as property of the Church, making it possible to enclose and define the location exclusively as a site for religious activities (Eiper 2007).

---

14. These dimensions are separated analytically, but in practice they may overlap.
15. Although hundreds of Marian apparitions have been reported since the early nineteenth century, only a handful of cases were investigated by diocesan commissions, approved by the local bishop, and thus officially recognized by the Church, at least at the local and regional levels (Zimdars-Swartz 1991, 11).
16. In addition, a hostel was built to host the many sick coming to the shrine for healing.

Purification

The purification dimension, as part of the governance of sacrality at the Fátima shrine, implied keeping unsullied the messages and behaviour of Lúcia, the only surviving member of the visionary children, as the other two had died in the Spanish influenza epidemic of 1918–20. Soon after the visions, she was removed from her hamlet and taken to a private school regimented by the Dorothean nuns, becoming an enclosed Carmelite nun some years later. Long before that, however, any contact with her mother, relatives and neighbours and the outside world was dramatically and strategically limited. Lúcia had become a saintly figure touched by God, separated from normal life forever.

Her seclusion (she only had contact with her confessors) also prevented new revelations or distortions of her older pronouncements, thus preventing modifying the apparition in uncontrolled ways. The message had to be kept pure and as unaltered as possible.

The risk of inflationary and distorted visions was not trivial. The importance of the isolation of Lúcia becomes clearer when Fátima is compared, for example, to the apparitions of the Virgin Mary in Garabandal, Spain, where the number of visionaries and the variety and character of their visions grew uncontrollably, becoming successively modified, inflated and baroque, until even the devil himself was included among the celestial/infernal visitors. This took place with uncontrolled media involvement, and ultimately the credibility of the apparitions was ruined (Christian 1989, 1999).

Another form of the purification of the sacrality of Fátima was the printing of the *Manual of the Fátima Pilgrim*, written in 1926 to provide instructions to pilgrims and to formalize the rules of proper behaviour in the precinct of the shrine. The *Manual* was important because it delimited the social boundaries of the shrine, dramatically breaking with accustomed cultural mores around Portuguese sanctuaries and the traditional festivities of the saints (*romarias*). There was to be no selling of any kind of merchandise or food in the shrine except religious items, no popular tunes to the Virgin, and no dancing or partying. Eating and drinking could take place outside the shrine, and modest dress and behaviour were required in the area of the sanctuary. In this way, Fátima as a space for meditation and prayer became unique, distinct from existing popular local shrines, where the sacrality of the precinct was clearly defined and maintained.

Legitimation

In 1922, the Bishop of Leiria wrote a letter indicating his approval of the miracles of Fátima, thereby commencing the official legitimization process.[17] In 1930, the journal *Voz de Fátima* was founded, becoming the quasi-official voice of the sanctuary. Its circulation would reach up to 392,700 newspapers in 1938, which proclaimed that thousands "miracle cures" had taken place in Fátima. That same year, the Bishop of Leiria declared the miracles in Fátima as a proof of Christ's divine mission, thus simultaneously providing stronger support and legitimation of Fátima's sacrality. Eventually, more and more Portuguese bishops would support it.[18]

In 1929, Fátima was legitimized by the local bishop as an "authentic revelation," and it was ratified by the Patriarch of Lisbon the following year.[19] A large basilica was constructed between 1927 and 1954 to receive the increasingly large number of pilgrims arriving at the shrine. In 1931, the Patriarch of Lisbon, Cardinal Cerejeira, presided over a procession to the Virgin of the Rosary (i.e., Our Lady of Fátima) and defended Fátima openly (Barreto 2002).

The official legitimation of the Church was essential. The emergence of visionaries and saints with a direct line to Heaven had the potential of challenging the organization of the Church, which was structured into hierarchical circles of authority (i.e., sanctity and legitimacy), with the least degree of holiness at the local level and the highest at the top (the Pope at the top of the hierarchical pyramid holds the ultimate charismatic power). Integrating visionaries into the Church made for a renewal of charisma, provided that this new contact with divinity could be framed in the tradition of the religious institution (Cardoso Reis 2001). If the Catholic Church had not from the start possessed the ability to present itself as the mediating authority of the apparitions, the sacrality of Fátima could, at least theoretically, have become diluted into a form of popular piety, either in parallel or in competition to other Portuguese shrines (Cardoso Reis 2001). After the canonical enquiry and approval, the visions of Fátima were officially declared "worthy of belief" in October 1930 by the Bishop of Leiria.

There is also a national political dimension to Fátima. An authoritarian, conservative police state had been established in Portugal under the leadership of Salazar from 1932–1968 and his successor, Marcelo Caetano, from 1968–1974. The new corporatist/fascist state, which counted the support of the more conservative faction of the Portuguese Church, harnessed the significance of Fátima. Salazar himself was not instrumental in recognizing Fátima, but as Minister of Finance since 1928, he was supportive of its

---

17. The shrine was the target of a bomb attack (on the chapel) in 1922. Paradoxically, they gave a tremendous boost to Fátima support.

18. Not all bishops or priests supported the apparition—ever. Officially, the head of the Portuguese Church, Cardinal Cerejeira, said that he did not believe it at first.

19. Approval of the Vatican would follow later; it became a sacred place for multitudes and a sanctuary that would be visited by several popes devoted to Fátima.

development, financing the construction of the electrical infrastructure of the shrine and the urbanization of Fátima. All these projects made possible both increased pilgrimage and opening Fátima into a major spiritual centre.[20] As part of the conservative elite connected to Portuguese Catholic Action, Salazar was also associated with the Catholic project of the re-Christianization of Portugal. The clerical conservatives, who around 1917 were still sympathetic to the monarchy, accepted the authoritarian Salazar state after the defeat of the secular Republic, at least initially. That is, in the words of Almeida (Almeida 2008, 23, quoted in Dix 2010): "The Estado Novo (1933-1974) can be understood as the institutionalization of a nation 'essentially Christian' and where the Catholic Church became like in Spain, (alongside the military) ideologically and institutionally a leading support for the Estado Novo." The sacrality of Fátima became tied to the sacrality of the nation, to a chosen people guided by God.[21]

International Legitimation: Fátima as the Altar of the World

After the local bishop declared that the visions of the three children were credible and the veneration of the Blessed Virgin was made official in 1930, most Portuguese bishops approved the genuine supernatural nature of the event (Salgado de Matos 2001). The Vatican responded by granting indulgences and permitting special Liturgies of the Mass to be celebrated in Fátima. One year after World War II started, Sister Lúcia asked Pope Pius XII to consecrate the world and Russia to the Immaculate Heart of Mary (Bromley and Bobbit 2011). She repeated this request on 2 December 1940, stating that the Blessed Lady had requested the consecration of Russia to her Immaculate Heart. She promised the conversion of Russia from its errors.[22]

In her later memoirs, Lúcia revealed that during her appearances, the Virgin Mary had revealed secrets, which later became known as the Three Secrets of Fátima.[23] The secrets include visions of the hells that

---

20. Salazar was present as Minister of Finance at the inauguration of the electrical infrastructure of Fátima in 1929, together with then-President of the military government Óscar Carmona.
21. Thus declared the Patriarch of Lisbon: "Since Our Lady of Fatima appeared in 1917 in the skies of Portugal a special blessing of God descended on earth to the Portuguese. With Fatima ends the cycle of violent religious persecution and begins a new era of peace and restoration of Christian conscience" (Flunser Pimentel 2010).
22. In response to this plea, in 1942 Pope Pius XII consecrated the "peoples of Russia" to her Immaculate Heart, and in in1952 the world to it; the world was consecrated to her Heart by Pope John Paul II in 1982 and 1984 and Pope Francis in 2013.
23. Lúcia's first testimonies are from 1917, but she gave testimonies on other later occasions. She wrote a recollection of the apparitions, dating from 1929 up to 1941. She started writing her memories in 1935 (Dos Santos 2006).

await sinners, a prediction of the early death of the other two children visionaries, the imminent end of World War I, and the need to consecrate Russia to the Immaculate Heart of Mary in order to stop the spread of communism in the world. The "third" revelation was to be kept a secret until after the 1960s, or after the death of Lúcia.[24] In fact, the messages of the Virgin to the visionaries in Fátima were rather dramatic and apocalyptic, predicting devastations if the world did not repent and pray. The whole world was portrayed as if on the brink of a chasm.[25]

In particular, Pope Pius XII was an ardent believer of Fátima. Not only did he consecrate the world to Mary's Immaculate Heart in 1942, but in 1950 he also declared the assumption of Mary to Heaven in soul and body as a dogma of faith, reaffirming the centrality of the Virgin in Christian theology. It also gave the Fátima shrine a special place in the Catholic world as the holy centre of anti-communist crusades at the time of the Cold War and as a bastion of traditionalist Catholic groups (Barreto 2002, 502).

Fátima progressively transcended Portuguese national boundaries, acquiring an international dimension as the champion of the conservative Catholic faith in modern times and becoming regarded as the archetype of a political apparition (Matter 2001).[26] Finally, Pope Paul II made a pilgrimage to Fátima and declared it "the Altar of The World."

---

24. Much of the large popularity of Our Lady in this century came as a result of the messages from Fátima made public in the 1940s and "the secrets" revealed to the visionary (Horsfall 2000). The apocalyptic nature of the visions—together with the third, unrevealed secret—aroused fears. Many assumed the worst, speculating that the third secret prophesized horrifying catastrophes, the assassination of the Pope and the end of the Church, or even the end of the world. The third secret was finally revealed in 2000 by the Vatican (Ratzinger 2000).

25. The social and socio-political environment of the time of World War II and the Cold War implied a deep crisis. The diaries (*Memórias*) of Lúcia revealed a strongly anti-Soviet character in the messages, describing communism as the primary adversary of the Catholic Church, and a time of uncertainty, threat, and instability. Apocalypticism is not an uncommon message in threatening or crisis situations (Dos Santos 2006).

26. From 1936–37 to 1941 during the Spanish Civil War, Lucia revealed that the messages of the Virgin had also included pronouncements against Russia and communism, as well as a request to consecrate Russia to her Immaculate Heart in order to convert the country and promote world peace, or else war and hunger would follow. These texts reached international diffusion, including the famous three secrets. Another turning point in the internationalization of Fátima was in October 1942, when Pope Pius XII pronounced via Vatican radio that the intervention of the Virgin of Fátima had not only restored Portugal to the Church, but had averted the "Red menace" in Spain. Also in 1946–48, the statue of the Virgin was sent on a European tour, increasing her celebrity. After World War II, during the Cold War, Our Lady of Fátima became known in the U.S. and Europe. Being central to Marian Catholic movements with a political anti-communist thrust, these gatherings of

Conclusion: A Note on Authenticity

Even when we can analyse and map the processes of institutionalization of authenticity as externalization and stabilization, purification and legitimation, a question remains: did something special happen there?

Understandably, the question of whether the Virgin truly gave messages to the visionaries is far from trivial. After all, Church commissions were established to verify the authenticity of the apparitions. Hearing commands from Jesus or Mary and experiencing visions and visitations of saints, angels and devils and so on are not recognized as "normal" phenomena. They are rather signs of mental disturbance than authentic messages from Heaven; this is recognized by local priests today (Konopasek and Palecek 2012) as well as by the Portuguese Inquisition in the past.[27]

Furthermore, not only political but also economic considerations are involved in the creation of a holy shrine. The possibility of income that pilgrims could provide to a remote and poor parish (pilgrims can significantly improve the economy of a parish) may have tempted many a priest to encourage a local visionary to see the Virgin or a saint (interview with Rev. Mario Oliveira). Aside from these considerations, however, thousands of Catholic pilgrims provide testimony on the astonishing power of the Virgin Mary for healing, mobilizing masses of people, and providing a stabilizing, symbolic centre for religious and spiritual practices among Catholics.

Nevertheless, Marian apparitions, including the apparitions of Fátima, are rather *controversial* and *ambiguous* events within Catholic theology.[28] Most of the voluminous literature on the Fátima apparitions tends to be divided between an apologetic camp, which regards them as divine interventions, and a sceptical camp, which focuses on their being a result of overenthusiastic and vivid imaginations or crowd phenomena, combined with more or less intentional forms of manipulation (Keith 2004). Here the issue often centres on defending versus questioning the authenticity and, consequently, the sacrality of the apparitions. In spite of their differences, scholarly studies of Fátima (such as those by Barreto, Torgal or

---

millions of devotees included the Blue Army, Rosary Crusades, the Legion of Mary, the Immaculate Militia and many others (Kselman and Avella 1986; Vowinckel et al. 2012).

27. There is a long history in the Catholic Church of assessing the authenticity of visions, apparitions and miracles. One of the concerns of the Spanish Inquisition was feigned sanctity and raptures, the focus being on "policing the borders between the natural and the supernatural" (Keith 2004).

28. The Catholic Church is rather ambivalent towards expressions of popular religiosity, in many situations trying to distance itself from what can be regarded as superstition and popular magic (Weber 1988).

Espiritu Santo), as well as the scholarly literature on apparitions in general (like that of Zimdar-Swartz or Harris), focus on the culturally and/or politically constructed dimensions of the Marian apparitions, bracketing questions of any particular sacrality they may possess.[29]

The authenticity of the apparitions may be thus understood as reflecting intersubjective and emergent social psychological/spiritual states of mind. Instead of trying to analyse these forms of sacrality as subjective versus objective phenomena (Keith 2004), apparitions can be studied as examples of exceptional intersubjective emotional and cognitive states of mind, which intensify and heighten the participants' sensitivity and sense of participation, detaching them from everyday routines and perspectives.

In this way, sacred places, sacred rituals and sacred objects can be understood as *nodes of structural agency*, anchoring and channelling the numinous through the medium of meaningful symbolic words and chanting, a saintly relic endowed with the power to heal, a consecrated holy statue, and the potency of a charismatic visionary (Latour 2005; Davis and Boles 2003).

The emotional and mental state that the believer experiences in the presence of these objects and sites is in itself regarded as a proof of their spiritual power and efficacy (i.e., their sacrality). Thus they constitute important elements in religious enactment, being part of the religious

---

29. The sceptical Portuguese literature presents alternative explanations to those of the official Catholic version of Fátima. Particularly the older Portuguese literature (see T. da Fonseca, *Na Cova dos Leões* (1957); João Ilharco, *Fátima Desmascarada* (1971); and Mário de Oliveira, *Fátima Nunca Mais* (2000)) rejected claims of sacrality and focused on the intentional fabrication of the apparitions for political or status quo purposes. Portuguese scholarly analysis of the apparitions in the social sciences includes that of Torgal (2002, 2011), centring on Fátima as the result of active promotion of the Portuguese Catholic Church in 1920, led by the bishop of Leiria and the cleric M. Formigão. J. Barreto (2002) also presents a cultural and historical study that acknowledges a political factor in the expansion of the shrine; Steffen Dix' work (2010) places Fátima in a context of a particular re-Christianization of Portugal; and Moises Espirito Santo gives a new interpretation of the visions based on the Islamic roots of the culture and metaphors in the area of Leiria (2006). A fascinating non-mainstream interpretation of the apparitions is found in the work of D'Armada and J. Fernandes (Fernandes *et al.* 2010 and other texts), where encounters at Fátima did not involve heavenly figures but extra-terrestrial forces, which were then interpreted as saintly visitations. A large number of interpretations of popular apparitions explain them as reactions to periods of cultural crisis, coinciding with times of war or similar catastrophes, without discussing particular mechanisms (for an example, see Mestrovic 1991, 136). Similarly, for other general studies of apparitions that include Fátima, see W. Christian's *Visionaries: The Spanish Republic and the Reign of Christ*, in which Fátima is presented as a symbolic tool of the traditionalists' resistance to the First Republic in Portugal (Christian 1996).

experience and mobilizing an emotional resonance with the believer. In this way, a momentous performance and a transformation takes place (Latour 2005). When provided with the appropriate symbolic, emotional structure, awe is evoked in both the officiant (spiritual virtuoso or charismatic) and in the followers, whose collective effervescence functions as a mode of sacrality (Nocera 2009). The utterances of visionaries and their gestures did not "inform" the people assembled at the site about the messages of the Virgin. Being transformative rather than informative (Latour 2005), the messages were examples of collective performances and the sharing among participants of a very particular, special time and space.

Important elements in the sacred performative are the holy scripts: the vision of the Lady brighter than the sun seen by the innocent children, the unrelenting messages on the importance of praying the Rosary, the requests of penance for the sins of the world. All of these presented the believers with a recognizable format of the divinity, a genuine sign of entering the realm of the numinous and communion, a key that opens the numinous place (Goffman 1974, 63). The sacred is then re-cognized by its brightness, by the elevation, by the feeling of awe that many reported feeling during the visions, and by the miracles and healing. In this way, the recurrent scenography of the divine does not have to be understood as a staged libretto to manipulate naïve simpletons, but a sacred performance, a recognizable and recognized language that positions the believer in a shared religious state.

All of the elements of a configuration such as Marian sacrality were present in Fátima, enacted by the trance of the visionaries, agents who were recognized as appropriate. These elements included the utterances and bodily expressions of the three children, the ritual performances with their rhythms, moments of elevation and signs, and the multitude of followers and visitors hoping to see or—perhaps more precisely—to be in communion with the visions.

Thus, the sacrality of the apparitions of Fátima can be analysed as an emergent effervescence resulting from a contextual configuration or configurations where specific agents and objects, as well as patterns of agency, are interwoven in specific historical and mythical environments. It is in this way that psychological and phenomenological factors relate to a whole complex of social and temporal processes. Thus, the truth of the apparition does not consist of what happened somewhere "inside" the visionaries (inside their souls, hearts, minds or brains), or at least not just that. Rather, it is in practice produced and reinforced by innumerable subsequent contributions of "many hands" (i.e., by empirically observable presences, actions, and mediations)(Konosek and Palecek 2012).

The many hands, actors and configurations that co-created Fátima, weaving diverse interests and perspectives in time, slanted and/or added new forms of the sacred to the shrine. In this way, the sanctity of Fátima underwent different sacred configurations and different alignments during its history. The local piety of the children visionaries, the miracles and the local priesthood are the larger figures of the early phase in 1917. Different is the later scenario of sacrality, where actors and forces were mobilized in a second phase (from 1917 to 1945) in order to keep the short-lived flare-up of the sacred of 1917 as alive and undiluted as possible, vitalizing the faith of believers and the Portuguese Church, as well as giving the Portuguese the sense of a united and chosen Christian nation with a large and magnificent shrine. This was followed by a third phase after 1945, in which the shrine of Fátima was transformed into the sacred "Altar of the World," with Mary as the Heavenly Queen commanding the forces of light against the forces of darkness, a symbol of Vatican and Catholic conservative and anti-communist forces during the time of the polarized ideologies of the Cold War.

References

Barreto, J. 2002. *Religião e Sociedade – Dois ensaios.* Lisboa: Imprensa Do Ciencias Sociais.

Bromley, D.G. and R. S. Bobbitt. 2011. "The Organizational Development of Marian Apparitional Movements." *Nova Religio: The Journal of Alternative and Emergent Religions* 14(3): 5–41.

Burns, T. R. and P. Hall, eds. 2012. *The Meta-Power Paradigm: Impacts and Transformations of Agents, Institutions, and Social Systems. Capitalism, State and Democracy in a Global Context.* Frankfurt am Main: Peter Lang.

Cardoso Reis, B. 2001. "Fatima: the Reception Catholics in the Diaries from 1917 to 1930." *Social analysis* 36: 249–299.

Christian, W. 1996. *Visionaries: The Spanish Republic and the Reign of Christ.* Berkeley: University of California Press.

———.1989. *Apparitions in Late Medieval and Renaissance Spain.* Princeton, NJ: Princeton University Press.

Davis, P.W. and J. Boles. 2003. "Pilgrim Apparition Work: Symbolization and Crowd Interaction when the Virgin Mary Appeared in Georgia." *Journal of Contemporary Ethnography* 32(4): 371–402.

de Santa Maria, F.A. 1711. *Santuario Mariano e historia das imagens milagrosas de Nossa Senhora e das milagrosamente apparecidas.* Lisboa: Officina de Antonio Pedrozo Galram.

Dias Coelho, G. 1987. "A devoção do povo português a Nossa Senhora nos tempos modernos." *Revista da Faculdade de Letras: História, II Série* 4: 227–256.

Dix, S. 2010. "As esferas seculares e religiosas na sociedade Portuguesa." *Análise Social* 65(194): 5–27.

Documentação Crítica de Fatima. 1992/1917. *Vol 1. Interrogatorios aos videntes.* Ed. Santuario de Fátima.

Dos Santos, L. (Compilación del P.L. Kondor). 2006. *Memorias de la Hermana Lúcia.* Volume I. Imprimatur Fatimæ.

Eiper, C. 2007. "Moving Statues and Moving Images: Religious Artefacts and the Spiritualisation of Materiality." *The Australian Journal of Anthropology* 18(3): 253–263.

Espírito Santo, M. 2006. *Os Mouros Fatimidas e as Aparições de Fátima.* Porto: Assirio & Alvim.

Fernandes, F., J. Fernandes and R. Berenguel, eds. 2010. *Fátima Revisited: The Apparition Phenomenon in Ufology, Psychology, and Science.* San Antonio, TX: Anomalist Books.

Flunser Pimentel, I. 2010. *Cardeal Cerejeira: O Príncipe da Igreja,* Lisboa: A Esfera dos Livros.

Goffman, E. 1974. *Frame Analysis: an Essay on the Organization of Experience.* New York: Harper and Row.

Horsfall, S. 2000. "The Experience of Marian Apparitions and the Mary Cult." *The Social Science Journal* 37(3): 375–384.

Ilharco, J. 1971. *Fátima Desmascarada. A Verdade Histórica acarca de Fátima Documentada com Provas.* Coimbra: Edição do Autor.

Keitt, A. 2004. "Religious Enthusiasm, the Spanish Inquisition, and the Disenchantment of the World." *Journal of the History of Ideas* 65(2): 231–250.

Kenna, M. 1985. "Icons in Theory and Practice: An Orthodox Christian Example." *History of Religions* 24(4): 345–368.

Konopasek, Z. and J. Palecek. 2012. "Apparitions and Possessions as Boundary Objects: An Exploration into Some Tensions between Mental Health Care and Pastoral Care." *Journal of Religion and Health* 51: 970–985.

Kselman, T. and S. Avella. 1986. "Marian Piety and the Cold War in the United States." *The Catholic Historical Review* 72(3): 403–424.

Latour, B. 2005. "'Thou Shall Not Freeze-Frame' or How Not to Misunderstand the Science and Religion Debate." In *Science, Religion, and the Human Experience*, edited by J. D. Proctor, 27–48. Oxford: Oxford University Press.

Lima, J. S. 1997. "Santuários, lugares de peregrinação em Portugal." *Communio: Revista Internacional Católica* XIV(4): 345–362.

Matter, E.A. 2001. "Apparitions of the Virgin Mary in the Late Twentieth Century: Apocalyptic, Representation, Politics." *Religion* 31: 125–153.

Meessen, A. 2003. "Apparitions and Miracles of the Sun." International Forum in Porto "Science, Religion and Conscience", October 23–25, 2003.

Nocera, P. 2009. "Los usos del concepto de efervescencia y la dinámica de las representaciones colectivas en la sociología durkheimiana." *Revista Española de Investigaciones Sociológicas (Reis)* 127: 93–119.

Pereira, P. 2007. "Peregrinações pouco católicas: o locus religioso das peregrinações a pé a Fátima." *Revista de Ciências Humanas* 41(1–2): 179–193.

Ratzinger, J. 1959. *The Message of Fátima.* From the diary of John XXIII, 17 August. <www.vatican.va/roman_curia/congregations/cfaith/documents/rc_con_cfaith_doc_20000626_message-fatima_en.html> [Accessed 23 February 2016].

Salgado de Matos. 2001. "Luís, Cardeal Cerejeira: universitário, militante, místico." *Análise Social* 36(160): 803–837.

Weber, E. 1988. "Religion And Superstition In Nineteenth-Century France." *The Historical Journal* 31(2): 399–423.

About the Author

Nora Machado des Johansson is associated with the Centre for Research and Studies in Sociology, Lisbon University Institute, and with the Department of Sociology, University of Gothenburg in Sweden. Machado's main areas of research and teaching are cultural sociology, social psychology and institutional & governance analysis. Her publications include articles in *Public Administration: An International Quarterly, Canadian Journal of Sociology, Social Science and Medicine, Death Studies, Human Systems Management* and a book *Using the Bodies of the Dead: Ethical and Organizational Dimensions of Organ Transplantation* in 1998 about the cultural-organizational factors of organ transplantations. She is currently completing a book about Marian sacrality in Fátima, Portugal.

— 9 —

Protection through the Invocation of Shared Thirds: Sacralization without Iconoclasm

PEIK INGMAN

This chapter engages in speculation on the notion of iconoclashes (Latour 2010) by drawing on insights garnered from three sources for which iconoclasm has become a central challenge: Bruno Latour, relational psychoanalysis and my ongoing research with queers in Christian families. The central question I wish to entertain is whether and how it might be possible to protect relationships against iconoclasm non-iconoclastically. A corollary to this question is another: could such a defence be meaningfully referred to as (a form of) sacralization? As Giorgio Agamben has argued, profanation involves negligence. It is the character of this negligence that is under question in an attempt at a non-iconoclastic defence against iconoclasm. Is protection against the accusation of sacrilege possible to achieve through non-iconoclastic sacralization?

Introduction

Bruno Latour's discussion of modernity and iconoclasm facilitates a shift of attention away from concerns pertaining to capital-T Truth or capital-J Justice onto concerns about the management of the quality of relationships. This focus enables a speculative discussion of sacralization as a specifically relational matter of concern emerging in relationships. I understand sacralization here as the act of invoking "divinities" and,

---

Keywords: Iconoclash, impasse, commensalism, antibiosis, negligence, pharmakon

more generally, the act of invoking something that evokes reverence. By insisting that all people, including Moderns, have their own divinities, Latour has managed to establish the necessary symmetry for recognizing instances of iconoclasm as what he calls "iconoclash," controversies where one sacred encounters another. "With iconoclasm, one knows what the act of breaking represents, and what the motivations of apparent destruction are. For *iconoclash*, one does not know: one hesitates, one is troubled by an action for which there is no way to know, without further enquiry, whether it is destructive or constructive" (Latour 2010, 68). Latour wants to render the status, the character and the quality of iconoclastic gestures a question mark for those involved.

This is a profound move that goes beyond recognition that modernity has related to its others iconoclastically. Establishing symmetry, however, tends to lead to a predictable outcome: an impasse. In the vocabulary of relational psychoanalyst Jessica Benjamin, such impasses are characterized by a challenging complementarity in which both parties come to relate to the other in terms of "done to" (Benjamin 2004):

> The idea of complementary relations (Benjamin 1988, 1998) aims to describe those push-me/pull-you, doer/done-to dynamics that we find in most impasses, which generally appear to be one-way—that is, each person feels *done to*, and not like an agent helping to shape a co-created reality. The question of how to get out of complementary twoness, which is the formal or structural pattern of all impasses between two partners, is where intersubjective theory finds its real challenge.
>
> (Benjamin 2004, 9)

Profound insights have been developed in the field of psychoanalysis concerning the intersubjective relations of child and caretaker as well as analyst and analysand, respectively. While concerns over transference and countertransference have been debated in psychoanalysis for decades, there has been a stubborn insistence on the analyst's non-professional subjectivity posing a threat for therapy (Clarke *et al.* 2008). Relational psychoanalysis challenges this notion and adds to the focus on the analysand attention to the quality of an emerging, therapeutic relationship. Because such a shift disavows the solution of leaving the analyst's subjectivity outside the treatment, relational psychoanalysis has needed to address concerns over the analyst's ability to protect themselves and the quality of the relationship *without* invoking their divinities (psychoanalytic dictums) iconoclastically, as that would disconnect them from a mutually composed relationality, or what Benjamin refers to as a "shared thirdness."

The move recognizes theory as a kind of actor; the analyst's relationship to this actor is thereby rendered recognizable as potentially excluding for the analysand. Here Benjamin notes the problem: "the central couple may become the one the patient is excluded from, rather than the one that analyst and patient build together" (Benjamin 2004, 20). However, Benjamin is not simply noting the inherent violence of invoking psychoanalytic dictums in ways that disqualify or override the analysand's concerns. She is asking questions about what is at stake in trying to overcome complementarity.

I would argue that these concerns are relevant for conceiving of and appreciating non-iconoclastic sacralization—a practice of invoking something as a defence against iconoclasm *without* shattering or disqualifying another's faith. A decisive point for appreciating such sacralization is that it is non-teleological. The focus is not on establishing universal justice, consensus or truth. Insofar as these are invoked as an independent judge, they iterate the inherent problem of iconoclasm. This is why the focus is instead on opening up impasses, so that the involved parties can "keep talking."

In order to really appreciate Benjamin's endeavours, we need a better understanding of: 1) what characterizes specifically Modern iconoclasm and 2) how such characteristics entail that iconoclashes tend to develop into impasses. The move to understand instances of iconoclasm as iconoclashes is not made in order to congratulate ourselves over having overcome our imperialist tendencies, but in order to develop a better understanding of what is at stake in overcoming complementarity. These concerns have become central for me in my research. I have been talking to queer family members of conservative Christian families who want to maintain a good relationship with their family members, yet bemoan their family members' iconoclastic gestures. What is striking to me is how their position as previous insiders who have to some extent become outsiders affords them an acute understanding of their own potential to simply respond in a complementary, iconoclastic way. Hence, the question of how to get out of an impasse is of paramount importance to them.

Iconoclashes are generally characterized by reciprocal indignation over sacrilege. What do I mean by this? Giorgio Agamben writes: "Children, who play with whatever old thing falls into their hands, make toys out of things that also belong to the spheres of economics, war, law, and other activities that we are used to thinking of as serious. All of a sudden, a car, a firearm, or a legal contract becomes a toy" (Agamben 2007, 76). Agamben refers to this act as profanation. It is characterized by an ambiguous negligence. The child's use of an object is deemed inappropriate because the "proper" use of the object has been sacralized. We (the adults) say "Put that down! It's not a toy!," implying not only that treating it as a "toy" represents misuse, but also irreverence—a sacrilegious insult to its correct use. What happens here is that the child's use of the object is disqualified in the name of the use to which it has been consecrated.

The child's use of the object *is* a form of negligence, but it is interpreted as a form that is deemed irreverent. What too seldom interests us is what the child made of it (beyond characterizing it as misuse). Once an object has been used in a negligent way, its status needs to be recognized as a question mark on which a number of concerns converge. Should we really be surprised to find the child outraged at the belittlement of her innovative use, as well as confused about the notion that her use is deemed hurtful? The question that interests me is: What are the child's prospects in defending herself against the accusation of sacrilege? More generally speaking, what can you do when someone is dead set on taking offence, when someone insists on your profanation as amounting to a negligence that is, if not malicious, at least callous?

My final question is, insofar as a defence against such accusations manages to remain non-iconoclastic—that is, not of a kind that simply aims to attack the accuser's divinities in turn—might it, under some circumstances, still make sense to call such resistance sacralization?

Modern and Nonmodern Stances to the *Pharmakon*

As the philosopher of science Isabelle Stengers has argued, what haunts Moderns is our inability to "culture the *pharmakon*" (Stengers 2010). The ancient Greek notion of the *pharmakon* represents an object characterized by ambivalence: it can be a remedy or a poison. Inherently, however, it is neither. This can be understood in terms of recognizing that the character and quality of attachments to it co-determine its effect on us and others. In ancient Greek culture,

> a *pharmakon* could be a remedy used in medicine or an ointment applied as a part of bodily training, but it could also be the basis of a spell, charm, or talisman used in sorcery or divination, and it could be an analogue to the power of the spoken word and its ability to place an audience under the influence of the speaker. What is more, in the ancient worldview understanding of these activities was deeply interwoven.
>
> (Rinella 2011, xxii)

When Stengers claims that the *pharmakon* haunts modernity, she means that modernity can be characterized by its intolerance to the ambiguity that the *pharmakon* represents. Stengers's discussion of the relevance of this intolerance takes us directly to Latour's discussion of the problem of iconoclasm, of disqualifying one's other:

> The contemporary scene is literally saturated with the "modern" heirs of Plato. Each of these heirs denounces his "other," just as the philoso-

pher denounced the sophists, accused them of exploiting that which he himself had triumphed over. They include not only the heirs of Plato, but those philosophers who, following the sophists, were used as an argument to demonstrate the need for a foundation. What, in Plato's text, can be read as a network of analogies isolating the terrible instability of the sophist—*pharmakon* has today split into a number of "modern practices" (scientific, medical, political, technological, psychoanalytic, pedagogical) that have been introduced, just as Platonic philosophy in its time, as disqualifying their other—charlatan, populist, ideologue, astrologer, magician, hypnotist, charismatic teacher.

(Stengers 2010, 29–30)

Let us consider four caricatured responses to controversy that can help us understand the significance of iconoclasm and why it is so problematic. The first three caricatures are aimed at clarifying what it means to be Modern; the last one is aimed at speculating on what is at stake in overcoming this temptation to respond in Modern ways. It is important to note that these caricatures represent *stances*. We may come to take the first three—the Modern stances—in relation to others or they may be projected on us, but most importantly, they are stances that we may be *tempted* to inhabit in part because they allow us to escape responsibility.

First, we have the caricature of the Modern religious person who wishes to surrender to being a vehicle of the benevolent force of God. He acknowledges evil in the world, but this evil never comes from God. God is not a *pharmakon*. Evil comes from "the Tempter," whom we may willingly or carelessly come to serve, while good comes from God; the caricature is basically a henchman of either. Except not quite. He is recognized to be in control in one sense. What he is considered to be in complete control of pertains to a choice: to choose between an allegiance to God or an allegiance to the Tempter. Beyond that choice, however, his fate is entirely out of his hands. Allegiance allows him to escape responsibility for anything that is done "in the name of religion," "in the name of God." While few people consistently take such a stance, my point is that we may be tempted to more or less momentarily do that or we may be related to as if this is a position that we do take (whether or not such actually is the case). This stance could be called fundamentalist. While most of us are not fundamentalist all the time, we may be tempted, from time to time and in particular circumstances, to adopt a stance that is fundamentalist.

Then we have the secular stance described by Max Weber of invoking the notion of an "in principle calculable world" through capital-S Science. Or, we could update this stance to accord with the figure of a "minion," as theorized by Stengers and Philip Pignarre. A minion aligns herself with neoliberalist arguments, which translate the negative effects of capitalism into a necessary evil, given the alleged lack of better alternatives (Stengers and Pignarre 2010). The minion surrenders (or falls prey) to an availability that aligns her as a non-resisting mediator of neoliberalism. The mechanism of capture involves accepting and proliferating a practice of categorically dismissing alternatives as "even worse." The *sense* of control emanates from taking pride in hard-line, utilitarian "realism" and berating those who would explore alternatives as idealists—allowing themselves to weakly fall prey to wishful thinking and thereby irresponsibly deflecting "what has to be done." Her allegiance allows her to escape personal responsibility for anything done "in the name of we-have-no-choice." Again, few people consistently argue this way, but many of us may be tempted to occasionally do so and we may be accused of occasionally or consistently doing so.

The third caricature is that of the critical mind, who prides herself on doubting and debunking everything except the power of critique. As Latour notes, "being an iconoclast seems the highest virtue, the highest piety, in intellectual circles" (2010, 69). This third figure may view the stances of the religious person, the believer in "an in principle calculable world," as well as the hard-line neoliberalist, with contempt. Her allegiance allows her to escape personal responsibility for anything done "in the name of critique."

What all of these stances have in common is a kind of allegiance that renders us intermediaries of our inculpable divinities. If problems are investigated, they are shown to be emanating from elsewhere, not from our allegiance to our divinities—God, the in-principle power of calculations, hard-line "realist" agendas or the curative power of critique—but from allegiance to the Tempter, superstition, wishful thinking/being "soft" and non-critical practices. The latter are portrayed as displacers of order, as enemies to be excluded or converted. Our own divinities' entanglement in problems is seldom investigated; the effects of the insistence on the divinities' inculpability are, likewise, seldom appraised. Of course, we could add several more caricatures, such as the do-gooder who escapes responsibility for anything done "in the name of Human Rights, Feminism, Gay Rights" or, simply, "Good Intentions." The point is that these are all examples where "a good cause" or even "a necessary evil" is invoked in a problematic way. My argument is not that they are always invoked in such a way. What is at issue here is the *relation* between Moderns and their divinities and how this relation protects Moderns against vulnerability *at the expense of others*.

In contrast, the fourth figure I want to consider is the "Nonmodern" person, whose divinities are recognized as *pharmacological*. This figure represents a stance that does not believe in "a stable distinction between the beneficial medicament and the harmful drug, between rational pedagogy and suggestive influence, between reason and opinion" (Stengers 2010, 29). For the nonmodern devotee of *pharmaka*, all of the attachments that she hopes will provide her and others with a sustainable enchantment also hold the potential of rendering those involved disenchanted and possibly possessed (that is, entirely unable to resist). Although all of her attachments are recognized as pharmacological (= risky), she understands that she needs attachments (divinities) in order to act. While Moderns keep insisting that they can only ever be held responsible for the things they *intend*, a nonmodern understanding of personal responsibility does not have access to the modern trick of translating responsibility from a question of involvement to a question of personal intention or "culture." A nonmodern invocation of doing things "in the name of *pharmaka*" does not have the power to deny complicity, because *pharmaka* are only as effective or detrimental as the compositions that they co-compose allow them to be, and the invocator is part of that composition.

Commensalism and Antibiosis

What I think we need is a vocabulary that will allow us both to maintain the nonmodern ontology of actor-networks, where an actor is a node in a network that allows her to act, and to recognize the effects of stances that refute such interdependence. I will argue that such refutations are based on our anxiety about dependence, and, more precisely, anxiety over our limited control in determining the character and quality of what we give and what we receive. It is this anxiety that tempts us to deny our complicity. Why might this anxiety be so intense among Moderns? The psychoanalyst Lynne Layton provides the following description, which highlights the issue of modern autonomy:

> The division of the worlds of work and government from the domestic sphere encouraged a psychic split between two sets of human capacities that ought not be separated. I refer to relational and autonomous capacities. [...] The form of *autonomy* that this split encourages is one that repudiates dependency and vulnerability, fostering an attitude of domination toward other people and the natural world. The form of *attachment* encouraged by the split is one that repudiates all versions of autonomy as selfish. The public/private split, in other words, produces hostile and submissive versions of dependency on one hand, hostile and omnipotent versions of agency on the other. This has the effect of impeding the chances of what Fairbairn (1954) considered a hallmark of psychosocial health—mutual interdependence. (Layton 2006, 147)

What are the relational effects of an autonomy that repudiates dependence and of attachments that repudiate autonomy as selfish? Let us return to the caricature of "the Modern." To further nuance this caricature, I will draw on additional concepts from biology that are considered sub-categories of symbiosis. These categories involve attachments that explicitly de-emphasize mutuality. The first one is *commensalism*. Unlike a parasitic relation, where one species feeds off another in a harmful way, in a commensal relation one species benefits and the other is neither harmed nor benefited. The species that benefits, which can be thought of as a freeloader, is referred to as the commensal in the relation. In order to understand my argument here, we need to appreciate the relational production of commensals. An individual who refuses to receive anything in return co-produces a commensal; the individual whose gifts are not accepted thereby becomes a freeloader/commensal, not because she does not want to contribute, but because the other refuses to acknowledge the possibility that they could want or need anything from the commensal.

Think now of the caricature of the ideal modern actor: the self-sufficient, yet non-selfish, contributor. She is productive and helpful, yet she refuses to render herself vulnerable to receiving (or needing) anything in return. She is not at risk of being harmed, but, much more importantly, she is protected from concerns about reciprocity by treating others as commensals: they benefit from her, but she needs no one. The obvious confusion here is that she actually needs others *as* a benefactor, to reap the rewards of her non-selfish autonomy. Moderns want people to depend on them on their (on the Modern's) terms. Not only do I consider this an accurate description of the ideal Modern, I would also claim that it is a good description of the Modern's divinities, such as God and Science: by their nature, they deny any role of dependence, and insist that what they have to offer is entirely up to *them*. Furthermore, our relationship to them is purely commensal (we benefit and they remain unaffected).

Stengers and Pignarre write about the arrogance of the Modern stance:

> When we send missionaries, teachers, armies—and nowadays smart bombs or the bureaucrats of the IMF and the World Bank—into distant countries, it is always a work of "pacification": we aren't destroying enemies, we don't have enemies. It is our backwards cousins we are rescuing—should we really leave them to their fate?
>
> (Stengers and Pignarre 2010, 41)

When our demonstrations of non-selfish autonomy are presented as remedies to other people's problems or controversies and the effect is other than what was intended, we insist that we are only responsible for what we intend. Such a stance is captured by the symbiotic term *anti-*

biosis, which refers to a relation where one organism has a detrimental effect on another organism's ability to metabolize. Crucially, antibiosis is not specifically targeted. As we all know, antibiotics do not limit their attacks to the identified pathogens. Their effect is very general. As a recent article in *BBC Earth* put it: "[Antibiotics] often kill a broad spectrum of microbes in order to eradicate the one that is problematic. Of course, at times antibiotics are necessary to save lives, but it would be 'nice to have something a little more judicious and targeted', [Betsy] Foxman adds" (Wilson 2015).

Antibiotics represent a *modus operandi* where the means justify the ends, and the positive effects are usually deemed to outweigh the negative ones. The intended effect of antibiotics is to get rid of a problem. The way it works, however, is often disturbingly invasive towards the operations of the immune and metabolic systems. When something goes wrong, the general use of antibiotics is seldom questioned, much less how it may interfere with alternative ways in which the immune and metabolic systems might tackle a problem. Instead of Modern solutions being treated as *pharmaka*, they are celebrated when they work as if they alone achieved it, and excused when they do not, on the grounds that any criticism against specific antibiotics is a criticism against the general use of antibiotics, a pillar of the miracle of modern medicine.

Antibiotic Iconoclasm

What I would like to suggest is that the Modern insistence on non-selfish autonomy and a utilitaristically justified science both function antibiotically. Treating others as commensals whose gifts, unless they are extensions of our glory, are a threat to our autonomy has a noxious effect, one that we refuse to take responsibility for on the grounds that the negative effects were not our intention. Commensalism and antibiosis describe the ways in which Moderns deal with their vulnerability in becoming complicit in unintended, negative effects.

Think of how Truth, Justice, God and Science are all invoked to disqualify concerns over any negative effects that Modern practices have on their heirs and fellow Earthly inhabitants. Due to the peculiar relationship Moderns have with their divinities, "it is possible to innovate without taking any risks, without accepting any responsibility or being exposed to any danger. Others—later, elsewhere—will pay the price, will feel the impact, evaluate the fallout, and try to contain the damage" (Latour 2010, 32). The issue is not about religion versus science, belief versus fact, but about how we evaluate the effects of our associations and what difference this makes. Consider the following comparison between two descriptions, one of religion, the other of science.

After having recounted a traumatic incident with her family members, a research participant, Sara, said the following about religion:

> I've like realized that religion is horribly dangerous. It's a way to fully and totally not give a shit about what harms people and what is good for people. [...] Basically you're discharged from all responsibility through it. You don't need to think about what you *do* to other people... by... you have your religion and that's what takes it all... it explains everything and makes it so that you don't need to ask for forgiveness for anything you've done—in the name of religion.

Here she is referring to the actions of her family members. She is noting that there is a fundamental problem with considering oneself unaccountable for what one does "in the name of religion." Latour provides an example of how modern science affords a similar exemption of personal responsibility, recounting an encounter with a researcher at the Institut Pasteur, "who introduces himself to me innocently, saying 'Hello, I'm the coordinator for beer yeast chromosome 11'" (Latour 2010, 32):

> When beer yeast chromosome 11 appears in the world, it will simply add one element to the furnishings—all at once, by surprise—of nature alone, on top, in plain sight. On the other side, caught by surprise, others will suddenly have to take care of the consequences—ethical, political, and economic—of this action. The researcher himself does, will have done, will do, "only science." (Latour 2010b, 32)

Sara is not only referring to acts of indignation, but to acts that were aimed to help her. A recurring incident involved Christians responding to her concerns with "Have you asked Jesus?"

The problem is not that the researcher presents the world with the gifts of science or that a religious person wants to share his enthusiasm about Jesus. The problem is that the coordinator and the proselytizer seem to understand themselves as doing "only science" and "only religion" and thereby not needing to consider how their gifts are received. The problem has to do with the relationship between the giver and the receiver and with recognizing the receiver's right to co-compose the character and quality of the gift. "Right" is perhaps not the best word here. I would like to say, rather, that denying that it matters how something is received is an act that merits our attention.

From Iconoclash to Impasse

Another research participant, whom I will call Mathias, told me a story that allows us to explore iconoclashes. First of all, Mathias emphasized that, unlike his boyfriend David, he was very religious. As we will see, once again shifting our attention away from the religious versus secular distinction to concerns over control and protection against iconoclasm, both David and Mathias can be understood as Moderns. He framed the story he told me as being about how his faith "crumbled." Something had happened that was different from earlier times when he had discussed religion with friends. He said, "I have always been able to discuss my faith with people, both believers and non-believers, in various contexts and ... with people who think differently than I do ... and it hasn't crumbled anything in me." Actually, he said he had discussed religion with his boyfriend on previous occasions without the discussion leading to a crisis. This time, however, his boyfriend had argued by wielding "scientific facts" that refuted the existence of God.

Yet there was more to it than that. Mathias told me that early on in their relationship, they had discussed their expectations and views about what happens when people die. David had emphasized that death is "the end."

> We talked about death and we talked about life and he talked about how he was prepared to die the day that he is supposed to die, like if that's how it is then that's how it is. And then I cried 'cause, I mean, I loved him so much, and he said "but you don't need to be worried, then I'll come down as an angel to you." Oh, and that was just so beautiful to hear.

As I interpret this, David's reference to coming down as an angel comes across as an attempt to respond—in a rather sweet way—to Mathias becoming upset over the prospect of never seeing David again. However, when David appeared to be arguing that God does not exist, Mathias confronted him by asking what he had meant when he said he would come down as an angel. David responded by saying that he meant that because Mathias believes in angels, he would *experience* Mathias coming down as an angel, even if, "in reality," he would not be one. Mathias said, "For me it was horrible to hear him say this... that it's just something made-up that I choose to believe somehow."

> I felt betrayed or *scammed*! Just really *disappointed* like "*what the hell are you saying?*" How can you say stuff like that? This is serious stuff for me. I felt that I was scammed somehow, which I have since understood that wasn't really the case but rather that he just said stuff without worrying too much about what he said.

Note that what Mathias is accusing David of here is precisely negligence. At this point he said he felt his faith crumble. He told me that David tried to console him by saying that "your faith has after all done so much good, for you and others, so there has to be *some* truth to it."

Although he was somewhat soothed by this, David's words about existence continued to haunt him.

I find it interesting how the way David's wielding of Science accords quite well with how Latour presents Moderns. David does not shatter Mathias's God, but his faith. Correspondingly, "He thought he was breaking the fetish, but it was the factish that broke" (Latour 2010, 27). Here, invoking Science works like an antibiotic, indiscriminately attacking the metabolism of its host, while relying on the narrative of Science being inherently neutral and emancipatory. But then something remarkable happens.

At first God was presented in terms of whether or not He exists at all, but then Mathias's attachment/association is described by David in rather different terms, that it "has after all done so much good." David seems to revert to a nonmodern understanding of divinities, viewed not in terms of their independence from us, but in terms of the quality and effects of our attachment to them. There are apparently two *different* questions being addressed at the same time: whether or not something exists (Modern) and whether or not something can do good (nonmodern). David appears to be saying that God does not exist, but faith in him might still *do* good. I find it intriguing to speculate that Mathias could have asked David an eminently nonmodern question: "What about your faith in Science? Has your faith in it done good?," thereby shifting the whole conversation away from "what exists?" to "what can our faith in X achieve?" (a pharmacological question). Such a move may have shifted the focus more symmetrically onto defusing the antibiotic effects of "only science" and "only religion/belief."

In the long run, this incident propelled Mathias into an abysmal depression in which he felt stuck on the Modern question of whether or not God or angels *exist*. Eventually he overcame his depression and his subsequent emphasis was consistently on the responsible management of relationships, not only with God, but between him and his parents, him and David, and so on. I also had a chance to ask David about this conflict. David's retrospective assessment of their relationship was:

> I think that nowadays I hesitate a little more getting involved with persons who are in one way or another religious. For me to be able to do that [get involved] I have to know that there is a mutual respect for our differing worldviews and a kind of "inner stability" in the other.

I take this to mean that David felt that Mathias did not manage to be as respectful towards David's views as he expected David to be of his views and that he felt that Mathias had responded to the impasse by positioning himself as a victim (and, by extension, David as a perpetrator).

It seems to me that their accusations of one another capture two of the most common responses emerging in modern iconoclashes: indignation over sacrilegious negligence, that is, frustration over antibiosis ("he just said stuff without worrying too much about what he said") and a presumption that the solution involves the other showing more respect towards an overarching principle ("mutual respect") invoked in defence. First we find the response that something (a reference to angels) is "not a toy." In defence we find an invocation of seemingly neutral justice, which is nonetheless typically invoked antibiotically. It is as if our only option would be to ask Solomon to cut the baby (the story of the angel) in half.

If we recall the situation in which David had initially said that he would come down as an angel, we can see how Mathias was extracting the story from a situation in which its quality and character was strikingly different than in a debate over the existence of God. As Isabelle Stengers notes:

> Once the neutrino, the atom, or DNA move away from the very specific site, the network of labs, where they achieved their existence, once they are taken up in statements that unbind existence, invention, and proof, they can change meaning and become the vectors of what might be called "scientific opinion"—scientific factishes have a very pharmacological instability. (Stengers 2010, 31)

While Stengers notes here that the appropriateness of invoking facts depends on whether or not we unbind the conditions that allowed them to emerge *as* facts, that is, the questions and criteria they managed to effectively respond to, the same point applies the other way: Mathias seems to be referring to the story of the angel *as if* it had been presented as a commitment to a specific, modern, Christian understanding of angels that, by extension, affirmed the existence of God. However, insofar as David then responded by phrasing the matter in the modern terms of "in reality" and "your experience," it seems that he became complicit in this use of the story as the battleground of an iconoclash.

What kinds of prospects might there have been for resolving the consequent impasse? One could argue that Mathias made a mistake in taking David's talk about science "too seriously." After all, there is "nothing personal" about Science. As I see it, however, the problem is not that he objected or asked questions. One could also argue that David's situation was hopeless once Mathias's feelings had been hurt. At this point, his negligence had tipped over into irreverence and now he could either admit to sacrilege and appear to denounce his faith in Science or hope that Mathias would "get over it" by realizing that "it wasn't personal."

I would like to remind the reader that the goal here is not to find the correct solution for David and Mathias, or evaluating who is to blame, but appreciating what is at stake in these kinds of controversies. What if David had noted the inappropriateness of utilizing the story for arguing about reality and objective existence and instead insisted that when he had originally said that he would come down as an angel, it was an expression of love and concern, not a statement about whether or not angels exist? Let us return to Agamben's discussion of the child's playful use of an object. He writes:

> This, however, does not mean neglect (no kind of attention can compare to that of a child at play) but a new dimension of use, which children and philosophers give to humanity. It is the sort of use that [Walter] Benjamin must have had in mind when he wrote of Kafka's *The New Attorney* that the law that is no longer applied but only studied is the gate to justice. Just as the *religio* that is played with but no longer observed opens the gate to use, so the powers [*potenze*] of economics, law, and politics, deactivated in play, can become the gateways to a new happiness. (Agamben 2007, 76)

What was arguably needed was recognition that Mathias was (originally) using "the object" of the angel story in a way *other than* sacrilegiously, as something *other than* irreverent disqualification. In the end, both of them seemed to affirm that it was a story about the *existence* of angels. Once this had occurred, David would have needed to distinguish between his disqualifying use ("in reality") and his original use. Such attempts can be tricky, however. Simply pointing out that Mathias was guilty of a category mistake might risk coming across as, once again, invoking a higher power aimed to disarm the other.

Protection against iconoclasm, if protection is to also be protection against the trap of complementarity, seems to demand more than the "demystifying exposure" of critique so characteristic of modern scholarship. As Eve Sedgwick has argued, contemporary faith in such exposure operates as if

> the one thing lacking for global revolution, explosion of gender roles, or whatever, is people's (that is, other people's) having the painful effects of their oppression, poverty, or deludedness sufficiently exacerbated to make the pain conscious (as if otherwise it wouldn't have been) and intolerable (as if intolerable situations were famous for generating excellent solutions). (Sedgwick 2003, 144)

Certainly David could have simply disqualified Mathias's interpretation, calling it a category mistake. But would such a move not again have invoked a divinity that Mathias was expected to bow down to? The question is, can we conceive of any non-violent alternatives?

Suppose that either of them had asked the other for forgiveness. Forgiveness for what?

To alleviate iconoclastic effects, it would appear that we need to shift our focus away from our relationship to our divinities and onto the relationship(s) in which the injury has emerged. Asking for forgiveness for unintended injuries, however, seems to be very difficult for Moderns. Why? It seems that we have trouble distinguishing between, on the one hand, acknowledging our involvement and our responsibility even for unintended consequences, and, on the other hand, submission.

Exploring Alternatives to Submission and Consensus

The problem was that the story of David turning into an angel had transformed into an iconoclastic hammer. Originally it had been introduced to act as comfort and, arguably, as a gesture of goodwill aimed to contain a risky discussion. The trouble is that once the problem became framed in terms of "beliefs" versus "facts," it easily seems as if the only solution would have been to arrive at some kind of consensus. Such consensus would, however, have risked disqualifying their divinities, to invoke an impartial judge, whom they could both bow down to—or again risk being accused of sacrilege. It is this "solution" that I think we need to question.

Stengers writes about a "symbiotic agreement," distinguishing it from consensus:

> The "ecological" perspective invites us not to mistake a consensus situation, where the population of our practices finds itself subjected to criteria that transcend their diversity in the name of a shared intent, a superior good, for an ideal peace. Ecology doesn't provide any examples of such submission. It doesn't understand consensus but, at most, symbiosis, in which every protagonist is interested in the success of the other for its own reasons. The "symbiotic agreement" is an event, the production of new, immanent modes of existence, and not the recognition of a more powerful interest before which divergent particular interests would have to bow down. Nor is it the consequence of a harmonization that would transcend the egoism of those interests.
>
> (Stengers 2010, 36)

Ecological perspectives allow us to think about problems in terms of dispelling impasses instead of relating to problems teleologically, demanding solutions that are fixated on the relations between means and ends. The "symbiotic agreement" allows individuals to co-exist without needing to either align their goals uniformly or disconnect in order to avoid conflict. What needs to be affirmed is that we *can* and often *do* genuinely care about one another's well-being for our own, mutually differing reasons. What got lost along the way in the conflict between Mathias and David was the mutual concern and appreciation that they had for one another. It had not mattered that they had different views on death, God and angels. It *came to* matter once such views were presented as disqualifying other views. Subsequently, it was "either your divinities or mine!" While the temptation here would be to suggest some overarching divinity that would restore peace, the problem is that invoking *any* divinity (be it the principle of equality, or mutual respect or whatever) risks being iconoclastic. The challenge lies not in finding the perfect divinity, but in the nonmodern question of whether our use of our divinities is/does good or bad.

Indeed, Benjamin notes how impasses may even take the form of both parties trying too hard to be "good," so that "both members of the dyad become involved in a symmetrical dance, each trying not to be the bad one, the one who eats, rather than being eaten" (Benjamin 2004, 27). The problem is that such "goodness" translates the other into a commensal. Such "goodness" may be (antibiotically) iconoclastic, disqualifying what is at stake for the other in service of guaranteeing one's own inculpability.

What to do then? Benjamin writes of a common dilemma facing analysts:

> The analyst, like a mother, may feel that her separate aims, her being a person with her own needs, will kill the patient. She then cannot distinguish between when she is holding the frame in a way that is conducive to the patient's growth and when she is being hurtful to the patient. How can she then bear in mind the patient's need to safely depend on her, and yet extricate herself from feeling that she must choose between the patient's needs and her own? (Benjamin 2004, 14)

Benjamin provides an example of an analyst-analysand relation where the need to resist the sense of threat co-composed by the analysand's attacks and the analyst's insistence not to counter-attack is explored. The example is interesting because it involves explicit efforts to avoid simply invoking an impersonal solution, what Stengers called "a more powerful interest before which divergent particular interests would have to bow down."

> As Mitchell (1997) contended, transformation occurs when the analyst *stops trying to* live up to a generic, uncontaminated solution... [and, instead] reveals "the transparency of the analyst's own working process..."(Goldner 2003). [...] Thus, the patient sees in the analyst a vision of what it means to struggle internally in a therapeutic way. The patient needs to see his own efforts reflected in the analyst's similar but different subjectivity, which, like the cross-modal response to the infant, constitutes a translation or metabolizing digestion. The patient checks

out whether the analyst is truly metabolizing or just resting on internalized thirds, superego contents, analytic dictums. (Benjamin 2004, 41)

Let us recall the research participant who accused religious people of being irresponsible. Sara's concerns about "religious people" not taking responsibility for what they do "in the name of religion" seemed to involve resentment over such lack of vulnerability, over not needing to metabolize because of a non-problematic access to dictums.

Benjamin provides the example of

> a patient whose highly dissociated experiences of her parents' homicidal attacks materialized as a death threat toward me. After I told her that there were certain things she absolutely could not do for both of us to safely continue the process, she left me a phone message saying that she had actually wanted me to confront her with limits, as she never had been before. In effect, she was searching for the symbolic third, what Lacan (1975) saw as the speech that keeps us from killing.
> (Benjamin 2004, 41–42)

Let us explore the nature of the limits that the analysand was confronted with, specifically in order to distinguish such limits from "criteria that transcend their diversity."

Thirdness was originally introduced into psychoanalytic theory by Jacques Lacan. Benjamin insists that Lacan's "law of the father" is not sufficient to achieve what she calls thirdness, arguing that "unless the third person is also dyadically connected to the child, he cannot function as a true third. He becomes a persecutory invader, rather than a representative of symbolic functioning, as well as a figure of identification and an other whom mother and child both love and share" (Benjamin 2004, 12). She notes that many contemporary Kleinians understand the third in terms of the analyst's relation to theory. Britton (1988, 1998), for instance, holds that "the patient has difficulty tolerating the third as an observational stance taken by the analyst because the theory represents the father in the analyst's mind" (Benjamin 2004, 19). Benjamin, however, contends that

> thirdness is not literally instituted by a father (or other) as the third person; it cannot originate in the Freudian oedipal relation in which the father appears as prohibitor and castrator. And, most crucially, the mother or primary parent must create the space by being able to hold in tension her subjectivity/desire/awareness and the needs of the child.
> (Benjamin 2004, 13)

The father who appears as prohibitor and castrator is precisely analogous to Latour's modern iconoclast: disqualifying and insisting that

1) he only means well and that 2) any resistance represents a disrespectful negligence. In the example provided, in contrast, Lacan's "symbolic third" "had to be backed up by a demonstration that I could participate emotionally, that is, could identify with her feeling of sheer terror and survive it" (Benjamin 2004, 42).

> The patient added in her message that she needed me to do this from my own instincts, not out of adherence to therapeutic rules. I came to realize that she meant that I had acted as a real person, with my own subjective relationship to rules and limits. And that this had to be demonstrably based on a personal confrontation of the reality of terror and abuse, not on dissociative denial of it. She needed to feel the third not as emanating from an impersonal, professional identity or a reliance on authority, such as she had felt from the church in which she had been raised, but from my personal relation to the third, my faith. (Benjamin 2004, 42)

Benjamin's metabolizing of the sense of threat created a connection that allowed the rule (that some things were off limits for being destructive towards their relationship) to act as a *shared* third. However, it was not the rule itself that was crucial; it was Benjamin's invocation of it in service of the quality of their mutual relationship.

The implication of this story, as I see it, is that it appears to be possible to say "no" without transforming into a prohibitor or a castrator, an iconoclast resisting submission to other iconoclasts. What is striking about Benjamin's story, however, is how risky it was. There were no guarantees that the analysand might not simply insist that the analyst "killed" her ("You're just like everybody else!"). Let us try to put Benjamin's stance into the vocabulary used in this chapter: "I will not bow down to your god(s) but I will not disqualify them either. I insist that my negligence is not iconoclastic. What I invoke, instead, is the sanctity of the relationship between *us*."

Resistance as a Gift

Note how Benjamin's resistance towards her analysand turned out to be a gift. Gifts, however, are tricky. They can wound. Modern iconoclasm is precisely the offering of gifts that wound. The anthropologist Michele Stephen has reconsidered Marcel Mauss's famous question "What force is there in the thing given which compels the recipient to make a return?" (Mauss 1954, 1) in terms of another, related question: "Why do gifts wound?" (Stephen 2000). Mauss's answer to this was: "To give is to show one's superiority, to show that one is something more and higher, that one is *magister*. To accept without returning or repaying more is to face subordination, to become a client and subservient, to become *minister*" (Mauss 1954, 72). Stephen's conclusion, based on object relations theoretical perspectives, is:

> Because they place the recipients unconsciously in the position of the guilty, cannibalistic child. Why do the donors triumph? Because they can unconsciously identify with the powerful mother, the source of all wealth. [...] The giving of gifts is confirmation at a deep level of the capacity to make reparation. (Stephen 2000, 144)

To give is to triumph, perhaps, but does it have to be? Stephen's emphasis on "the capacity to make reparation" affords another interpretation. The more fundamental concern involved is over either party winding up in a position where they are not capable of giving back, hence becoming a commensal or a parasite—one who only receives and never gives; one who is thereby forced to struggle with the guilt over taking and intermittently harming without being able to repair.

Consider the central story for object relations theory, as interpreted by Melanie Klein. Initially, the child is presumed to consider the breast an extension of herself, or at least not something entirely separate from her. Whenever she feels hungry or in need of comfort, the breast seems to magically appear. This tempts her to think that she is making it appear by herself, or, shall we say, that the breast is not significantly different from, say, parts of her own body that increasingly respond to her will. However, at some point she is bound to suffer disappointment in this regard. The breast does not consistently behave as an extension of her will. She is hungry or upset, but the breast is nowhere to be seen. Again, it seems helpful to imagine the child responding as one might respond when part of one's own body is not working the way it usually does. The breast is ruthlessly disciplined in an effort to control it again. Or, since it was never actually controlled in the way that is now imagined, the need to control it arises when it is no longer magically available.

As the child matures, it is assumed that at some point she will experience what for her amounts to a painful epiphany: the breast is really a part of her mother. This realization is imagined to be devastating, because it initiates a difficult process of coming to terms with having hurt the mother whom the child loves. The child's actions have jeopardized the quality of this relationship, and this now becomes an explicit concern for the child. How can she repair the damage which has been done?

When the infant realizes that, in her frustration, she has attacked her mother—she has attacked something she loves—the crucial endeavour that the mother/caretaker needs to facilitate is a reparative one. The caretaker needs to be attentive and responsive to the child's initially clumsy efforts to "make up." It is these reparative or integrative gifts that modern stances have difficulties in recognizing and distinguishing from either expressions of non-selfish autonomy or signs of submission. It is the ability to recognize another's relationship-nurturing gifts (and to distinguish them from gifts that wound or a triumphal giving) that we forfeit by relating to others as commensals.

Benjamin writes:

> If [the analyst] gives from a position of pure complementarity (the one who knows, heals, remains in charge), the patient will feel that because of what the analyst has given him, the analyst owns him; in other words, the analyst can eat him in return. Further, the patient has nothing to give back, no impact or insight that will change the analyst. The patient will feel he must suppress his differences, spare the analyst, participate in pseudomutuality or react with envious defiance of the analyst's power. (Benjamin 2004, 14)

Her patient was eager to give back, to share her insights and acknowledge Benjamin. Moreover, both emphasized not having bowed down to impersonal, therapeutic rules. What the analysand had learned was something that Benjamin certainly facilitated, yet something that she realized by appreciating how Benjamin's resistance was not coercive.

Stengers recounts a story by the famous neopagan feminist, Starhawk:

> Starhawk tells about her own experience, when she was part of group of activists who were mobilized to help Native Americans fighting for their rights. An old woman asked: "You are nice people, you who come and help us, but where are you coming from?" Which meant for Starhawk: "We can tell you who we are, and what we defend, but who are you, and how can we connect?" What Starhawk understood was that the answer could not be made in terms of generalities, presenting herself as an anonymous, self-sacrificing, righter of wrongs, but required being able to tell about her own attachments, in order to meet in dignity.
>
> (Stengers 2008, 57)

Telling about her own attachments entailed telling how her engagement in a shared endeavour involved connecting for her own reasons. This does not mean that there are two completely separate sets of endeavours. That we have access to invoking (concern for) compositions that we share with people we sometimes disagree with and need to resist allows us to negotiate respect without getting stuck in impasses where one sacred is pitted against another.

Whatever we offer as resistance to iconoclasm, if we are to overcome the inherent violence of modernity, we will need to consider what it does to others. What kind of position will it put others in? What kind of relationality will be composed through it? Is our help antibiotic (do we follow through on our good intentions?) Are our demonstrations of competence such that others are related to as commensals? These kinds of questions are not about bowing down to shared norms of "the common good" but ask us instead to consider the effects of our entanglements with those we co-compose relations with.

If and when we are (implicitly or explicitly) accused of sacrilege, instead of reverting to protecting our rights or invoking an impersonal principle, we might endeavour to exhibit reverence in service of the continued possibility to "meet in dignity." Instead of managing our relational vulnerability by invoking inculpable idols (that both provide guarantees and are never held accountable), we might channel our hopes in the endeavour of protecting ourselves against iconoclasm and complementarity by invoking shared thirds: "in the name of the continued possibility of being able to meet in dignity."

Acknowledgments

I would like to thank Ann-Helen Sund and Pekka Valkealahti for insightful and challenging commentary on an earlier version of this chapter.

References

Agamben, G. 2007. *Profanations*. Translated by Jeff Fort. New York: Zone Books.

Benjamin, J. 2004. "Beyond Doer and Done To: An Intersubjective View of Thirdness." *Psychoanalytic Quarterly* 73(1): 5–46.

Britton, R. 1998. *Belief and Imagination*. London: Routledge.

———. 1997 [1988]. "The Missing Link: Parental Sexuality in the Oedipus Complex". In *The Contemporary Kleinians of London*, edited by R. Schafer, 242–258. Madison, CT: International University Press.

Clarke, S., H. Hahn and P. Hoggett, eds. 2008. *Object Relations and Social Relations: The Implications of the Relational Turn in Psychoanalysis*. London: Karnac Books.

Freud, S. 2010 [1939]. *Moses and Monotheism*. Eastford, CT: Martino Fine Books.

Goldner, V. 2003. "Gender and Trauma: Commentary on Michael Clifford's Case Presentation." *Progress in Self Psychology* 20: 223–230.

Lacan, J. (1975)1991. *The Seminar of Jacques Lacan, Book I, 1953-54*. Translated by J. Forrester. New York: Norton.

Latour, B. 2010. *On the Modern Cult of the Factish Gods*. Translated by H. MacLean and C. Porter. Durham, NC: Duke University Press.

Mauss, M. 1954. *The Gift. Forms and Functions of Exchange in Archaic Societies.* Translated by I. Cunnison. London: Cohen & West Ltd.

Mitchell, S. A. 1997. *Influence and Autonomy in Psychoanalysis.* Hillsdale, NJ: Analytic Press.

Rinella, M. A. 2011. *Pharmakon: Plato, Drug Culture, and Identity in Ancient Athens.* Plymouth, UK: Lexington Books.

Sedgwick, E. Kosofsky. 2003. *Touching Feeling: Affect, Pedagogy, Performativity.* Durham, NC: Duke University Press.

Stengers, I. 2010. *Cosmopolitics I.* Translated by R. Bononno. Minneapolis: University of Minnesota Press.

———. 2008. "Experimenting with Refrains: Subjectivity and the Challenge of Escaping Modern Dualism." *Subjectivity* 22: 38–59.

Stengers, I. and P. Pignarre 2011. *Capitalist Sorcery: Breaking the Spell.* Translated and edited by A. Goffey. Basingstoke: Palgrave Macmillan.

Stephen, M. 2000. "Reparation and the Gift". *Ethos* 28(2): 119–146.

Wilson, N. 2015. "Surprising Benefits of Sexually Transmitted Infections." <http://www.bbc.com/earth/story/20150828-STDs-that-are-good-for-you> [Accessed 15 October 2015].

Peik Ingman:

Interviews by Peik Ingman, kept in the Cultura archive at Åbo Akademi University.

Sara: IF mgt 2012/004

Mathias: IF mgt 2012/001

David: in author's archive

About the Author

Peik Ingman is a PhD candidate in Comparative Religion at Åbo Akademi University. He is currently working on a doctoral thesis with the working title "Sacralization and the Gift: Queer Family Members in Christian Families." His research combines actor-network theory, philosophy of science and object relations theory.

PART III

Academic Concerns

— 10 —

Enchanted Sight/Site:
An Esoteric Aesthetics of Image and Experience

JAY JOHNSTON

This chapter proposes an "esoteric aesthetics" as enabling a rethinking and reformulation of aesthetic relations that distinctly takes into account varieties of material agency. It takes seriously the question of how we are to understand aesthetic engagement if we are *not* interacting with purely empirical material. This approach has potentially radical implications for the concept of subjectivity, artistic agency and interpretations of the *role* of image or object *and* the viewer. Therefore, the argument draws together several academic disciplines: in particular, post-structural philosophy, Western art historical discourse and the Western esoteric tradition. The objects selected for analysis are an image found in a Coptic magical handbook (p. 12 of P. Macq. I, c. VIIth century CE) and *Crow Stone* (Dumfriesshire, April 1998), a work by the contemporary artist Andy Goldsworthy. Through analysis of these examples, this chapter argues that an esoteric aesthetics requires not only attention to the possible agency of image or object, but also attention to one's own embodied experience and the multiple frameworks through which meaning is made.

Introduction

A dry stonewall enclosure. A familiar enough sight amongst Cumbria's undulating, sheep farming landscape. Look again. Look longer. There is

Keywords: esoteric aesthetics, material agency, cultivation of perception, subtle bodies, ontology, other-than-human agency, intersubjectivity

no entrance, only a stone step to take one up over the unbroken wall. In the square enclosure sits—almost smugly—an enormous stone boulder. It inhabits the centre space, a space usually occupied by sheep. What is the relation of stone and sheep? The artist, Andy Goldsworthy, writes of the work "Drove Stone, Sweet Riggs, Fell Gate Farm" that the stone does NOT "represent sheep," but rather that he hopes viewers will "momentarily see the stone as something living." As he explains: "My stones are not trying to represent sheep but to touch on the life, movement and energy that are in both animal and stone" (Goldsworthy 2007, 74). Here, then, is the core question: how do we perceive stone liveliness? "The energy and space around a rock are as important as the energy and the space within" (Goldsworthy 1985).

Over the past few decades, numerous post-structural, phenomenological, anthropological, archaeological and cultural studies methodologies and theories have challenged interpretative schemas of aesthetic experience that prominently encompass the heritage of Kantian aesthetics and the dominant form of disembodied vision which it advocates. The viewer's body has been firmly placed back in the consideration of aesthetic exchange, and the aesthetic exchange itself is opened to be understood as a markedly more multisensory, subjective, creative experience. From the dynamic philosophy of Gilles Deleuze to the anthropology of Alfred Gell, and including the art historical work of Hans Belting and David Freedberg, the intersubjective relations between viewer and object have been given increased recognition and predominance in interpretative methodologies.[1] Furthermore, these developments have raised questions concerning the agency of image/object. They challenge interpretations of images as static representations or illustrations by attributing various degrees of activity—and even agency (including ontology)—to them. In short, the boundaries between subject and object, between self and image, have become blurry, inconsistent, and even incoherent.

This chapter enters into the field opened by these developments; in particular, it aims to identify and demonstrate (with requisite brevity) a methodological approach that is distinctly furnished by theories and concepts found within the discipline of Western esotericism. It will be argued that the proposition of an "esoteric aesthetics" (outlined further below) enables a further reformulation and re-thinking of aesthetic relations *per se*. This approach has potentially radical implications for the concept of subjectivity, artistic agency and interpretations of the *role* of

---

1. See Gilles Deleuze, *Francis Bacon: Logique de la sensation*. Paris: Éditions de la Différence, 1981. Gell, A., *Art and Agency: An Anthropological Theory*, Oxford: Clarendon Press, Oxford, 1998. David Freedberg, *The Power of Images: Studies in the History and Theory of Response* (Chicago and London: University of Chicago Press, 1989).

image or object *and* the viewer. Therefore, this chapter draws together several academic disciplines: in particular, post-structural philosophy, Western art historical discourse and the Western esoteric tradition.

The selection of objects for analysis and discussion here mirrors this approach of "bridging" realms that are often—but by no means always— held apart. First, it includes elements of a visual culture usually considered within the corpus of Western esotericism's "objects"—an image found in an early Coptic magical handbook (p. 12 of P. Macq. I, ca. VIIth century CE)[2]—although the study of ancient magic in the field has to date been eclipsed by a rich focus on the Medieval and Renaissance periods; studies of ancient magic and ritual are more commonly found in the discipline of ancient history and, more recently, particularly within the strongly emerging field of Late Antiquity studies. Secondly, with over one and a half thousand years separating their creation, also included is a selected work from the contemporary installations of Andy Goldsworthy, specifically *Crow Stone* (Dumfriesshire, April 1998), a piece that has no "obvious" or superficially conceptual or material heritage from the Western esoteric tradition. This work in particular has been chosen because of its secular context and its aesthetic agenda, which extends beyond the borders of the page or painting into and encompassing the environment, because of its use of animal and geological materiality.

Together, these make—I hope—an incongruent selection. These two examples are included because of the diversity of their historical periods, materiality and purpose in an effort to demonstrate the predominant subject of this paper: the consideration of what an esoteric aesthetics— as a form of subject-object engagement—might "look" like, what experiences it might yield, what questions it might ask.

I have previously articulated my concept of esoteric aesthetics in more detail (2008, 2010); however, it is possible to summarize its core features, all of which do not need to be concurrent (which are also further explicated and exemplified in the case studies below), as follows: i) the relationship between viewer and object is radically intersubjective and co-constitutional; ii) this relationship is constitutive of other-than-human agencies which may not be perceptible to the five senses, but may be perceived by forms of extrasensory perception; iii) an esoteric aesthetics requires the utilization of a range of scopic regimes, some of which may require conscious cultivation; iv) an esoteric aesthetics is an embodied and self-reflective relationship that often requires elongated periods of time to cultivate; v) it requires continual questioning of socio-culturally defined concepts of "materiality," "subjectivity" and their interrelation; and v) it embraces epistemological

---

2. See Choat, M. and I. Gardner, *A Coptic Handbook of Ritual Power*, Turnhout: Brepols, 2013. I thank the authors for access to the pre-published edition.

plurality in the understanding of subject-object relations; vi) because the aesthetic relationship is built upon a radical form of intersubjectivity. Thus, an esoteric aesthetics is also an ethics. That is, it constitutes active worldviews which direct behaviour and response-ability (Oliver 2001).

The two examples discussed here focus on two different aspects of the proposed engagement of esoteric aesthetics: the ontology of the image (an illustration in a magical handbook) and the kinesthetic/synaesthetic relations between artwork and viewer (Goldsworthy's installations). Prior to discussing each example in turn, modes of visuality and ontology—the image/objects and the viewing subjects—are explicated. Vision is, of course, never neutral. Furthermore, as I have argued elsewhere, perception is an ethical choice (Johnston 2008, 215). That is, there is a spectrum of perceptive capacities potentially available to any individual; however, these are not necessarily culturally innate and may require conscious cultivation via a range of mind-body practices.

Disinterested Vision and the Body's Sight:
Debates on Iconography and Experience

> Everyone must allow that a judgement on the beautiful which is tinged with the slightest interest, is very partial and not a pure judgement of taste. One must not be in the least prepossessed in favour of the real existence of the thing, but must preserve complete indifference in this respect, in order to play the part of judge in matters of taste.
>
> (Kant 1790 [1982] §2, 43)

"Traditional" art history—and indeed even our "everyday" vision—has been strongly influenced by this appeal to the "objective" viewer: a viewer that is entirely (both physically and emotionally) distinct from their object of study. Such an approach assumes that an individual perceives with disinterest and that such a disinterested scopic regime is potentially universal. Of course, images utilized as a focus for religious veneration are not approached in their ritual context with an agenda dominated by disinterested aesthetics. In fact, the embodied and "interested" forms of engagement associated with such religious imagery may explain the derisory attitudes toward religious art articulated by some critics. For example, James Elkins commented: "Most religious art—and I am saying this bluntly, because it needs to be said—is just bad art" (2009, 71). In the discipline of art history, this disinterestedness has been correlated with connoisseurship and the possession of refined aesthetic sensibilities (such a "cultivated" individual is associated with particular social and class formations).[3]

---

3. For example, see Martha Woodmansee, *The Author, Art, and the Market: Rereading the History of Aesthetics* (New York: Columbia University Press, 1994).

Accompanying this perspective, and of crucial importance to the development of art history, is the agenda that images can be evaluated on the basis of purely aesthetic criteria (internal to the object); indeed, the disinterested relation is requisite for such an evaluation. Desire and attraction, being "unrefined" emotive responses, have no place in this type of aesthetic exchange. Finally, as signalled by the reference to connoisseurship, over time these ideas of *aesthetic engagement* became intertwined with ideas about personal development and morals and teleological concepts of the development of civilization (obviously Hegel's aesthetics demonstrates the latter). A personal and social cultivation, it should be noted, was designed (and responded) to take place within a Christian cultural milieu. The pure, universal aesthetic value of an object could be witnessed by those who were suitably cultivated, and this approach has persisted predominantly in the "art for art's sake" of interpretive methodologies. The autonomous nature of the art object is taken as primary (at least for that which is deemed "good" art).

Critiques of this approach have come thick and fast, and they are now quite numerous. However, the degree of ontological ascription—the degree to which the image/object is ascribed capacities to *do* and *elicit* particular effects and relations—varies. This chapter is concerned with the more extreme ontological interpretations: interpretations that not only challenge the supposed "empty" space between viewer and object, or the "static" and representative nature of the image/object itself; but which ask questions regarding the nature of materiality itself. Before turning to consider materiality more directly, a brief—and inductive rather than comprehensive—overview of some of the challenges to disinterested relations will assist in situating the esoteric considerations detailed below in an interdisciplinary context.

The rise of material cultural studies and its emphasis on the object, image and tactile experience has helped to raise questions about the viewer-object in a number of disciplines. In the archaeology of religion, Timothy Insoll, Richard Bradley, Colin Renfrew and Ian Hodder have each in their own individual ways considered the complexities of visuality and material culture. While generalizations necessarily erase the richness and specificity of their individual arguments, note should be taken of the questioning of schematic and historical categories, as well as the disciplinary bias shown towards certain materials and processes—and certain cultures and not others.[4] The work of Christopher Tilley in theoretical and phenomenological archaeology has been especially focused on the *materiality* of images and objects through a kinaesthetic approach.

---

4. For example, see Bradley's discussion of the category of "prehistoric art" in *Image and Audience: Rethinking Prehistoric Art* (Oxford: Oxford University Press, 2009).

Indeed, a scholarly turn towards the examination of the role of the senses in perception—and the epistemologies with which they are associated—has provided a particularly rich vein of analysis in cultural studies, which builds on (but also critiques) phenomenological approaches (for example, the work of David Howes or Constance Classen).[5] Critiques of historical methodologies developed on the basis of textual evidence alone are also developing rapidly, leading to works where the incorporation of material evidence is being taken alongside the written, and eliciting new—and at times confronting—interpretations of the past. Lotte Hedeager's *Iron Age Myth and Materiality: An Archaeology of Scandinavia AD 400-1000* is a prime example of this approach. Of particular importance is her discussion of the agency of animal motifs and their transpecies subjectivity (2011).

However, perhaps anthropological discourses have had the most enduring impact on rethinking the role of art/objects and their relations; most evident is Alfred Gell's now iconic *Art and Agency: An Anthropological Theory* (1998). Gell does not attribute ontological status to images, but he does suggest that they are active, proposing an "anthropological theory in which *persons* or 'social agents' are [...] substituted for by *art objects*" (1998, 5), thus initiating a diverse and continuing conversation on the art-anthropological interface. In the discipline of religious studies, Caroline Walker Bynum's *Christian Materiality: An Essay on Religion in Late Medieval Europe* (2011) is a recent example. Taking up the concept of "holy matter," Walker Bynum investigates the agency ascribed to sacred material objects (for example, relics, images, and statues) with a focus on the (expanded) concepts of materiality and body specific to Christianity of late-medieval Europe. However, she side-steps (by way of her introduction) the concerns of this chapter by specifically choosing not to enter into debates about recent ontological definitions of materiality (while also acknowledging that her use of "agency" does "parallel" the works of Gell and Latour, amongst others) (Walker Bynum 2011, 31). Also in the field of religious studies, religious aesthetics has emerged strongly in northern Europe over the past five years or so. It is characterized by an emphasis on the sensory experience of material culture (pertaining to religious practice), rather than the traditional Kantian aesthetic categories of the sublime and the beautiful.[6] Whilst it can be considered both an outgrowth of, and challenge to, phenomenology of religion, a consideration of religious aesthetics at its most basic level aims to ask questions

---

5. David Howes, *Sensual Relations: Engaging the Senses in Culture and Social Theory* (Ann Arbor: University of Michigan Press, 2003; Constance Classen, *The Colour of Angels: Cosmology, Gender and the Aesthetic Imagination* (London: Routledge, 1998).

6. Mohr, H., "Material Religion/ Religious Aesthetics: A Research Program," *Material Religion: The Journal of Objects, Art and Belief* 6.2 (2010), 240.

about what modes of perception and visuality are presupposed by particular cultural formations, and what this says about the ways that individuals and cultures conceptualize time, space and subjectivity: "how a particular community utilizes certain perceptions, media, senses, artefacts, signs etc. to present [... a] religious dimension." (Schüler 2010, 247). Thus, the production and use of religious material culture both creates and maintains shared metaphysical worldviews. As I have argued elsewhere (2008), this is not a matter of simple apprehension but an embodied cultivation of perception. Such a perspective considers the relation to image to be not purely ocular (just to do with the eyes), but an embodied perceptual relation utilizing a range of senses and inherently based in metaphysical concepts of self and other.

As material culture studies boomed, very few questions were asked of the *concept* of materiality that forms the cultures analysed Indeed, as I have also noted elsewhere (2013), even in New Materialism the type of "thing power" articulated is far from "new"; indeed, esoteric traditions are replete with examples of such other-than-human agency. This is inclusive of not only considering images as ontological, but also as enchanted to various degrees, and, further, as comprised of a type of materiality that is simultaneously tangible and elusive: subtle material. In regard to Western esoteric "examples" of such a materiality, the concept is often requisite for understanding specific phenomena (for example, the efficacy of magic or the ontology of angels). The subtle relations afforded by such nebulous concepts of matter are discussed below in relation to both the image from the Coptic ritual handbook and Goldsworthy's *Crow Stone*.

I do not advocate that iconographical analysis be eschewed—indeed it is a feature of the analysis of the "magical image" that it is afforded a less dominant place, with the initial emphasis being placed on considering the subject-object encounter (the aesthetic exchange) and the ontological foundation of such. As anthropologist and archaeologist Christopher Tilley writes in advocating a kinaesthetic approach to interpreting rock art, "Iconographic approaches are usually primarily cognitive in nature. They grant primacy to the human mind as a producer of the meaning of the images through sensory perception" (2008, 18). For Tilley, due attention is not paid to the whole-body perceptive encounter, nor the way in which perception is induced and limited by our particular visceral selves. Further to this, and presaging a point detailed later, it pays no credence to one's own capacity to knowingly cultivate perception.

While taking into account the aforementioned attitudes towards materiality and image, it is also requisite to note that some art historical analysis has considered seriously the idea that images have power or agency: in particular, Hans Belting's superb *Likeness and Presence* (1994) and David Freedberg's equally erudite *The Power of Images* (1989). Of special note here is the large degree to which the images they discuss are orientated towards ritual, spiritual and religious functions. That is, they originally existed in very particular metaphysical contexts that directly informed not only the "reading" of iconography but their materiality and ascriptions of agency. Turning to the discipline of Western esotericism, a number of scholars have also engaged with image agency, most notably for this chapter's purpose Gyorgy Szonyi (1996) (who works with Gell's schema), Kocku von Stuckrad and Wouter Hanegraaff.

It appears that increasingly (and delightfully) more scholars are now responding to Hanegraaff's (and my own) bafflement about this lack of discussion: that is, whether those images found within the corpora of Western esotericism are animated. Indeed, "The full history of the animation of images in Western culture still remains to be written" (Hanegraaff 2007). Hanegraaff also curtailed the limits of such discussion when he wrote: "there is simply no other way of understanding images 'on their own terms' than by following Wittgenstein's advice, disappointing though it may be: remain silent about what cannot be spoken but can only be shown" (2007, 134). As I have signalled elsewhere (2010) the expression "on their own terms" seems to evoke an "art for art's sake" style of analysis—that somehow the purpose and meaning of these images lies locked within, an internal quality of the image/object. Perhaps it is not so much the deployment of silence that is requisite for respecting these images' alterity and difference, but a methodological position that acknowledges that any contemporary interpretation is a necessarily incomplete one. The acknowledgment is not so much of a resonant silence as of a partial voice, tentative suppositions created and informed by the methodological program detailed at the close of this paper, and which also informed Kocku von Stuckrad's analysis of "Renaissance" pagan iconography (2006, 59–85).

As von Stuckrad recounts, Gombrich identified how attitudes to images are profoundly imbricated in an individual's "whole idea about the universe" and discussed styles of "representation" and "symbolization" as "strategies of 'distancing' the presumed inherent power of images" while not venturing to consider this as an ontological problem (2006, 62). The consideration of "image acts" is a central concern:

> If we take seriously the notion that religious ideas, convictions, and traditions are "acted out" in the public sphere, that they form part of people's identities in a unity of image, message, and body, and that the materiality of religion is something to move to the center of scrutiny, we will perhaps arrive at a better understanding of the status of paganism in post-ancient Europe. (von Stuckrad 2006, 75)

According to von Stuckrad, such an orientation is a challenge to the primacy of text in religious studies scholarship, placing emphasis on the sensuous, lived nature of an individual's encounter with image or object.

One way of approaching such "image acts" within an esoteric corpus is to be mindful of the *mundus imaginalus*—creative imagination—as an epistemological attitude. In regard to the selected objects of analysis herein, there is admittedly some "flouncing" of historical boundaries and contexts, if Ficino's or Corbin's[7] sense of the term is invoked. However, if a broader conceptualization is applied, one that takes into account an esoteric aptitude for reading relations between the human and the divine—the unseen in between—then the evocation is of a perceptual experience that can read invisible relations, invisible sympathies, and perhaps even the "energy and space" that Andy Goldsworthy perceives as surrounding and internal to the material with which he creates his contemporary installations. Therefore, a creative imagination could embrace epistemologies of kinetic and synesthetic perception, of affect relations—whether understood as psychological, spiritual or ontological—and interrelations between subject and object. What can be "seen" with empirical certainty is accompanied by an unseen exchange filtered and understood within specific ideological contexts. Such an aesthetic experience requires not only attention to the possible agency of image or object, but also attention to one's own embodied experience and the multiple frameworks through which meaning is made.

If, for example, the invisible relations of exchange are understood to be comprised of subtle matter—neither empirical matter nor pure spirit/consciousness—then no ontological distinction is drawn between subject and object; rather, both are set in complex, nebulous and dynamic relation to one another. As prescribed by a variety of esoteric texts and traditions, such relations can be apprehended by the employment of various epistemologies, including that of *mundus imaginalus* or intuitive forms of perception. Such modalities are affective in a broad sense and involve more than a mental translation of perceptive experience: a whole-body "listening" and response, being a conscious cultivation of alternative modalities of perception.[8] The attribution of a particular ontology results

---

7. On creative Imagination, see Henry Corbin, *Creative Imagination in the Sufism of Ibn 'Arabi* (Princeton: Princeton University Press, 1969); Antoine Faivre, *Access to Western Esotericism* (Albany, State University of New York, 1994) and *Theosophy, Imagination, Tradition: Studies in Western Esotericism* (Albany: State University of New York Press, 2000); Marsilio Ficino, *The Book of Life* [1489], trans. Charles Boer (Woodstock, CT: Spring Publications, 1996); and Jay Johnston, *Angels of Desire: Esoteric Bodies, Aesthetics and Ethics* (London: Equinox, 2008), 107–122.

8. For a more detailed discussion of subtle relations between subject and object, see Johnston's *Angels of Desire*.

in a specific concept of matter (subtle matter), which in turn enables a re-reading of the mode of aesthetic experience.

Therefore, in a respectfully cheeky manner, this paper now turns to discuss—in a necessarily partial and incomplete manner—that which might indeed have best been left unsaid.

Script and Spirit-being:
Considering an Image from a Coptic Handbook of Ritual Power

Over the past twenty years, the scholarship on ancient ritual practices—particularly those commonly classified as "magical"—has developed rapidly, leading to a re-evaluation of their influence and role. Indeed, there is an increasing tendency to abandon the former term as misleading or carrying vestiges of colonial and Christian discourses and agendas. This has been the result of many factors: an increased recognition and more holistic understanding of popular religious and social practice beyond the traditional emphasis on textuality and the word (due in part to the interaction between anthropology and historical studies); major developments in the history of medicine and science, together with the birth of the academic study of Western esotericism as a discrete discipline; substantial new finds; and integrated international publication projects or databases for the great mass of material now available. This recent scholarship has significantly enriched the understanding of the cultures of Late Antiquity.

However, the majority of studies of magical papyri and ritual artefacts still focus on the translation and interpretation of the written word to the exclusion of a more integrated understanding of these objects.[9] The approach herein seeks to be more holistic by considering the images as integral to the magical papyri's purpose, agency and ritual function. Elements of art and design warrant the same type of critical scholarly examination. This is to take seriously the common formula in the papyri: "This is the drawing you have to draw" (e.g., *PGM II* 170). In order to do this, an interdisciplinary approach is needed; and, in addition to that, the ontological nature of these images needs to be more centrally addressed.[10]

Figure 1 is a complex (but fairly typical) image, taken from a Coptic ritual handbook on parchment (viz. p. 12 of P. Macq. I, ca. VIIth century CE). It illustrates some of the ways in which text, art and design elements are

---

9. An example of an exception to this is Attilio Mastrocinque, *From Jewish Magic to Gnosticism*. Studien und Texte zu Antike und Christentum 24. Tubingen: Mohr Siebeck, 2005.

10. This is the topic of the project "The Function of Images in Magical Papyri and Artefacts of Ritual Power from Late Antiquity" by J. Johnston, I. Gardner, J. Kindt, H. Whitehouse and E. Hunter, funded by the Australian Research Council (2012-2015).

Enchanted Sight/Site

Figure 1 Analysis example. From M. Choat and I. Gardner, *A Coptic Handbook of Ritual Power*. Image reproduced with permission of Museum of Ancient Cultures, Macquarie University.

deployed together in magical papyri. The translation of the text by Choat and Gardner (forthcoming)[11] provides detailed identification of and commentary on invocations and textual parallels, but it necessarily lacks the means to understand the functional aspects of the practice or issues of agency. One must suppose that the placing of sections of text in relationship to the images was deliberate, although in standard editions this would hardly be discussed. Indeed, the entire purpose of the page is both an aid and an instruction to the practitioner. We must consider all the elements of design, including the relationships established between the images and the text, and then the visual and functional aspects, as well as the oral and aural effects caused by the repetition of letters and syllables. To give an example, the text located on the chest/body area of the central figure starts with a repetitive syllabic pattern that requires chanting and rhythmic breathing. It then lists the four "light-aeons" of Sethian

---

11. My thanks to Iain Gardner for discussion of the handbook's textual elements and Sethian context.

tradition (an earlier ritual community from which various details such as the names of these spirit-beings were borrowed and re-used), followed by the technical instruction that this is a spell. As such, we can interpret the anthropomorph (*orans*) as an image of the ritualist invoking each of the named spirit-beings (which needs to be done orally) which are then visually "present" in the figures of the four disc-like designs that appear beside and in the hands of the figure (these are what we could understand as ontological; that is, they presence the named "spirit-beings").

Furthermore, questions can be asked about placement: Is the text written on the chest because that is the seat from which invocation was understood to be physically generated? Or is it because the practitioner understood the light-aeons as coming to inhabit his/her physical being during the ritual? Are they present "in" the image in a similar way? The very asking of such questions is, in itself, unusual in the methodology of studying such material. It illustrates the significance of the holistic approach to image *and* text that I advocate. Similarly, the lower figure, which I identify as a scorpion, contains a palindrome of sacred names and the word for spell. The 'n' of one name in line 3 is turned around and shapes the mouth or pincers of the creature, providing clear evidence that both text and image were conceptualized as working together and therefore must be considered by means of an integrated analysis.

Furthermore, the text and design elements in the upper-left corner provide information about the metaphysical hierarchy of the belief system. The letters deliberately hide the name of the "great invisible spirit whose name cannot be pronounced," and the design elements are a visual representation of that "hidden" name. The positioning of both epithet and image above and behind the central figure is a visual indication that this was an overarching being considered superior to the anthropomorph depicted below it, which itself stands above the zoomorph. This is, I must stress, a provisional reading that I hope to further substantiate by comparative analysis across different types of magical corpora. What I wish to emphasize here, however, is that such a reading—and the questions it poses—can only be answered if we view the image as active, not only an instructive diagram or representation, but also having power—*of doing*—in and of itself. Teasing out what this doing is/was can only be attempted by locating it as thoroughly as possible within the conceptual, philosophical and religious context of production. This is not only a case of examining the image within its specific cultural context; it is also includes consideration of the intersubjective dynamic between the viewer-object and a wider range of scopic regimes. For this, no form of universal or disinterested vision will do.

Ontological Slippages: Animal and Earth in Goldsworthy's Landscape Installations

The image is of a photographed landscape: a velvet blue-black feathered "rock" sits in the mid-foreground. Of substantial breadth, it dwarfs its foundation of smaller, grey rocks. These appear as if an immense cairn had tumbled, or are the remnants of broch or a great stone wall. In the background are rolling green hills, chequed by fencing, gentle peaks and an undulating horizon. This is, no doubt, an inadequate description of the visual elements of Andy Goldsworthy's contemporary art installation, *Crow Stone* (1998). The vibrancy—the aliveness—of the "crow stone" is alarming. Is it animal? Is it earth? If disturbed, will the feathered mass unfurl its being? Or is the simple pleasure of passing silenced feathers across the palm as one feels its "body" a type of aliveness? It is these very questions of ontological status, of the slippage between states (animal-rock), that the installation invokes.

The contemporary British artist Andy Goldsworthy (b. 1956) is well known for his installations that utilize elemental materials (water, wood, stone, and so forth) and are often temporal and strongly linked to specific environments. His work has been discussed within the framework of "spiritual art," including Suzi Gablik's *The Reenchantment of Art* (1991), in which she emphasized nature as the subject of his work and his specific processes of engagement, specifically the process of "tuning in and adapting to different landscapes and seasons, establishing a dialogue with the place, cooperating with its subtle web of interrelated processes" (1991, 91). More recently in *Refiguring the Spiritual: Beuys, Barney, Turrell, Goldsworthy* (2012), Mark C. Taylor has sought to position Goldsworthy as an overlooked artist (a highly debatable conjecture) whose practice is "committed to the materialization of the spiritual." In particular, he notes, "The northern Scottish lowlands and hills are haunted by Celtic ghosts that quietly roam through Goldsworthy's even when they are not explicitly involved" (Taylor 2012, 162; 190–191).

Crow Stone has no obvious magical intent—although at a stretch its location in the border region of Scotland evokes the role that magic stones held in Gaelic cultures, as well as the crow's symbolic role as a portent of the magical arts. This boulder, however, has been wilfully transmogrified. It is richly and thickly covered in crow feathers. Hence, the work plays with a number of dominant dualisms: the air element and flight of the bird contrasted against the land and stability of the rock; the weight of the rock contrasted against the ethereal lightness of feather. *Sheep Stone* (June 1998) is a piece of very similar visual construction, which provides a counterpoint to the abyssal black of *Crow Stone*. As the title implies, here the rock is covered with shaggy, white fleece—a static sheep amidst its hereditary landscape. To leave aside this obvious chromatic black-white dichotomy and return to merely contemplating *Crow Stone*, it appears clear that Goldsworthy's comments about the energetic context of an artwork are brought to the fore with this piece. Its very materiality evokes a more multisensory consciousness from the viewer. The feathers are seductive in both colour and tactility; their obscure placement emphasizes their material qualities. Although feathers are natural on a bird's body, one looks quite differently at them when amassed on stone in a landscape.

The landscape placement itself makes the viewer conscious of their corporeality and scale. Where one is positioned in the landscape to view the work inherently affects the aesthetic experience, as do features like the weather and the duration of the "looking" process. In the cultivation of a subtle perception, a perception which would glean the energetic relations that exceed a work and circulate in its environment—whether attributed an organic or spiritual framework, the length of time required for the experience of the work may be longer than a quick glance or single circumnavigation of the sculpture. It may require a "sitting with/in" the piece for hours, or multiple times.[12]

And what of the photographic image, that which "remains" of the installation itself? Can the same style of energetic exchange be cultivated with this caught moment of time? An esoteric aesthetics would require more than a mere cursory glance: a reading that considers in detail the multiple relations between object, its constituents and the landscape as represented. It could also involve the multisensory response that the photograph itself invokes in the viewer, an image of a held movement held in the moment.

Goldsworthy can be considered an elemental artist due to the centrality of natural elements in his works.[13] Stone, water, snow, wood—these are all cultivated into installations that draw attention to the agency of the natural world, the agency of the human and their intersection. His interest in energetic and special relations lend themselves to be read not so much as in the tradition of *Naturphilosophie* in a strict sense, but rather in the capacity of *material* to defy human expectation. He brings attention to its empirical material aspects—colour, shape and form—and works with them in such a way as to re-enchant them, to make their familiar properties strange and powerful via position, action, displacement and pattern. The initial oddity of a feather-covered boulder in a

---

12. For a longer discussion of duration and aesthetic experience, see Johnston, *Angels of Desire*, 2008.

13. See, for example, Andy Goldsworthy, *Stone* (New York: Abrams, 1993) and Andy Goldsworthy, *Wood* (New York: Abrams, 1996).

field is soon replaced by considerations of materiality and location, thus drawing the viewer into a multisensory aesthetic relation. This experience need not be interpreted via specific spiritual or esoteric frameworks—although, as indicated, it could be. However, the work certainly does call on epistemologies privileged within the tradition of Western esotericism, including those often positioned in dominant culture as "alternate" (for example, intuition, *mundus imaginalus* as previously discussed, and forms of associative correspondence). It draws attention to "thinking" with the whole body (and its energetic interrelations) by means of intuitive and subtle perceptive responses, to asking questions of the ontological capacity of materials and of the dominant logic with which they are usually categorized and understood. The enchantment is achieved via selection and placement. *Crow Stone* evokes specific material associations as well as calling into question the ontological divisions between animate and inanimate material: the very "in between" space that an active enchantment inhabits. An esoteric aesthetics would foreground—in multiple multisensory ways—a consideration of that space.

Esoteric Aesthetics: An Animate Methodology

> One of the most unfortunate problems of public — and academic — debate is the misunderstanding that relativism means arbitrariness. Against this biased presentation of the "postmodern" cultural analysis and philosophy, I want to stress that relativism takes seriously the *relation* of an identifiable object with its surrounding structure. Relativism, thus, is the very opposite of "anything goes," because it addresses the influences that define the positions of actors, opinions and currents in a field of networks. (von Stuckrad 2010, x)

The issue of context and one's own positioning within it becomes even more acute when trying to speak of/on/about cultures different from one's own, whether the difference is social, cultural, racial, gender-based or historical. The recognition of such differences and the way in which they have informed knowledge formation and interpretation constitutes, of course, the salient moment of many an academic insight. However, it remains that one is often more adept at spotting another's oversight than one's own. The consideration of the relative nature of knowledge—both another's and one's own—is an acknowledgement (however necessarily incomplete) that the position one conducts research from is as political as it is philosophical. The same holds true for aesthetic experience.

The emphasis on relations is, I argue, the key element of an esoteric aesthetics broadly conceived: viewer-object relations and their aesthetics of engagement. The understanding of any such process is inherently tied to the concept of "self," "materiality" and the world that underpins the phenomena being considered. This is not a universal self, but a deeply located one; not a universal concept of matter; but one predicated upon beliefs of the period and socio-cultural group of the time; and, of course, a specific and located worldview. These things are particular and processual.

Just as how one thinks—and the capacity and limits of any such thinking, its "unthought" predicates—is culturally determined, so too is vision. To look is not an innate process; one is taught how to view, and our scopic regimes shift, given changes in context and expectation. Here then are the two core aspects of an esoteric aesthetics as I have approached it in this paper: first, the proposition—well-evidenced in esoteric practices from meditation and ritual to creative imagination—of an individual's capacity to perceive on a broad spectrum and in response to various body-mind techniques and training; and secondly, a call to pay greater attention to *matter* (that is, the very physicality of the images/artefacts under study). The magical papyrus draws attention to the conceptualization of matter, and especially its potential interrelationship with concepts of ontological agency, while Goldsworthy's *Crow Stone* highlights the subtle energetic relations between objects and viewers, and the animate slippage of "liveliness." Of course, these are places where an esoteric approach is the most controversial and also potentially productive. How are we to understand aesthetic engagement if we are *not* interacting with purely empirical material? It would seem that the discipline of Western esotericism with its inherently transdisciplinary remit is singularly well-placed to ask questions of the *matter* and *agency* of image, object and the aesthetic experience itself. Enchanted matter is simultaneously *material* and *relation* and all that takes place between.

References

Belting, H. 1994. *Likeness and Presence: The History of the Image before the Era of Art*. Translated by E. Jephcott. Chicago, IL: University of Chicago Press.

Bradley, R. 2009. *Image and Audience: Rethinking Prehistoric Art*. Oxford: Oxford University Press.

Choat, M. and I. Gardner. 2013. *A Coptic Handbook of Ritual Power*. Turnhout: Brepols.

Classen, C. 1998. *The Colour of Angels: Cosmology, Gender and the Aesthetic Imagination*. London: Routledge.

Corbin Henry. 1969. *Creative Imagination in the Sufism of Ibn 'Arabi*. Princeton, NJ: Princeton University Press.

Deleuze, G. and F. Guattari. 1987. *A Thousand Plateaus: Capitalism and Schizophrenia*. London: Athlone.

Elkins, J. 2009. "How Some Scholars Deal with The Question." In *Re-Enchantment*, edited by J. Elkins and D. Morgan, 69–78. London: Routledge.

Faivre, A. 2000. *Theosophy, Imagination, Tradition: Studies in Western Esotericism*. Albany: State University of New York Press.

———. 1994. *Access to Western Esotericism*. Albany: State University of New York Press.

Ficino, M. 1996 [1489]. *The Book of Life*. Translated by C. Boer. Woodstock, CT: Spring Publications.

Freedberg, D. 1989. *The Power of Images: Studies in the History and Theory of Response*. Chicago, IL: The University of Chicago Press.

Gablik, S. 1991. *The Reenchantment of Art*. London: Thames and Hudson.

Gell, A. 1998. *Art and Agency: An Anthropological Theory*. Oxford: Clarendon Press.

Goldsworthy, A. 2007. *Enclosure*. New York: Abrams.

———. 1996. *Stone*. New York: Abrams.

———. 1993. *Wood*. New York: Abrams.

———. 1985. Brochure, *Rain Sun Snow Hail Mist Calm: Photo Works by Andy Goldsworthy*. The Henry Moore Centre for the Study of Sculpture, Leeds City Art Gallery and Northern Centre for Contemporary Art, Sunderland. <http://www.goldsworthy.cc.gla.ac.uk/extracts/> [Accessed 22 February 2016].

Hanegraaff, W. 2007. "The Trouble with Images: Anti-Image Polemics and Western Esotericism." In *Polemical Encounters: Esoteric Discourse and Its Others*, edited by O. Hammer and K. von Stuckrad, 107–136. Leiden: Brill.

Hedeager, L. 2011. *Iron Age Myth and Materiality: An Archaeology of Scandinavia AD 400-1000*. London: Routledge.

Howes, D. 2003. *Sensual Relations: Engaging the Senses in Culture and Social Theory*. Ann Arbor: University of Michigan Press.

Johnston, J. 2013. "Subtle Subjects and Ethics: The Subtle Bodies of Post-Strcuturalist and Feminist Philosophy." In *Religion and the Subtle Body in Asia and the West*, edited by G. Samuel and J. Johnston, 239–248. London: Routledge.

———. 2010 "Prolegomena to Considering Drawings of Spirit-Beings in Mandaean, Gnostic and Ancient Magical Texts." *ARAM* 22: 573–582.

———. 2008. *Angels of Desire: Esoteric Bodies, Aesthetics and Ethics*. London: Equinox.

Kant, I. 1982 [1790]. *The Critique of Judgement*. Translated by J.C. Meredith. Oxford: Oxford University Press.

Mastrocinque, A. 2005. *From Jewish Magic to Gnosticism*. Studien und Texte zu Antike und Christentum 24. Tubingen: Mohr Siebeck.

Mohr, H. 2010. "Material Religion/ Religious Aesthetics: A Research Program." *Material Religion: The Journal of Objects, Art and Belief* 6(2): 240–242.

Oliver, K. 2001. *Witnessing: Beyond Recognition*. Minneapolis: University of Minnesota Press.

Schüler, S. 2010. "From the Material to the Imaginative: An Outline of the Aesthetics of Religion Program in Münster." *Material Religion: The Journal of Objects, Art and Belief* 6(2): 243–244.

Szönyi, G.1996. "The Powerful Image: Towards a Typology of Occult Symbolism." In *Iconography East and West*, edited by G. E. Szönyi, 250–263. Leiden: Brill.

Taylor, B. 2010. *Dark Green Religion: Nature Spirituality and the Planetary Future*. Berkeley: University of California Press.

Tilley, C. 2008. *Body and Image: Explorations in Landscape Phenomenology 2*. Walnut Creek, CA: Left Coast Press.

Von Stuckrad, K. 2010. *Locations of Knowledge in Medieval and Early Modern Europe: Esoteric Discourses and Western Identities*. Leiden: Brill.

———. 2006. "Visual Gods: From Exorcism to Complexity in Renaissance Studies." *Aries* 6(1): 59–85.

Walker, B.C. 2011. *Christian Materiality: An Essay on Religion in Late Medieval Europe*. New York: Zone Books.

Woodmansee, M. 1994. *The Author, Art, and the Market: Rereading the History of Aesthetics*. New York: Columbia University Press.

About the Author

Jay Johnston is an interdisciplinary scholar (religious studies, art history, philosophy, gender studies, Norse and Scottish studies) who investigates ritual and its use in identity formation, healing practice and cultural exchange. She is particularly interested in Late Antiquity; pre-1400 Scottish and Norse cultures; complementary and alternative medicine and its historical precedents; and human-animal-environment relations. Her publications include *Religion and the Subtle Body in Asia and the West* (ed. with G. Samuel), Routledge 2013, and forthcoming *Stag and Stone: Religion, Archaeology and Esoteric Aesthetics* (Equinox). She is Chief Investigator on "The Function of Images in Magical Papyri and Artefacts of Ritual Power from Late Antiquity," a project funded by the Australian Research Council (2012–2015).

— 11 —

From Religion to Ordering Uncertainty: A Lesson from Dancers

Milan Fujda

This chapter is based on an ethnography of dance improvisation. It analyses instances of handling unpredictability and fragility in ordinary life. It shows that such situations are common and that people are well-skilled in dealing with them without recourse to the idea of a clearly defined order. While the imperatives of modernity seem to lead to a preference for clear orders and calculable means, people in ordinary practice handle disorders arising from unpredictability and complexity by developing and mixing strategies which acknowledge the lack of order. It seems that no practical distinction arises between modern and non-modern people in this case. Furthermore, due to the human tendency to mix various "rational" and "irrational" strategies to overcome unpredictable and fragile situations, the theoretical notion of separated spheres of "secular" and "religious" also loses any practical relevance. Managing chronic illness and pain with its demand for traversing evidence-based medical practices, traditional science, magic, prayer, and so forth in order to gain control over a patient's situation is a key example of this. The point of the chapter is fourfold: 1) analysing such situations leads the study of religion(s) beyond such binaries as "religious" and "secular," or "traditional" and "modern"; 2) it moves the study from marginal, exotic themes towards the core issues of human behaviour in culture and society; 3) it helps the study grasp the meaning and significance of what once

---

Keywords: unpredictability; improvisation; ethnomethodology; ordering practices; study of religion

used to be called "religion" with a practical relevance for actual human (inter)action(s); and 4) it thus helps the discipline to stop being "the marginal discipline of the margins, picking up the crumbs that fall from the other disciplines' banquet table," as Bruno Latour once said about anthropology, and to begin to address the important issues of life of societies and cultures.

An Introductory Note: Refocusing the Study of Religion(s)

The following analysis is based on my ethnography of dance improvisation. The presented descriptions deal with "instructed action,"[1] or more precisely, agency in instructed action. I formulate the question of agency as a question of how and by what means an action is enacted. The aim is to demonstrate one possibility of doing the study of religion(s) without "religion" by studying the practical management of uncertainty. This understanding of agency derives from Bruno Latour's (1996, 2005) respecification of the sociological concepts of action and actor.

> The competencies of the actor [...] must not be confused with the idea that the actor acts, as if actualizing some potentiality. [...] Now to act is to be perpetually overtaken by what one does. [...I]t is simply a recognition of the fact that we are exceeded by what we create. To act is to mediate another's action. But what holds upstream for manufacture also holds downstream for manipulation. [...] There are only actors—actants—any one of which can only "proceed to action" by association with others who may surprise or exceed him/her/it. (Latour 1996, 237)

Put differently: "To use the word 'actor' means that it's never clear who and what is acting when we act since an actor on stage is never alone in acting" (Latour 2005, 46).

In dance improvisation such ambiguity is ubiquitous, hence providing rich opportunities to study unpredictability, vulnerability and uncertainty. A deeper understanding of the *fragility*, *complexity* and *ambiguity* of life *in vivo* is vital in order to reorient the study of religion(s) so as to bring it closer to the idea that organization, ordering and sense-making of the (social) world—all endeavours involving the management of the fragility of life—actually occur in quite ordinary situations.

Ordinary Ordering Practices and Doing Away with "Religion"

Shifting the focus of interest towards ways of managing life in the making entails a move towards paying attention to ordinary *ordering prac-*

---

1. As a study of instructed action, this analysis was inspired not only by the dancers' work in their improvisation project, but also by the studies initiated by Harold Garfinkel (see especially the second part of Garfinkel 2002, 197–285).

tices[2] in a broad sense. In the context of studying religion, it might be also a move away from "religion" as a domain of practice analytically separated from other human activities. Such a move, I think, is necessary in order to overcome serious drawbacks pointed out time and again by the critics of the concept "religion." Building on arguments by Timothy Fitzgerald (1997, 2003), Talal Asad (1993, 2003), Richard King (1999), and S. N. Balagangadhara (2005), I would like to emphasize that "religion" is a fundamental tool of *ordering*, utilized by the moderns[3] to distinguish themselves from *others*: their non-modern ancestors ("*orientals*," "*primitives*," etc.). Bruno Latour (1993) analysed this construction of the "Great Divide" in terms of a practice based on two complementary processes called *translation* (or mediation) and *purification*. He explains

> that the word 'modern' designates two sets of entirely different practices *which must remain distinct if they are to remain effective* [my emphasis], but have recently begun to be confused. The first set of practices, by 'translation', creates mixtures between entirely new types of beings, hybrids of nature and culture. The second, by 'purification', creates two entirely distinct ontological zones: that of human beings on the one hand; that of nonhumans on the other. Without the first set, the practices of purification would be fruitless or pointless. Without the second, the work of translation would be slowed down, limited, or even ruled out. (Latour 1993, 10-11)

In this narrative, nonhumans play an important role in maintaining the boundary between Nature and Culture. The reason why the two processes "must remain distinct if they are to remain effective" is that objects and the rules of Nature are constructed in dominant modern discourses so that they stand independently on their own in relation to the activities of humans. We only need to discover them. They form reality, which only needs to be laid bare.[4] They are neither manufactured nor

---

2. Ordering practices in a broader sense refers to practices of creating order at numerous levels, ranging from making sense of a situation and providing meaning to what was said or done, through making things ordinary by following rules in communication and interaction, up to organizing reality through analysis or politically negotiating problems and subsequently solving them through organizational means. Such a list of topics can be studied by ethnomethodology or actor-network-theory. In both cases the aspect of temporality and process is strongly emphasized (see Garfinkel 1967). I have borrowed the concept of ordering from John Law (1994, 1-9), who emphasizes that it is more useful to approach social order in terms of doing something than in terms of some stable object—of processes going on in a messy environment. Law has emphasized that order is quite often an occasional and temporary "product, outcome, effect, of a lot of work" (Law 1994, 5).
3. An expression borrowed from Bruno Latour (1993).
4. I borrow this metaphor from Jean Baudrillard (1995).

negotiated. Negotiation takes place within the sphere of politics. This sphere is a domain of culture. While nature is a domain of the non-negotiable "reality" of facts, negotiation within the domain of culture creates a space for fantasies and errors. The domains of nature and culture are kept separated by the practice of ordering that Latour calls *purification*, but, at the same time, one needs only to accidentally open a newspaper (as Latour demonstrates in his narration) to encounter the "proliferation of hybrids":

> On page four of my daily newspaper, I learn that the measurements taken above the Antarctic are not good this year: the hole in the ozone layer is growing ominously larger. Reading on, I turn from upper-atmosphere chemists to Chief Executive Officers of Atochem and Monsanto, companies that are modifying their assembly lines in order to replace the innocent chlorofluorocarbons, accused of crimes against the ecosphere. A few paragraphs later, I come across heads of state of major industrialized countries who are getting involved with chemistry, refrigerators, aerosols and inert gases. But at the end of the article, I discover that the meteorologists don't agree with the chemists; they're talking about cyclical fluctuations unrelated to human activity. So now the industrialists don't know what to do. The heads of state are also holding back. Should we wait? Is it already too late? Toward the bottom of the page, Third World countries and ecologists add their grain of salt and talk about international treaties, moratoriums, the rights of future generations, and the right to development.
>
> The same article mixes together chemical reactions and political reactions. A single thread links the most esoteric sciences and the most sordid politics, the most distant sky and some factory in the Lyon suburbs, dangers on a global scale and the impending local elections or the next board meeting. The horizons, the stakes, the time frames, the actors—none of these is commensurable, yet there they are, caught up in the same story. (Latour 1993, 1)

As Latour points out, our ordinary experience is that hybrids proliferate and things are richly mixed together as in any other collective, or, as Latour puts it, in any other nature-culture. But at the same time, this collective's self-representations, its mythology produced by experts (including philosophers, sociologists, students of religions, etc.) do not acknowledge these hybrids. Instead, they appear to actively conceal them. The narrative about moderns and their others emphasizes a significant difference: while others strangely mix (or fail to distinguish between) culture with nature, moderns have a Culture and a Nature that are considered entirely separate. Following Baudrillard's metaphor, one could say that the moderns have this privileged access to the strip show of Reality, which lays itself bare to them through their exceptional way of seeing and doing things. This artful combination of purification and translation makes moderns invincible to outside critique. Consider Latour's imagined exchange between the moderns and anyone considered an outsider, through which he demonstrates the pervasive double standards of "the modern critique":

> Native Americans were not mistaken when they accused the Whites of having forked tongues. By separating the relations of political power from the relations of scientific reasoning while continuing to shore up power with reason and reason with power, the moderns have always had two irons in the fire. They have become invincible.

> You think that thunder is a divinity? The modern critique will show that it is generated by mere physical mechanisms that have no influence over the progress of human affairs. You are stuck in a traditional economy? The modern critique will show you that physical mechanisms can upset the progress of human affairs by mobilizing huge productive forces. You think that the spirits of the ancestors hold you forever hostage to their laws? The modern critique will show you that you are hostage to yourselves and that the spiritual world is your own human—too human—construction. You then think that you can do everything and develop your societies as you see fit? The modern critique will show you that the iron laws of society and economics are much more inflexible than those of your ancestors. You are indignant that the world is being mechanized? The modern critique will tell you about the creator God to whom everything belongs and who gave man everything. You are indignant that society is secular? The modern critique will show you that spirituality is thereby liberated, and that a wholly spiritual religion is far superior. You call yourself religious? The modern critique will have a hearty laugh at your expense!

> How could the other cultures-natures have resisted? They became premodern by contrast. They could have stood up against transcendent Nature, or immanent Nature, or society made by human hands, or transcendent Society, or a remote God, or an intimate God, but how could they resist the combination of all six? Or rather, they might have resisted, if the six resources of the modern critique had been visible together in a single operation such as I am retracing today. But they seemed to be separate, in conflict with one another, blending incompatible branches of government, each one appealing to different foundations. What is more, all these critical resources of purification were contradicted at once by the practice of mediation, yet that contradiction

had no influence whatsoever either on the diversity of the sources of power or on their hidden unity. (Latour 1993, 38)

This *modus operandi* marginalizes others and makes us unable to understand them. At the same time it makes us unable to understand ourselves.[5] Particular kinds of institutionalized power relations are thereby created and maintained, and "religion" serves this order of power. Fitzgerald summarizes its role in a concise formulation:

> I argue that "religion" is one of a pair, the other half being "non-religion" or "the secular." The formation of the modern notion of religion needs to be seen initially in relation to privatized Protestant piety and the separation of church and state, whereby an apparently demystified human nature and fully rational modern civil society was made possible. But the application of the religion-secular distinction to an increasing number of colonies has resulted in "religion" becoming a catch-all container for indigenous institutions and practices that impede progress (i.e., impede realization of secular rationality by the natives).
>
> (Fitzgerald 2003, 259)

The trouble "arises because the boundary between religion and non-religion constantly shifts depending on context" (Fitzgerald 2003, 210). Scholars studying religion effectively serve the purpose of maintaining the Great Divide.

The concept "religion" (together with its other, the "secular") should be abandoned, because it "systematically hides what it seeks to find."[6] But what to do then? Fitzgerald (2007) turns from the study of religion to the study of "religion." Such a move may be meaningful, yet it does not inspire everyone, including myself. I prefer to build on the initial intuition of the founding fathers of the discipline. I understand this intuition as a presumption about the cultural and social significance of the activities, notions, and symbols referred to as "religion." The problem was that "religion" was delimited and designated as a relatively separate domain of action, thinking, and symbolism. Instead of respecting this separation, I propose to redirect research towards the study of *ordinary ordering practices* (henceforth OOPs) without respecting any *a priori* distinctions. "Ordinary" here has nothing to do with "folk" or "popular." "Ordinary" implies something commonly practised or familiar to the competent member of the collectivity. Its familiarity indicates, furthermore, that it is somehow *ordered* or *orderly*. "Practices" do not imply "religious prac-

---

5. With reference to this, see the chapter "Small Mistakes concerning the Disenchantment of the World" (Latour 1993, 114–120) and Mary Douglas (1996, 18).
6. Allan Radley (1995, 21) used this expression with reference to "power" and "discourse" as a theoretical tool for researching the body in social constructivism.

tices," but just that making things familiar, orderly, or ordered demands an investment of effort.[7] So this would not mean that praying or wearing a charm is irrelevant. While praying is quite universally familiar, making *religion* is not so universal! As Fitzgerald (2007) shows, some people and collectivities, mostly in Europe and the US, differentiate and position themselves into asymmetric power relations against others by doing "religion," "secularity," and so forth.

Relatively universal OOPs like a prayer can become culturally important for very different reasons. For instance, it may become a dominant alternative therapy in the process of healing disease (Tovey *et al.* 2006, 234), where it may be found side by side with the practice of taking pills and other biomedical (as well as complementary and alternative) medical approaches. In such cases, an in-depth anthropological understanding of the practice of healing and managing the quality of life of a diseased person cannot arise if either of the pair, biomedicine or prayer, is neglected. The significance of OOPs lies then in their capacity to focus our attention on smaller things than religion and to follow how such smaller things intermingle with practices and objects that we would customarily ignore were we studying religion. What are we studying then? Well, that depends, but the point is to allow ourselves to find something else than the "religion" we are presuming to find.

In the following text, the smaller thing I want to begin with is an *instructed action*. I will present three vignettes, all concerning various aspects of what is involved in following instructions. The stories are reconstructed from my field notes, recorded during a study of dancers in an improvisational dance project. During the whole project I was allowed to attend and participate in all the training sessions, all the choreographers' strategic meetings, all meetings in a café or pub after the training sessions, all the weekend workshops, and all the performances. I became a part of the project and even played an active role during the second public performance. The vignettes are thus based on participatory observation and on members' reflections of what was going on at various occasions and during various time periods. The stories elucidate the role of chance, complexity and lack of control, and they serve to illustrate the quite ordinary practices of their management.

Story 1: The Story of the Intervening Mirror and the Creation of a Shared Skill

The first story begins with a simple instruction. It is the evening of the third training. The warming up slowly evolves into the first training

---

7. On making commonplace scenes familiar and on sociologically making sense of practices, which make this familiarity possible, see Garfinkel (1967, 35–75).

activity: simple walking with an appeal to react to one another's movements. The instruction by a choreographer is described in my field notes thus:

"I´ll try what I am able to achieve."

"How far I am able to attune [with others]."[8]

After the relief of the head, rolling down and the stretch into the [position of] "the roof" [i.e., during the continuing guided warm-up]:

"I look who all is here."

"Let´s walk."

"So that you don´t just hang around, so that you know where you are going, which trajectory you choose."

"You can go faster, slower, play with tempo."

"Realize what, in this particular space, with these people, you can do."

"And try **not to use the mirror**."[9]

Monika is smiling—she seems to have been using it—[she says:] "Shot goose."[10]

(Tr-14022012)

The activity is slowly led to a conclusion, and some other tasks are added to the initial instruction to walk and pay attention to others. The instructions get more complicated. Markéta [one of the two choreographers] continues instructing:

"Take it just as information. You don´t need to SPECULATE about it."

Lenka: "And I cannot then also check the mirror. Yes?"

Markéta: "You don´t need to, try not using it, don´t look at it."

(Tr-14022012)

Markéta observes them carefully. After a while, the activity comes to an end. She explains that the aim was simply to work on developing sen-

---

8. Each line of direct speech in the field notes is separated by a time gap between the individual instructions. Due to making notes exclusively by hand (not audio recording), I was not able to record the length of these time gaps. Each line, therefore, represents a position of the instruction in the sequence but not the exact timing of the instruction in the sequence.
9. All the bold letters and italics are my emphases. In the field notebook I used only words written in capital letters to mark emphases by the participants. I also consistently used quotation marks to distinguish exact quotations and maximally precise paraphrases of members' speech from my own remarks and descriptions.
10. "Potrefená husa" ["shot goose"]: an expression that the one to whom a general comment was targeted proved himself guilty by reacting to that comment. The English equivalent would be "a guilty conscience needs no accuser."

sitivity to relations in the space. She emphasizes that she wanted ordinary walk, **not any special hopping**, and iterates that next time they **should check themselves in the mirror** *even less.* Because they will not have one on stage, they need to become sensitive to one another's movements without [watching them in] the mirror.

> Monika complains that it is not possible and shows how she was discreetly checking the mirror. The girls start discussing what to do with the mirror: cover it with paper or cloth? Maruška maintains that the problem is not the mirror, but the fact that Markéta was standing on the mirror side [of the room] while instructing. (Tr-14022012)

What Can We Learn?

What can we learn from this story? First of all, that things normally do not go as planned. Forbidding the use of the mirror was an *ad hoc*, situational instruction. It was not planned. We come to appreciate this fact in the second story. While it is quite common that dance studios have mirrors installed to allow dancers to be able to observe themselves, it is not difficult to grasp how mirrors may also interfere in the development of desired stage skills. Indeed, Monika's complaint suggests that the mirror may interfere quite strongly. The training aims to prepare dancers for actual performances, yet it is an activity of a special kind, in many ways different from the performance. The histories of the two places are divergent. The dancers are aware of the trouble and manipulate the training space when possible. They proposed some changes in this case as well. What is interesting is that in this case the proposals never led to any measures being taken to fulfil them. There is not a single note on covering the mirrors in my later records. What should we make of that? The mirror lost its agency. In the beginning the mirror was a veritable attention-seeker, risking to disrupt the training, but thanks to the intransigence of the choreographer, these "efforts" were deflected. The dancers learned to ignore the mirror and direct their attention elsewhere. As far as I can remember, Markéta or Šárka (the second choreographer) did not stop instructing with the mirror behind their back. Instead it appears that the agency shifted from the mirror to the shared skill of the dancers. People learn such things quite easily and adjust by shifting their attention. It is not very surprising. It is rather ordinary.

Story 2: The Story of Inevitable Distortions of Shared Experience and Difficulties in Gaining Shared Knowledge and Habitus

The second story also involves a situation where things did not go as planned. It is a story of more complex, yet still rather simple, instruction.

To begin with, the dancers are asked to use less than a quarter of the training hall in order to encourage them to interact. The choreographer instructs seven dancers occupying different parts of this restricted space in an activity she calls "the tree":

> Šárka: "**Make your legs deeply rooted**, stand as comfortably as you can, breathe deeply, feel the air coming through your nose. And imagine the tree—on the rock. Not very fertile soil, but enough; it stays solid and reliable. Notice its shape, the directions of its roots, its stem, the stem's structure, [imagine] how the sap flows [through it], how the tree moves. Try to be **as believable as you can** [in representing] **its movement by your movement**. […] Try to make your movement **the closest possible to your vision**. Represent its largest as well as its most tiny movements, which you can notice. […] And **make sure that your movement resembles as accurately as possible the movement in your imagination**. […]" During that, Šárka moves around (…) and speaks, and inspects what is going on. "**Notice if the tree moves still the same way.**" This she says after I have myself noticed that Lenka and Martina, once again, create much more expressive—outstretched, outwaved—movements than the others. "And as you are getting your movement to resemble the tree, start slowly leaving your vision so that you can divide from your tree. The tree will remain available to you; you can come back to it whenever you like. And at the moment you can do it, move out."
>
> (Tr-13032012)

Once the dancers "move out," the subsequent instructions direct them to go **their own way** to locate something they need. They are told it can be anything—maybe food, maybe something else, it does not matter. "Go, collect it, and get back to your tree." So for a while all the dancers move around, searching for something, and then return. To the surprise of the choreographer, none of the dancers engaged with one another when crossing paths. A passage from the subsequent discussion reads as follows:

> Šárka: "Good. Let´s take it one by one. First of all: **It does not have to be an aesthetic movement**, not at all."
> Lenka: "*Yes, as one feels it*, isn't it?"
> Šárka: "Yes."
>> "**The second thing: have your legs rooted even deeper.**"
>
> And Lenka stares into nowhere, as if she was thinking of something.
>
> (Tr-13032012)

It appears that Šárka felt disappointed especially by Lenka. Indeed, all the special *ad hoc* added instructions are addressed particularly to her:

"**To get deeply rooted**" was a response to Lenka moving around, as was her emphasis on not needing to care for **aesthetics**. Šárka seems to express doubts about whether Lenka was "really feeling the tree moving like that," hence her emphasis on needing to "try to **be as credible as you can** [in representing] its movement in your movement" and to "**make sure that your movement resembles as accurately as possible the movement in your imagination**." When none of this has an effect, she tries "**notice if the tree moves still the same way**."

What is important about this? Šárka is issuing general instructions seemingly addressed to all the dancers, but in actuality she is directing them primarily at particular dancers—ones who seem to fail (too much) to align themselves to her expectations. Due to the setting, she cannot navigate each dancer separately; she does not have any tool to do that. I suspect that she also wants to avoid creating more tension between her and Lenka, as there already is some. For example, my notes say:

> Markéta [the second choreographer] switches off the music, and Šárka takes on her part [of the training session]. And Lenka says immediately: "I am already afraid of what you'll say." (Tr-13032012)

So Šárka issues her instructions carefully and generally, in part to avoid singling out Lenka. This is inevitable in a given situation. However, it creates confusion, similar to the confusion that surprised Šárka when the dancers did not engage one another in the second part of the activity. Helena and Maruška discussed this confusion after training. While Helena at first seemed to have simply understood the instruction "**your own way**" as "my way in which nobody interferes," Maruška explained that she had expressly avoided contact with anybody for another reason. She had understood the issue of contact in technical terms related to a special dance form called contact improvisation or contemporary partnering, where having contact, put very simply, is thought of as "sharing weight." She said she had avoided contact because she did not feel like performing this kind of contact at the time. Helen agreed and added that "sharing weight" did not seem to fit the situation. Further discussion revealed that in this case, Šárka's notion of "contact" was not so technical. She meant whatever kind of contact or interaction the dancers were already experimenting with in previous sessions.

During the previous training session, Šárka had noticed that some dancers (having more experience with ballet and modern forms) were not familiar with principles of contemporary partnering. She had decided therefore to slightly change the training program and guide dancers through some activities designed to develop the relevant skills. As Maruška and Helena argued, this experience framed their understanding of Šárka's instruction concerning "contact." Coming back to Lenka, we find in the café discussion that her understanding of the tree activity derived from an activity conducted seven and a half months earlier, during a weekend workshop for interested dancers, long before the project officially began. A tree activity then had been guided not by any of the choreographers, but by Alena, a person who had introduced the idea of the project, invited the choreographers to carry it forward, and participated herself as a (visual) artist responsible for the stage design. But not only that, deeper analysis of the data shows that both Lenka and Alena diverged significantly from Šárka in their aesthetic theory of dance. While Šárka described the aesthetic quality of dance in terms of the ability to provide a visible expression of emotions and feelings in interaction, Lenka (and Alena) stated that the quality of dance depends on its ability to create a visually attractive composition in space. This turned out to be a serious problem, due to the fact that the discussion was not resolved by any kind of consensus. Instead, stuck in their exclusive positions, the women approved their mutual right to disagree on the point. Šárka clung to her expectations as a choreographer, while Lenka continued to perform her best as a dancer, not changing her habitus to harmonize with Šárka's creative thinking. As a result, their mutual frustration grew deeper until, in the last period of the project, Lenka withdrew as a dancer.

What Can We Learn?

While the first story taught us that an instruction may be internalized as a skill, the second story teaches us something about complex relations and agencies. The instruction is planned as well as improvised, and it is bound to numerous aspects of the ongoing situation as well as to incidents in the past. Situations are framed unexpectedly by the previous experiences of the people engaged in them. There is a carefully designed plan behind any instruction. The choreographers held a two-hour meeting before every training, where they discussed previous achievements in order to prepare for the following training session as well as possible. And yet, a lot of improvisation was demanded to enact this plan, because things usually went otherwise than expected. The plan and the situational interferences needed reconciliation, which had to be achieved then and there. Stability and full intersubjective consensus about the meaning of an instruction as a collectively shared experience is almost impossible to achieve. Or more precisely, it cannot be achieved as a permanently stable achievement. Agency is too dispersed and unpredictable. To be sure, shared experiences can be built; an awareness of the same aim is continually being achieved. All the dancers learned slowly "what it is all about," and thus their action gradually aligned to a collective purpose. Were this not the case, a dance improvisation like this could never have been successfully carried out as a performance. Yet, surprising actions never cease to arise. At best, the rate of unwelcome and welcome surprises is slow and in favour of welcome(d) innovations. In sum, people are remarkably good at—more or less successfully—*improvising*. It's their daily business. The conditions of acting, as well as the course of action, always contains a measure of unpredictability.

Story 3: The Story of Productive Uncertainty

Human action necessarily contains some confusion and uncertainty, a relative lack of control. Despite this, and sometimes even *due to* such confusion, action and performance do not come to a halt; they instead seem to morph and swerve. Some aspects of how people can go on performing in the face of uncertainty can be learned from the final story. Here we come closer to what scholars of religion understand as their field of interest. I am not going to frame this story in terms of "religion" or even "spirituality," however. My reasons for avoiding these terms will be presented throughout the story, which follows:

We are a few days before the premier. Šárka sits in the auditorium of the theatre, and the dancers are improvising on stage. Šárka stops the improvisation after 20 minutes, although it normally takes more than 40 minutes to finish the whole piece. Everyone, including the musicians and myself, gathers in a circle and discusses the situation. Šárka wants to hear what the dancers have to say and what they felt about what was happening on stage. They mostly seem surprised that Šárka stopped the performance so early. Of course, not everything went smoothly, they acknowledge. But most of them express that they felt something interesting was going on; they experienced it intensely. Šárka then formulates in terms of emptiness what she did not like about it: "I could not get any impression of who you are." Helena is quite surprised: "Now I already understand nothing. When we think it's quite fine and something is really happening, you say that it looks empty and useless, when we feel it's quite useless and empty, you say that it was perfect." Shortly afterwards, Helena posts a picture on the dance company's Facebook page and adds the following comment:[11] "Don't we want to change the text of the program? I think that this nicely expresses our semi-annual achievement :))." [And the photograph shared beneath the post contains the following text:]

> Theory is when you know everything but nothing works.
>
> Practice is when everything works but no one knows why.
>
> In our lab, theory and practice are combined: Nothing works and no one knows why.

---

11. The following quote from Facebook and the following paragraph preceding the next quote are borrowed from Fujda (2015, 60).

This Facebook status shows at least three things: first, that six months of hard systematic work does not necessarily deliver results by any kind of instrumentally rational means; second, that joking is an important means of handling the feeling that things are not under control; and third, that the dancers are not the first ones to deal with such problems and, accordingly, they can use publicly available (i.e., institutionalized) cultural resources for humour.

However, one more thing is implied in the situation and supported by further data: namely that joking is just one of the strategies for managing a situation, which is defined by unpredictability and a loss of control. While joking is a way of freeing some shared experience of tension, there are further ways in which people r tension, provide some measure of assurance, facilitate optimistic expectations, help to overcome stage fright, and enable themselves to move through events without having full control over them. They do this by acknowledging the existence of the insecurity and by anticipating possible complications.

Some of these practices are mentioned in another set of quotes from my field notes. These quotes concern the very last moments spent backstage before walking on stage:

> Before the performance started, standing in a circle in the changing room we held each other's hands. It was a ritual initiated by Šebestián [the musician and shaman]. Before, of course, he did not forget to smudge the stage with the smoke of the sage. [...] Anyway, now we were holding hands and Šárka said that she does not know what to do. Šebi replied: nothing. So we were just standing. (Per-14062012)

Before the second performance—carried out during a local dance festival after a few months and some revision of the piece—the backstage story was a bit different:

> and then [after a discussion following the final rehearsal] we ran to the changing room because it was almost 8pm. There Ester cheered us up strongly and spat on us for luck: "ptui ptui." Many of us were also hugging each other and wishing each other good luck. Monika proposed to form a circle as the last time, but the situation was already too hectic and disordered, so no circle was formed. (Per-19112012)

Lucky items were also distributed among the dancers on both occasions. It is important to note that the participants did not automatically have full faith in the efficacy of the reported items or in the actions that were aimed at securing good luck. They took part (as with the burning of the sage, the spitting for good luck and the forming of a circle) even without knowing how to engage correctly, nor did they necessarily ponder about any specific mechanisms that would explain their effects. Monika's unrealized proposal, nevertheless, reveals their significance.

There is hardly anything extraordinary in all this. That might be one of the reasons why scholars do not pay attention to such practices. But I think we ought to. They are so common that we are blind to their occurrence, despite the fact that if such activities were reported in a tribal or oriental context, we would be ready to analyse them as expressions of "religious" or "magical" behaviour. In the case of modern people, these pass unnoticed; we are modern people and we do not practice magic. The fact that some participants do not know exactly how to participate—and that the "real" efficacy of such activities is not necessarily presupposed, inquired about, nor analysed in terms of operating principles—might justify our silence.

But that, I argue, would be a mistake. As Mary Douglas pointed out long ago, the situation among the so-called "primitives" is the same. The only difference is our ingrained and stubborn presumptions concerning the beliefs of others: "Old anthropological sources are full of the notion that primitive people expect rites to produce an immediate intervention in their affairs, and they poke kindly fun at those who supplement their rituals of healing with European medicine, as if it testified to lack of faith" (Douglas 1966, 58). Douglas hits the nail on the head: combining rites with "rational" technical means of achieving goals is quite common and should not surprise us. As was already mentioned in the earlier stories, the dance project was full of rational planning, testing, and the hard work of developing skills and more or less reliable tools to help the performance be a success. As the beginning of the last story indicates, such efforts never result in full control. The situation is too complex and a measure of risk cannot be excluded, as is ordinarily the case for most of us in our daily lives.

Our ability to accurately predict and to control ordinary actions is always limited, but we are generally skilled in dealing with such challenges. When I was trying to gain access to the field during this dance project, my experience with two important leading participants was quite different. While the visual artist, Alena, had agreed to my participation immediately, Šárka (the choreographer) engaged me in a long and thorough interview. Her final decision to allow me to participate was based on the following reasoning: "OK, in fact in this case, I am more interested in *the process* itself than in the *result*" (Ent-Šár-07022012).

Alena, who had extensive experience with numerous exhibitions and performative interactions in the past, decided that trying to have things fully under her control would only drain her energy without bringing appropriate results. She had started to think about this project during a long illness which almost killed her. Not wishing to be stressed out and overwhelmed with responsibilities, she invited two choreographers to help her with the project. She gave them full creative freedom to bring their own ideas and work in the way they found most appropriate. In her opinion, things go best if they are allowed to progress on their own terms. She felt that stress and rigid effort is counterproductive. "God manages it," she told me over the phone during our first conversation (No-Ph-AL-10022012). From her point of view, I could easily become a part of the project because "the project itself is finding people it needs for its fulfilment" (Int-AL-23022012). Alena's and Šárka's strategies were apparently different. One might say that Šárka was much more rational and control-oriented in her strategy. Yet in both cases, the decisive moment of opening a space for one more unpredictable element in the project resulted from a relaxation concerning the outcome—namely, the idea that, after all, the result is not fully in our hands and that this is not a bad thing.

Of course, numerous details had to be organized and planned in a very timely and rational manner: the organization of training sessions, managing background issues at the theatre, fund-raising, and so forth. I have already mentioned the planning efforts of the choreographers, but the same applied to the dancers. The entire time they were elaborating on ways to improve their communication during improvisation, their sensitivity to what was happening among themselves, and strategies to maintain an overview of the situation (so that if the performance were to go astray, at least somebody would have an idea of how the situation appeared from the perspective of the audience and be able to appropriately intervene). The same idea concerned the musicians, who were also improvising. For example, the dancers used numerous strategies to make sounds themselves, in order to help the musicians become attuned to the performers. So while a lot of rational planning, preparation, and calculation took place, unexpected events demanding improvisation occurred time and again.

What Can We Learn?

Here I would like to offer some preliminary notes on the management of ambivalence, uncertainty and unpredictability. All three of the previous stories show that lack of control and the occurrence of surprising events and actions are very common. We are so habituated to managing such actions and events that we do not pay attention to them unless they are quite striking. We have also seen that we are generally skilled at managing this lack of control and we do it routinely most of the time. We habitually achieve control by improvising. Such achievements, however, have some degree of order, to which scholars of religion may be sensitive. This fact challenges all of our presumptions concerning divisions between rational and irrational, secure and insecure, intuition and calculation, technical and aesthetic, disorganized and structured, stable and unstable, order and disorder (see Montuori 2003, 239; Strauss 1993, 261), and religious and non-religious.

An interest in religion usually demands that the pairs mentioned above are separated. Religion is often associated with the "less modern" part of the pair. Yet, as my final story suggests, the ability to improvise and handle limited control is based on the capacity of participants to neglect such pairs, to ignore the divisions, and to pragmatically use all available means at their disposal: planning and analysis, as well as intuition, magic, and so forth. Regarding such skills as the ability to maintain awareness of an external perspective while still remaining engaged and present, we can hardly determine whether the skill is secure or insecure, rational or intuitive, or technical or aesthetic. To hold on to such distinctions does not make sense in such cases. Indeed, the efficacy of such skills most likely lies exactly in their not being reduced to such distinctions. Improvisation is beyond such polarities, and improvisation, I would argue, is our "daily bread."

I suggest that these points apply to all ordinary practices, including practices in the economy, politics, law, and science. That is the reason why 1) the day-to-day work in the economy, politics, law, and even science is never fully faithful to its ideological presumptions, and 2) the study of religion(s) cannot understand its subject matter until it stops being politically engaged in favour of maintaining Latour's Great Divide by serving the work of *purification*. Whatever needs to work efficiently in ordinary conditions (of ambivalence and uncertainty) cannot be really rational, or ordered *purely*. As Ernest Gellner reminds us: "No Delphic oracles for small issues, where reason prevails, but for really big questions, oracle-surrogates remain in use [in modern society]" (Gellner 1989, 210). In other words, everything really important cannot be rational, but only pragmatic, thus mixing means that transgress the modern sets of oppositions mentioned above. For the study of religion(s), this does not imply that everything is religious, nor that everything is non-religious. It implies exactly that everything is beyond the religious/non-religious (secular) distinction.

Carrying on everyday activities involves some experimenting and testing, devising reliable strategies of dealing with problems and employing those to repair things if they go wrong. However, only a few of these tested practices are truly *secure*. They can help to bring some measure of control, yet there are no guarantees. And they are treated as such—to some extent being inherently risky or unreliable. They can help, they can fail, and if they fail some other strategy can be used the next time around. In this way, ordinary life challenges remain open-ended and unsolvable by absolutely secure, calculable means. So the *insecure practices of pragmatic handling of unpredictabilities and ambivalence* (Fujda 2015, 58) are crucial for our management of daily life problems. At least when witnessing them among "others," we tend to call some of these practices "religious," "magical," "superstitious," "mystical" or "intuitive." These practices work on various levels, ranging from stress relief—creating optimistic expectations or coping by providing devices that help in spite of not necessarily being very reliable—to well-tested, more reliable (although never 100% sure) means to particular ends. People use more or less open-ended strategies, evaluate their momentary results and go on dealing with the situation. They generally do this very pragmatically; there is nothing particularly irrational or naïve about it. These practices do not necessarily demand being "believed in" fully. Indeed, an awareness that their employment is not foolproof allows a person to be able to take possible failures into strategic consideration, thereby becoming more realistic in their expectations concerning subsequent courses of action.

"Nothing Works but No One Knows Why" and the Study of Religion(s)

The notion that "nothing works and no one knows why" represents a specific way of ordering. It works because it does not hide or deny a measure of working disorder. It is a good and pragmatic way to handle insecurity, unpredictability and ambivalence. Modernity, the study of religion(s) included, is characterized by a preference for a purified, clear order—for "either-or." A horrifying example of such modern ways of ordering was analysed by Zygmunt Bauman (1989) in his *Modernity and the Holocaust*. Ulrich Beck (1986), on the other hand, has shown how such ordering attempts produce unprecedented measures of risks as their side effects. One could argue that these side effects are a result of the insistence on clear divisions and a denial of the existence of hybrids.

The conceptual and practical strategies of Helena and other aforementioned middle-class, university-educated dancers, living in a modern European city, handling unpredictability by way of open-ended ordering, refute the notion that order is only possible by eradicating disorder—and these strategies are not specifically European nor modern. David Kinsley (1987) provides some guidelines on the same issue in a completely different setting: the worship of protective village goddesses like Śītalā in India. These goddesses puzzle scholars of religion(s): they are worshipped as village protectors while being at the same time associated with diseases and even held accountable for spreading epidemics. They protect as well as endanger people; they kill them and endow them with new life. "The ultimate mystery and potency of these village/disease goddesses may well lie precisely in the fact that their ambivalent natures are not capable of being comprehended rationally," says Kinsley (1987, 208).

Trying to make sense of this common kind of worship, Kinsley discusses some attempts at explanation through speculations which locate these goddesses in terms of *purified* orders compatible with modern beliefs in rational control. One of these was Victor Turner's attempt. According to Turner, rituals, especially periodic festivals, are means through which society periodically participates in chaos in order to preserve the well-being of the society and culture (Kinsley 1987, 209). Such explanations, I would argue, fail to do justice to the fact that people are able to live with an awareness of the ambivalent features of reality. Kinsley's conclusion seems to me less speculative and much better empirically justified: "To worship Śītalā, to pay attention to what she represents, is to provide oneself with a more realistic, less fragile view of life, which in turn makes the inevitable outburst of disease or tragic occurrences less devastating." (Kinsley 1987, 211).

This view may be more compatible with anthropological accounts that exhibit more sensitivity towards complex ways of ordering:

> The strange opacity of certain empirical events, the dumb senselessness of intense or inexorable pain, and the enigmatic unaccountability of gross iniquity all raise the uncomfortable suspicion that perhaps the world, and hence man's life in the world, has no genuine order at all—no empirical regularity, no emotional form, no moral coherence. And the religious response to this suspicion is in each case the same: the formulation, by means of symbols, of an image of such a genuine order of the world which will account for, and even celebrate, the perceived ambiguities, puzzles, and paradoxes in human experience. The effort is not to deny the undeniable—that there are unexplained events, that life hurts, or that rain falls upon the just[12]—but to deny that there are inexplicable events, that life is unendurable, and that justice is a mirage.
>
> (Geertz 1973, 107–108)

Geertz's quote has its place in the context of his presentation of the problems of evil and justice. But, as I have tried to show, unpredictability, surprises, unexplained events, paradoxes and puzzles abound in almost all walks of life. Drawing a comparison with Reichard's account of Nav-

---

12. This line refers to a quatrain mentioned earlier in the text that sums up the problem: "The rain falls on the just/And on the unjust fella;/But mainly upon the just./Because the unjust has the just's umbrella" (Geertz 1973, 106).

aho religion, Geertz himself indicates that: "The Dinka are in a universe which is largely beyond their control, and where events may contradict the most reasonable human expectations" (Geertz 1973, 107).

The only thing that does not make sense in the previous account is speaking of "religion." It is not religion that makes reasonable human expectations fail, nor does religion serve to deny that there are inexplicable events. It is an unlimited scientific optimism, an opium of the moderns, which makes moderns believe that they can render the world controllable. This belief makes us less able to reflect on the measure of uncertainty in our world and our own ability to practically handle it by means of a pragmatic strategy, such as ordering practices that *allow for* disorder. Uncertainties, ambivalences and sudden disruptions are not confined to a particular sphere of life. Situations like disease, for example, are as much the domain of prayer as they are of evidence-based medicine. As a late-stage cancer patient explained his decision to try alternative therapy along with care in a system of evidence-based medicine: "I am looking for a cure. I just want to hear how well it works and the success rate. This would fit with what the evidence is. Evidence to me is the proof. There is a truth to the information. (...) If the person down the street drank this tea and is cured, then that is all I need" (Verhoef *et al.* 2007, 351). Disease is the domain of whatever practice can help. Help can also mean empowering patients by giving them more control over the disease, its treatment and their own life.[13]

This is why we need to seriously question our tendency to define religion in order to demarcate *a priori* our field of study, to employ it as an analytical category and as a dependent or independent variable. Complex (i.e., unpredictable or ambivalent) issues, which are our daily lot, always transcend the purified boundaries, and they can be successfully and pragmatically handled only by practices which do the same. Managing illness is a rather illuminating example; it reveals a junction where contemporary Western medical science intermingles with various forms of "traditional" sciences like Indian Ayurveda or Chinese medicine, traditional knowledges of healing herbs, and even numerous practices otherwise simply deprecated or disparaged as "magic" or "superstition," which work together in healing or at least providing some sense of well-being to the suffering person.

Marginality, Exoticism, and the Principle of Symmetry

Demarcating religion thus distorts understandings of how and why people behave in particular ways. But it also has another detrimental

---

13. Loss of control due to disease has been studied by Bury (1982), who introduced the concept of biographical disruption.

effect: believing that modernity is secular has transferred interest in religion either towards outdated or exotic cultures or towards marginal phenomena in modern societies. Classics by such scholars as Durkheim and Weber acknowledged the social or cultural significance of religion. For Durkheim it was the very source of solidarity in society, while for Weber it was a crucial variable in the formation of economic systems, modern and traditional alike. Both of them, however, proposed ideas inspiring theories that describe or explain, from various perspectives, the end of the social significance of religion in modernity. The study of religion in traditional contexts could touch the core of a society/culture (or nature-culture, in the Latourian sense), but in the modern context it has remained confined to marginal phenomena of culture only, never to be applied to the whole of modernity, modernity as a nature-culture.

Following the criticism of David Bloor, Latour reflects on this issue with reference to the sociology of knowledge (Latour 2005, 95). In this context, the issue turns into a question: why have sociologists been so reluctant to take on the task of explaining *true* scientific knowledge, limiting themselves to only explain scientific errors? Latour's answer reflects on the already mentioned distinction between nature and culture: while scientific error is a result of operating (too human) Culture, truths are justified by Nature itself (Latour 1993, 102). Bloor had traced the asymmetry in explaining true and false scientific knowledge in different terms back to a theological debate with Christian Baur on the study of orthodoxy and heresy. While the mainstream maintained that only a heresy needs an explanation regarding its deviation (based on greed, superstition, etc.) from the orthodox, because the orthodox needs no questioning due to its inherent truth, Baur maintained that orthodox and heretical ideas both needed to be explained on the same terms (Bloor 1991, 184–185). Bloor thus pointed out an interesting taboo in modern society and formulated a way to overcome it by means of a methodological principle: symmetry. This is a principle according to which methodological alignment with "invincible Moderns" (to use Latour's expression) is overcome by studying all societies in the same way as nature-cultures. For Latour, it is also a way to enable symmetrical anthropology to stop being "the marginal discipline of the margins, picking up the crumbs that fall from the other disciplines' banquet table" (Latour 1993, 101). The study of religion(s) has the same task to overcome its marginality. This task cannot be fulfilled by saying that modern society, once again, is religious. I have tried to show why this does not make sense. But I claim that studying the myriad ways in which human beings cope with uncertainties, fragility and complexity in their ordinary endeavours is one possible way to secure our discipline as one that deals with core issues—important and relevant matters of concern—rather than exotic but marginal issues characterized by their otherness to modernity.

Acknowledgements:

I would like to thank Peik Ingman and Måns Broo for their valuable feedback on a working version of this text. Their criticism of my argument, as well as Peik's suggestions concerning my English, helped to improve the chapter significantly. The research resulting in this text was supported by the project "ITMEPRE—Innovative Theoretical and Methodological Perspectives in the Study of Religions" (project No. MUNI/A/1148/2014), hosted at the Department for the Study of Religions, Faculty of Arts at Masaryk University.

References

Asad, T. 2003. *Formations of the Secular. Christianity, Islam, Modernity*. Stanford, CA: Stanford University Press.

———. 1993. *Genealogies of religion. Discipline and Reasons of Power in Christianity and Islam*. Baltimore, MD: Johns Hopkins University Press.

Balagangadhara, S. N. 2005. *The Heathen in His Blindness: Asia, the West and the Dynamics of Religion*. New Delhi: Manohar.

Baudrillard, J. 2001 [1995]. *Dokonalý zločin*. Translated by A. Dvořáčková, Olomouc: Periplum.

Bauman, Z. 2010 [1989]. *Modernita a holocaust*. Translated by J. Ogrocká. 2nd ed. Praha: SLON.

Beck, U. 1986. *Risikogesellschaft. Auf dem Weg in eine andere Moderne*. Frankfurt am Main: Suhrkamp.

Bloor, D. 1991. *Knowledge and Social Imagery*. 2nd ed. Chicago, IL: The University of Chicago Press.

Bury, M. 1982. "Chronic Illness as Biographical Disruption." *Sociology of Health and Illness* 4(2): 167–182.

Douglas, M. 2010 [1970]. *Natural Symbols: Explorations in Cosmology*. London: Routledge.

———. 1992 [1996]. *Purity and Danger: An Analysis of the Concepts of Pollution and Taboo*. London: Routledge.

Fitzgerald, T. 2007. *Discourse on Civility and Barbarity: A Critical History of Religion and Related Categories*. Oxford: Oxford University Press.

———. 2003. "Playing Language Games and Performing Rituals: Religious Studies as Ideological State Apparatus." *Method & Theory in the Study of Religion* 15(3): 209–254.

———. 1997. "A Critique of 'Religion' as a Cross-cultural Category." *Method & Theory in the Study of Religion* 9(2): 91–110.

Fujda, M. 2015. "What Would an Informant Tell Me after Reading My Paper? On the Theoretical Significance of Ethical Commitment and Political Transparency in the Symmetrical Practice of Studying Religion(s)." *Religio* 23(1): 57–86.

Garfinkel, H. 2002. *Ethnomethodology's Program: Working out Durkheim's Aphorism*, edited by A.W. Rawls. Lanham, MD: Rowman & Littlefield.

———. 1967. *Studies in Ethnomethodology*. New Jersey: Prentice-Hall Inc.

Geertz, C. 1973. *The Interpretation of Cultures: Selected Essays*. New York: Basic Books.

Gellner, E. 1989. *Plough, Sword and Book*. 2nd ed. Chicago, IL: The University of Chicago Press.

King, R. 1999. *Orientalism and Religion: Postcolonial Theory, India and 'the Mystic East'*. London: Routledge.

Kinsley, D. 1987. *Hindu Goddesses: Visions of the Divine Feminine in the Hindu Religious Tradition*. Delhi: Motilal Banarsidass.

Latour, B. 2005. *Reassembling the Social: An Introduction to Actor-Network-Theory*. New York: Oxford University Press.

———. 1996. "On Interobjectivity." *Mind, Culture, and Activity* 3(4): 228–245.

———. 1993. *We Have Never Been Modern*. Translated by C. Porter. Cambridge, MA: Harvard University Press.

Law, J. 1994. *Organizing Modernity. Social Ordering and Social Theory*. Oxford: Blackwell.

Montuori, Alfonso. 2003. "The complexity of improvisation and the improvisation of complexity: Social science, art and creativity." *Human Relations* 56(2): 237–255.

Radley, A. 1995. "The Elusory Body and Social Constructionist Theory." *Body & Society* 1(2): 3–23.

Strauss, Anselm L. 1993. *Continual Permutations of Action*. New York: Aldine de Gruyter.

Tovey, Philip *et al.* 2006. "Use of Traditional Medicine and Globalized Complementary and Alternative Medicine among Low-Income Cancer Service Users in Brazil." *Integrative Cancer Therapies* 5(3): 232–235.

Verhoef, M.J. *et al.* 2007. "Assessing the Role of Evidence in Patients' Evaluation of Complementary Therapies: A Quality Study." *Integrative Cancer Therapies* 6(4): 345–353.

Other sources

Milan Fudja:

Author's field notes.

Tr-14022012: note from a training [numbers indicate a date, i.e., 14th February 2012].

Tr-13032012: note from a training.

Per-14062012: Note from a performance.

Per-19112012: Note from a performance.

No-Ph-AL-10022012: Note to a phone call with Alena.

Int-AL-23022012: Interview with Alena.

About the Author

Formerly interested in an acculturation of Indian spiritual practices in Europe **Milan Fujda** has turned to studies of ordinary (organizing) practices under the influence of ethnomethodology and ANT. At present he studies how unpredictable and complex situations are handled. His ethnography of contemporary dance improvisation is the first project after his methodological and thematic shift. It opened to him the way to locate questions concerning social meaning and the significance of allegedly irrational aspects of human life in a theoretical framework defined by practical pragmatism rather than by concepts of modernization, secularization, and religion. He is the author of the following books: *Akulturace hinduismu a formování moderní religiozity: K sociálním dějinám českého okultismu 1891-1941* (*The Acculturation of Hinduism and Forming of Modern Religiosity: The Social History of Czech Occultism 1891-1941*) and *Oddaní Kršny. Hnutí Haré Kršna v pohledu sociálních věd* (*The Krishna Bhaktas: The Hare Krishna Movement in the Perspective of Social Sciences*, together with Dušan Lužný).

— 12 —

Co-composing a Village History in the Archipelago of Southwestern Finland

JAANA KOURI

Nostalgic narration as such is not religious, but it can be recognized as having an ontological function. I have conducted an oral history project in Lypyrtti, an old pilot village on the southwestern coast of Finland, where the inhabitants' fear of losing knowledge of their local history arises simultaneously with the fear of losing access to clean water. Time has passed and the future seems to promise the rather unwelcome change of eutrophication. Most likely due to this sense of impermanence, the past spatial practices or old ways of living in the reminisced village are almost sacrosanct. The nostalgic, enchanted village lives in the memories of the present inhabitants, and the present, ominously changing environment reminds them of it, prompting them to remember.

 This oral history project had two literal results: a history book on the village and my ongoing research project in comparative religion. It was a reciprocal signification process in many ways. The production of narrated data was an act of interaction and dialogue between the locals, the environment and myself. As I understand it, cultural knowledge, rather than being imported into the settings of practical activity, is constituted within these settings. Every step of the conceptualization—from the observation to the verbalization—is social. I combine the ideas, concepts and methodology of oral history and place research. I bring into the discussion the double agency of re-

---

Keywords: Actor-network-theory, environment, nostalgia, oral history, place research, textualization, autoethnography

searcher as experiencer (in the field) and as conceptualizer (in the textualization process). I draw inspiration mainly from the thoughts of the anthropologist Tim Ingold and sociologist Bruno Latour, in order to elaborate how various kinds of actants and actors mediated information in the process and influenced each other, thereby extending conceptualizations of agency from human to non-human actors.

Ethnographic Notes on a Meaning-making Process and Agency

I made most of the journeys to interview the villagers by rowing a little boat. One evening when I was returning home, I stopped to watch the waterways extending in five different directions. My geographical position was in the centre of the village. There was no church—as is customary in Finnish villages—only water.

The above description of a landscape experience is from my field diary of conducting oral history research in Lypyrtti, an old pilot village on the southwestern coast of Finland. It adheres to three themes concerning empiricism that I wish to discuss in this chapter, which is based on my ethnographic fieldwork. The first concerns the village itself as a *place* or as many places. The second concerns the researcher's *agency* among other agencies. The third is methodological and concerns the importance of local *practices of placemaking*, particularly in the environment of water, as an essential part of the study. These themes were also some of the main constituents of the textualization process, which had two literal results: a history book on the village and my ongoing research project in comparative religion. For this chapter, I draw inspiration mainly from the thoughts of the anthropologist Tim Ingold and sociologist Bruno Latour, in order to elaborate the co-composition of different agencies and my involvement as a researcher in this process.

The locals in Lypyrtti expressed their interest in collecting oral history on their village in 2006. As one of the local summer residents, I decided that I wanted to do this. I was also a postgraduate student planning to do dissertation work, so I decided to combine these two endeavours.[1] It was a reciprocal signification process in many ways. First, I was interested in meanings in terms of what Latour (2005, 114) calls "matters of concern." Latour writes: "The discussion begins to shift for good when one introduces not matters of fact, but what I now call *matters of concern*. While highly uncertain and loudly disputed, these real, objective, atypical and, above all, interesting agencies are taken not exactly as object but rather

---

1. I published a book of collected stories, *Lypyrtti-Lypertö—Kylä väylien varrella*, concerning the history of the village in 2011.

as *gatherings*." Secondly, my research was an experiment and "an exploration of a thing and its relationships, rather than an explanation of or for the thing," as Mika Lassander (2012, 246) has translated Bruno Latour's term 'network'. According to geographer Doreen Massey (2005, 28), village is "not a representation, but experimentation." As such, the production of narrated data was an act of interaction and dialogue between the locals, the environment and myself. I travelled on a horizontal plane, on a landscape, and in temporal spaces of narration. In this way of telling things, village is, to quote Massey (2005, 130) again, "the dimension of a multiple trajectories, a simultaneity of stories so far." Obviously, this article is not the whole story from the beginning to the end of that process, but it discusses some examples of my itinerary to the village, and it is an element of a more detailed description of marking interest in and co-composing the meaning of the village.

In his book *Reassembling the Social: An Introduction to Actor-Network-Theory*, Latour proposes the following definition or way of understanding "the social": "it doesn't designate a domain of reality or some particular item, but rather is the name of a movement, a displacement, a transformation, a translation, an enrollment" (Latour 2005, 64–65). For Actor Network Theory, the social "is an association between entities which are in no way recognizable as being social in the ordinary manner, except during a brief moment when they are reshuffled together" (Latour 2005, 65). Latour (2005, 114) emphasizes that this shift in focus should allow us to renew from top to bottom the very scene of empiricism—and hence the division between "natural" and "social." The sociologist John Law proposes the idea of method assemblage to broaden the notion of "method" to include not only what is present in the form of texts and their production, but also their hinterlands and hidden supports. It is "a continuing process of crafting and enacting necessary boundaries between presence, manifest absence and Otherness" (Law 2006, 144). In other words, what is central to such a view is an understanding of sociality and culture as a form of making, doing, and acting, as well as an understanding of sociality through pragmatic, sensuous intentionality and interaction between human actors and non-human actors (Vannini 2009a, 4).

A Dwelling Place

To begin with, I pull back to illuminate a panorama of Lypyrtti and describe how the "locals are *localized*" (Latour 2005, 187, 195, his emphasis; see also Oppenheim 2007, 478). Lypyrtti is an independent and distant part of another municipality, Kustavi, where the church is located. Lypyrtti is nowadays a village of about 50 houses on the coasts of three bigger and a couple smaller islands. The houses are located in an area of approximately two square kilometres, although the water areas of the village extend even further. In the archipelago, the borders of a village are actually drawn on the water. Since the time of the general parcelling out of the land in the 18th century, the area of the village has been about the same as the largest farm in the village. Lypyrtti has been first and foremost an uninhabited fishing and hunting area. After about 500 years of active piloting, small-scale farming and husbandry, hunting and fishing, it became "an island dwelling place," as one of the interviewees expressed it. In his book *The Perception of the Environment: Essays on Livelihood, Dwelling and Skill* (2000), Ingold discusses the relation between the concepts of building and dwelling. He refers to Heidegger's view of building as a container of certain life activities. If people are capable of dwelling, the people build (Ingold 2000, 186). In the part of the archipelago where Lypyrtti is located, this basically required—at the time when the first inhabitants decided to stay—two or three things at the same time and a good combination of them: enough land to collect hay for animals, good possibilities to fish, and access to extra income from piloting. Here we can see a kind of macro co-composition, a balance of survival maintained through several different sources of livelihood. With the passing of time, the more important piloting would become. Nevertheless, in 1961 the Finnish Maritime Administration decided to terminate piloting along the Strömi, which had traditionally been an important passage, and it closed the Lypyrtti pilot station, requiring deeper waterways for ships to safely carry more cargo. After this change, the history of the village has been—if I may simplify—a story of the depopulation of a vital community.

Both the idea of who belongs to the village and the areal idea of the village have changed over time, depending on what has been the centre of the villagers' activity (Kouri 2011). These perplexities reminded me of what Latour calls "the first source of uncertainty," from which one should learn that there is no relevant group that can be said to make up social aggregates, no established component that can be used as an incontrovertible starting point (Latour 2005a, 29). In any case, Latour's idea of a "center of calculation" affords the possibility of examining the village as not one place but many places. It is any concrete site where calculations—such as decisions for action, value judgments, and interpretations—are made about issues presently at hand (Latour 1999, 304; see also Lassander 2012, 248–249). In Lypyrtti, the centre of calculation has changed over time from the biggest farm and large sailboats to the pilot station and nowadays to the common wharf, where villagers keep their boats to get to other islands.

After 2008, when the mobile grocery shop stopped coming to the wharf (Kouri 2011, 208), there has not been a clear locus for a definitive centre of calculation, only those in memories or in the past. Furthermore, the identity of a summer resident today is more or less like a visitor in his/her ancestral home, as opposed to a local inhabitant.[2] Most of the 50 old houses are summer residences of relatives of the families that once lived in the village all year round. There are also some villagers whose parents were summer residents already in the 1960s, so these people spent parts of their childhood in the vibrant pilot village (Kouri 2011). There was neither one clearly defined village with boarders and inhabitants nor concrete centres of calculation. This was not the only ambiguous situation. Older associations mutating into slightly different ones became the rule—not the exception (see Latour 2005, 36). However, there were places to calculate in the narrative past. This nostalgically remembered village figured in my experience and observations as a "landscape of the soul" (*sielunmaisema* in Finnish), a place that was already infused with significance, not least because time has passed and the future seems to promise the rather unwelcome change of eutrophication. Most likely due to this sense of impermanence, the past spatial practices or old ways of living in the reminisced village are almost sacrosanct.

The Sacralization of a Landscape

Before discussing examples from my fieldwork, I shall focus briefly on two concepts of environment: "landscape" and "sacred." The relationship between religion, tradition and environment has enjoyed increasing recognition in the analysis of ethnographic data since the 1980s. Also, recent literature in religious studies includes a great deal of consideration about spatial categories such as landscape, location, place and space (see e.g., Anttonen 2003, 2013, 2014; Knott 2005; Tweed 2006). Adding "sacred" to this perspective renders the discussion even more complex. The process of sacralization of a landscape involves the landscape becoming, or being viewed, as sacred (e.g., Nordeide 2013, xix). In anthropology, the conventional dichotomy between naturally given and culturally constructed worlds is commonly expressed by means of the contrast between the "etic" level of objective description and the "emic" level, on which an environment is made meaningful by cultural subjects. Already in the 1980s, the Finnish folklore and comparative religion scholar Lauri Honko introduced what he called "the ecology of tradition," which distinguishes between two interrelated methods, perception and action, by means of which people interact with their environment. Honko concluded that an individual's concept of her or his environment proceeds

---

2. I ended up concluding that an inhabitant of the village was anyone who considered themselves as belonging to Lypyrtti or who talked about themselves or was referred to by someone else as a villager (see Latour 2005, 29–30, 32).

from subjective perceptions to objective concepts, actions and their results. In classifying his or her perceptions, communicating them or acting in nature according to his observations, an individual objectivizes the concept of his or her environment, whereby it becomes intersubjective. In this way, a subjective observation of the environment becomes social. A subjective observation needs and uses products of language and tradition, names and concepts (Honko 1985, 67, 69).

Honko's concept of "total" milieu thus calls for an outside observer and information that is often not even available in the culture under study. Honko (1985, 67) also points out that the researcher may have to assist in the description of the "effective" environment or the "perceived" milieu, particularly as regards the verbalization and systemization of ideas and attitudes that do not occur in the culture or tradition in verbal form. This is why there may be benefits to being a researcher who is an "anthropologist at home," an insider of the group and a practitioner of its dwelling places. As I understand it, every step of the conceptualization—from the observation to the verbalization—is social. Perception or observation is not only a mental operation in the human mind. It is one part of a social co-composition, where we also take other agencies than human minds into consideration.

The term "landscape" has been defined in many ways (e.g., Wylie 2007, 2). Certainly it is not easy to draw a distinction between landscape and environment, but the main distinction seems to be between diverse researchers' characterizations of the agency that they accord humans and cognition (Ingold 2000, 193). Ingold begins by explaining what landscape is *not:* it is neither "land," "nature" nor "space." He basically rejects the divisions between inner and outer worlds—respectively, of mind and matter, meaning and substance. For him, the focus is the familiar domain of our dwelling and how, through living in it, the landscape becomes a part of us, just as we are a part of it. It is this relational and compositional context of people's engagement with the world from which each place draws its unique significance. Thus, whereas with space meanings are *attached* to the world, with the landscape they are *gathered from* it (Ingold 2000, 190–192, his emphasis.) Or, as I prefer to conceptualize, *co-composed in* it. Although I pay attention to the agency of the ethnographer and the significance of the researcher's engagement and involvement, I want to emphasize that endowing spaces with value is not something that I do *alone*. Rather, I co-compose the meaning of the landscape in the space of negotiation. I recycle the metaphor of *conversation*, which the anthropologist Anna Lund and geographer Karl Benediktsson introduced as enabling recognition of the more-than-human character of all meaningful exchanges involving humans and landscape. It points towards a two-way communicative process and enables us to understand human and non-human life in more dynamic ways. They understand landscape as involving "a more-than-human materiality; a constellation of natural forms that are independent of humans, yet part and parcel of the process by which human beings make their living and understand their own placing in the world" (Lund and Benediktsson 2010, 1).

The Researcher's Agency among Other Co-composers

Anthropological theories of the nature-culture relationship have throughout their history centred on the topics of perception and cognition. Ingold (2000, 153) writes that the main question seems to revolve around the distribution of agency: is landscape or environment the world we are living in, or a scene we are looking at and giving meanings to? Two main assumptions have persisted as endpoints of the continuum. One of these is the assumption that people construct the world, or what for them is "reality," by organizing the data of sensory perception in terms of received and culturally specific conceptual schemata. The other, more recent assumption is the "practice theory." Its advocates argue that cultural knowledge, rather than being imported into the settings of practical activity, is constituted within these settings through the development of specific dispositions and sensibilities that lead people to orient themselves in relation to their environment and to attend to its features in the particular ways that they do (Ingold 2000, 153; see also e.g., Honko 1985, 59–60; Wylie 2007, 1). My aim with this chapter is to present parts of my fieldwork, the settings of practical activity, as examples of and in light of the latter perspective. I draw inspiration from Ingold's thoughts, particularly from the following description: "In way-finding, people do not traverse the surface of a world whose layout is fixed in advance—as represented on the cartographic map. Rather, they 'feel their way' *through* a world that is itself in motion, continually coming into being through the combined action of human and non-human agencies" (Ingold 2000, 155, his emphasis).

If the emic level is understood as reality constituted in *relation* to the beings whose environment it is, it is apparent that the world becomes a meaningful place for people through being *lived in*, rather than by having been constructed along the lines of some formal design (Ingold 2000, 168, his emphasis). Because my own position as a researcher was that of an "anthropologist at home," an insider and outsider in the village at the same time, exploring my own agency in composing the study became particularly important to address. In the field, the entire situation turned into a dynamic interpersonal experience, the world between me and others (Okely 1992, 1–3, 14; Skultans 2006, 2–3). My research context was produced by reciprocally localizing myself in the environment. I was—in Latour's terms—a full-blown *mediator* (Latour 2005, 128), as were the interviewees. The "social actors" began to include environmental phenomena and other non-human actors. I was in the position of a bifurcation, an event, or the origin of a new translation (Latour 2005, 108). Those events were temporally liminal spaces, one after another in the process of becoming. The social anthropologist Vieda Skultans explains that translation involves the personal engagement of the researcher. Translation is involved when we move from one modality to another, be that from culture to culture, from person to person, from orality to textuality, from experience to narrative, and from local embodied knowledge to generalization (Skultans 2006, 10).

The construction of knowledge in this analysis is based on my experiences in the field. It was built up in my process of reflecting those experiences by writing about the choices I made and the thoughts and associations I had during the research work. I realized that meaning is immanent in the contexts of people's pragmatic engagements with its constituents (Ingold 2000, 154, 168).[3] Next, I describe how I experienced present realities in the environment—"out-there," to quote Law—and as an ethnographer created knowledge of those realities as "in-here" (Law 2006, 13). With those mutually penetrating autoethnographical and reflexive practices, I was exposed to "a hinterland" of pre-existing social and material realities (Law 2006, 13). The history of a village is a "collection of narratives" (Massey 2005, 9) picked up from the stream of an ever-changing environment: events, voices and still indescribable experiences, such as intuition or "senses of place" (Feldt and Basso 1996). This stream is what Latour (2005, 242; see also Oppenheim 2007, 480) calls "plasma," namely something that "is not yet formatted, not yet measured, not yet socialized." "It is in between and not made of social stuff. It is not hidden, simply unknown" (Latour 2005, 244). Law defines (2006, 34) this unknown "hinterland" as "an overall geography" and "a topography of reality-possibilities." With the last definition he refers to his disagreement with the claim of Latour and Steve Woolgars that in its practice science produces its realities as well as describes them (Law 2006, 13; see also Oppenheim 2007, 482).

My focus here is to describe *how* various kinds of actants and actors participate in a meaning-making process, not to solve ontological questions concerning their applicability to the co-composition. I prefer to keep the perspective open for all possible realms and actants and actors, humans and non-humans. As a researcher of religious studies, I also take into

---

3. In these words, Ingold summarizes the psychologist James Gibson's (1904–1979) central ideas of "ecological psychology" (Ingold 2000, 165–168).

account beings conventionally referred to, for example, as "spiritual" or "supernatural." Therefore, as the ethnographer Phillip Vannini stresses, rather than focus on agency alone or on wherein it lies, it is best to turn the ethnographic attention to the creative ways of relating among and between humans and non-humans. Understood in this way, agency is not something that a human being has, but rather the diffused potential for action present in a social and material setting. In this sense, to speak of diffused agency is also to invoke an ecology of interaction from the level of practice to the level of conceptualization (Vannini 2009b, 76–78).[4] The interviews were a particular situation where the level of practice—in the form of reminiscences of past ways of living—met the level of conceptualization. Let us now take a closer look at them.

In the Space of Paying Attention

The oral history researcher Alessandro Portelli has reflected that "every interview is an *experience* before it becomes *a text*" (Portelli 1997, xiii, his emphasis). He has also stressed that narration in interviews deals rather with the meaning of the reminisced situations than with the situations themselves (Portelli 1991, 50). The meaning of the reminisced experience is not usually performed verbally, but quite often emotionally. In the interviews, I found new topics by listening with sensitivity to the interviewees. In particular, emotional "hotspots" or peaks and those things that aroused great interest during the narration, and which I reciprocally experienced more strongly, opened up meaningful dimensions of the history of the village. I had some kind of intuition or pre-understanding, which at the time was still an indescribable experience, of the place. However, only my own history of residing in the village, living there in the summer, doing the same things as the other villagers and listening to its voices and silences, I believe, helped me to better understand what it is to be a local of Lypyrtti and what is meaningful to such a person in that specific place. The way in which you recollect and react to things from the past depends, of course, on the place and time you are reliving. Humanistic geographers have argued that place is best understood as a locus of meaning. According to Yi-Fu Tuan (1977, 6), space is more abstract than place: "What begins as undifferentiated space becomes place as we get to know it better and endow it with value." The meaning was co-composed by all of the actors between the present interviewing event and the remembered situation. The experience of conducting

---

4. Ever since Clifford Geertz (1973) introduced the idea of "thick description," it has been a self-evident method in ethnography. Likewise, Bruno Latour (2005, 136–137, 184) also stresses that "the task of sticking to description is the highest and rarest achievement" (see also Lassander 2012, 245, 247).

the interviews was more like participating than witnessing. Together we produced the meaning of the village (as a place) in the space of negotiation of the village history.

As Lassander (2012, 249) stresses, emotions play an important role in the calculation, as do rhetoric and other means of influencing emotions.[5] In the interviews, I interpreted emotions as micro-historical footprints and as signals or clues to meaningful things (see Ginzburg 1996, 37–76, especially 39, 44, 48; Fingerroos and Haanpää 2006, 30–32). In narrational spaces, spatial and temporal orientations intertwine (e.g., Tweed 2006, 97, 123). Nostalgia is an emotion of longing, where the narrator and the listener move backwards in time to bring something into the present, something that the narrator has experienced before. Nostalgia (from the past) is to share (in the present) the fear of losing something (in the future). The interviewees picked things up from the past. By re-awakening memories and particular reminiscences and allowing them to speak again, the narrators brought them back from oblivion.

The place in the past is like an anchor, even though the environment changes as time passes. Jonathan Z. Smith (1992 [1987], 25) writes, "So it is with memory: it is a complex and deceptive experience. It appears to be preeminently a matter of the past, yet it is as much an affair of the present. It appears to be preeminently a matter of time, yet it is as much an affair of space." Nostalgic topics and the actors in those reminisced places, spaces in narration, were meaningful things, which the villagers wanted to commemorate and transform for the future. In Lypyrtti, the villagers' emotional and nostalgic narration primarily included three themes: childhood memories from the piloting days, stories about the earlier locals and their relationship with nature, and nostalgia for clear water. People described how the preceding generations had practiced the place: observed nature, rowed a boat or walked on ice during the wintertime. What has made those memories or events in the past particular or meaningful enough to be brought back? Why were they more meaningful than others? I presume that the nostalgic telling is a reaction or even an effort at solving ontological problems. To clarify what I mean, let me provide an example that illustrates one kind of practice of place, namely rowing.

Rowing as a Spatial Practice

In Lypyrtti, people have made watercourses or paths on the surface of water, so to speak. From a historical viewpoint, Lypyrtti was born in a junction of watercourses. The significance of the village is connected

---

5. Studies in oral history have also pointed to the importance of paying attention to emotions during narration (see e.g., Anderson and Jack 1998; Portelli 1991, 8–9).

not only to its geographical position but also to its "waterway" location, which together co-compose the experience of spatiality or sense of place. Moreover, water is the centre, the fairway and the all-around matter or essence of the village.[6] The historian Terje Tvedt and archaeologist of religion Terje Oestigaard write that water is unique as an element also in the sense that it is *both universal and always particular* (Tvedt and Oestigaard 2011, 16, their emphasis). Moreover, the surface of water is at the same time carrying and sinking, moving and changing the borderline between what is above and beneath it. This becomes evident by considering a particular situation on a particular physical platform, which Honko would call (yet another environmental term) the "micro-milieu" (Honko 1985, 69). It comes close to Ingold's concept of *taskscape*. The term serves to vitalize a landscape, which is very useful when examining more closely, for example, rowing in terms of practicing a place: "*[T]he landscape as a whole must likewise be understood as the taskscape in its embodied form*: a pattern of activities 'collapsed' into an array of features" (Ingold 2000, 198, his emphasis).

How to row depends very much on the winds, the direction and intensity of the current, the shape and weight of the boat, and the rower herself. This external world came into being through my experimental self (see Skultans 2006, 3). I made most of my journeys to interview the villagers by rowing a little boat. When you are rowing, you are sitting with your back towards your destination. But that's not all. If there is no wind, remaining aligned with your destination is relatively easy. Yet this is seldom the case. So you have to feel the winds and allow your body to sense how the waves are taking the boat downwind. You should not lose track of your destination; you need to constantly check your alignment between a shifting point of departure and destination. All the while, you need to *feel* the currents; you cannot know them by looking at the surface of the water, but through the immediate experience of your body's involvement in the compositional movement of wind, water, boat and body. Maintaining balance in following the trajectory is attained through a very corporal engagement and by observing everything at the same time (water, winds, currents and the environment as a whole) and co-operating with it. Rowing is a good example of the practice of co-com-

---

6. Naturally, drinking water is also essential for living. There is a lack of freshwater on land, although salty seawater is found all around. Previously people collected freshwater from distant rock holes and kept those holes clean. There is still a lack of freshwater, although there have been wells on the islands for years. At the time of my fieldwork, many summer residents brought drinking water from the city. In 2010, the villagers formed a water cooperative, which brought pipes from the nearby town to the islands.

posing in action, where the actor is the one who rows and the actants are all the phenomena of nature in the taskscape. I use the concepts of actant and actor as Latour does: the actor is anything that modifies a state of affairs by making a difference—or, if it has no figuration yet, it can be called an actant. The technical word originates from the study of literature. It could be a structural trait, a corporate body, an individual, a loose aggregate of individuals, morphisms or individuals (Latour 2005, 54, 71). The political theorist Jane Bennett (2010, 38) describes the same idea about agency through the analogy of riding a bicycle on a gravel road. She writes that even though agency is distributed across a mosaic, "it is also possible to say something about the kind of striving that may be exercised by a human within an assemblage."

In the textualization process, all of the aforementioned actants or actors, including myself, were narrators or voices in co-composing the meaning of the village. Some of the actants and actors of the taskscape became literal actors, while some participated only in the composing phase. Aside from all the phenomena of nature, like the wind and currents, the deceased locals also participated. There are some stories in which the skills of past villagers are described reverently as almost supernatural. For example, one interviewee laughed when she told me that a particular old woman could walk on ice so thin that not even a cat dared tread on it. When I interpret the narratives of practicing place—where a local is rowing, for example—he or she is simultaneously an actor in the past taskscape, an actant of the narration in this moment (during the interview), and the becoming actor in the composition of the written history of Lypyrtti. He or she is both human and non-human, according to the temporal space. What kind of actors are the deceased people in the narration? Are they spiritual non-humans, spiritual humans or supernatural humans? The historian of religions Jonathan Z. Smith addresses these questions in his description of the transformation of an ancestor among the Arandas in Australia:

> In the words used there, the transformation of an ancestor is an event that bars, forever, direct access to his particular person. Yet through this very process of metamorphosis, through being displaced from his "self" and being emplaced in an "other"—in an object, person, or mark— the ancestor achieves permanence. He becomes forever accessible, primarily through modes of memorialization.[7] (Smith [1987] 1992, 112)

---

7. Smith informs that he has been greatly influenced by N. Munn (1970), "The Transformation of Subjects into Objects in Walbiri and Pitjantjatjara Myth," in *Australian Aboriginal Anthropology*, edited by R. M. Berndt, 141–163. Nedlands (Smith 1992 [1987], 176, n. 64).

From the point of view of landscape, Ingold suggests that a landscape is constituted through an enduring record of—and testimony to—the lives and works of past generations who have dwelt within it and, in so doing, left something of themselves behind (Ingold 2000, 189). Tilley (1994, 40) considers landscape as a fundamental reference system in which individual consciousness of the world and social identities are anchored. How this anchoring is understood to be achieved varies. Ingold, for example, sees it quite concretely, stressing co-compositional agency: "Human beings do not, in their movements, inscribe their life histories upon the surface of nature as do the writers upon the page; rather, these histories are woven, along with the life-cycles of plants and animals, into a texture of the surface itself" (Ingold 2000, 198). The past generations of Lypyrtti participated in and contributed to the oral history of the village by providing testimony and meaning, something that I as a researcher made possible through a transformation process of oral to literal history of the village. In the history book, they survive in narrations from the past to the future. Another translation happens when a reader opens the book. With regard to my research, could we see here some antecedent for sacralization of the past taskscapes and landscape of the village, which I translated into a visible text? The reader gets the last word.

Water as a Place

An emotion which manifested itself in many of the interviews of villagers—along with the concern or fear of losing the knowledge of local history—was a sadness or nostalgia for the lost clear (sea)water. So far I have examined the landscape of the village of Lypyrtti, in Ingold's (2000, 193) words, "as a world, as it is known to those who dwell therein, those who inhabit its places and journey along the paths connecting them." Now I want to take a step forward, to elaborate Lypyrtti as a water environment, to explore water as an element or a place—under the surface. As noted before, it is not easy to draw a distinction between landscape and environment. Ingold (2000, 193, his emphasis) thinks of environment primarily in terms of *function*, of how it affords creatures—whether human or non-human—with certain capabilities and projects.

Many historical studies of environmental philosophy since the beginning of the 1980s, as well as the modern environmentalist movement, have been criticized for disregarding the fact that nature consists of different elements and that the relationship between society and nature varies, depending on which natural element is being focused on. Images of and ideas about water have been and are prevalent in religious texts from all over the world. They also seem to be an interminably gushing reservoir of linguistic metaphors. The literature on the history of perceptions and images of nature and the environment is extensive (Tvedt and Oestigaard 2011, 1-3). From the perspective of Actor Network Theory, it is not important to judge *a priori* whether an object of study necessarily has anything to do with religion (see Lassander 2012, 251). However, as a researcher of religious studies I have a particular interest also in the supernatural or spiritual—besides the deceased locals—actors or actants in the narration. There were only a few. One of them was a water spirit (*näkki*). The narrators had been told by their parents or grandparents that this was a spirit that lived in wells and by the seashore, places where children should not go for fear of drowning. The shore is a borderline between land and water. The surface of water is, similarly, a borderline. It is also a borderline between death and life, if you do not know how to swim, which was the case for most people in the archipelago before the 1960s. The scholar of comparative religion Veikko Anttonen assigns particular importance to sacred-making behaviour as a human tendency to invest special referential value and inferential potential to boundaries of temporal, corporeal and territorial categories. He argues that they are established in social thinking through the category of the "sacra" and that their illegitimate crossing or passing is made binding by references to supernatural dangers and sanctions (Anttonen 2013, 5). According to Anttonen (2003, 297), wells are documented in ethnographic accounts as ritualized spaces. Even though wells are not ritualized in Lypyrtti, the water in them is "spiritualized." The *näkki* was not a sacralized being, but a kind of guardian spiritual actant, whose function or agency was to frighten.

While there are plenty of stories about fishing and fishes in the oral history of Lypyrtti, another main theme of the nostalgic narration was eutrophication. This refers to a marked environmental change in the landscape, which has rendered many seasonal activities such as swimming or fishing almost impossible. The situation is worst in July, when many residents have their holidays. One of the interviewees lamented that there is no need for July. Many people mentioned that it is no longer possible to see the yellow flowering of seaweed through the water, as one could do in the 1960s. People today no longer caution about *näkki*—perhaps because most of them have learned to swim in their early childhood. Instead they warn about blue-green algae (*Cyanophyta*). It is almost as invisible as the *näkki* was. Water polluted by blue-green algae and bacteria could be interpreted as a non-human actant, a significant co-composer of their nostalgic narration.

As a term, "ecology" refers to the totality of relations among human agents, non-human agents, and their environment (Vannini 2009b, 73).[8]

---

8. According to Vannini (2009b, 74), an ecological way of conceptualizing their subject

In this chapter, I have explored Ingold's idea of a "dwelling perspective": humans are brought into existence as organism-persons within a world, environment or lifeworld that is inhabited by beings of manifold kinds, both human and non-human. Therefore, relations among humans, which we are accustomed to calling "social," are but a sub-set of ecological relations. (Ingold 2000, 5, 153.) Ecology is not a structure, but an ongoing process whose perspectives need to be sensitive to change, adaption, integration, reintegration and disintegration (Vannini 2009b, 75). Moreover, the same applies to the textualization of these ecological relations and the humans' perception of it through temporal space. Ethnography in the form of travel accounts directs attention to the process through various spaces. Any cultural operation might be represented as a trajectory, relating to the places that determine its conditions of possibility (Tweed 2006, 58). The relationship between emic and etic, for example, is reciprocal, and the product of that relationship is a dialectical landscape that is a resolution of environment and culture, of practice and theory, of reason and imagination, of biology and religion.

The researcher of religious studies Timothy Fitzgerald (2000, 137) has argued, "It seems likely that purity and danger, the protection of boundaries and structures from pollution and distribution from a vast range of imagined enemies, involve the deepest concerns for all societies and social groups." Some anthropologists similarly conclude that anything connected to matters of "ultimate concern" for a specific collectivity can involve religious experience (Tweed 2006, 50). Furthermore, the folklorist Lina Būgiene has pointed out (2012) that changes in the surrounding landscape also find their expression in narratives. The contemporary manifestation of narratives and general public discourse is an emergent ecological consciousness that perceives the preservation of the surrounding environment as a significant common value. Tracing back the reasons or actors of polluting, we witness human actions, both global and local.

Conclusion

My study began as a village history project, but transformed into an exploration concerning what kinds of practices can be considered relevant to place research, what kinds of actors participate, and how they participate in the co-composition of the meanings which local people give to their village and its environment. I also brought into the discussion the double agency of researcher as experiencer (in the field) and as conceptualizer (in the textualization process). The research process

---

matter is central, for example, to pragmatism, symbolic interactionism and performance theory.

directed my attention to the practices of place-making in their environmental context.

In the textualization process, the villagers of Lypyrtti engaged in nostalgia as a spatial practice of a place. However, at the time of the textualization of the village history, the forthcoming book was a space to calculate. Through narration, the villagers brought meaningful things back by verbalizing them. I continued the process by textualizing these, making them available for the future. As one of them and as a researcher, I transformed the history of the village, editing and writing a published space and, later on, my doctoral thesis. In the textualization process I was one of the actors. I was dependent (and continue to be dependent) on a flood of entities enabling me to do the work and influencing its development (see Latour 2005, 54, 212–213, 218).

In ethnographic texts, readers are already used to the idea of "polyphony" in ethnographic fieldwork—the many different "voices" present in the actual discussions and dialogues through which ethnographic understandings are constructed. In this chapter I wanted to examine how various kinds of actants and actors mediated information in the textualization process and influenced each other, thereby extending conceptualizations of agency from human to non-human actors.

The nostalgic, enchanted village lives in the memories of the present inhabitants of Lypyrtti, and the present, ominously changing environment reminds them of it, prompting them to remember. Their fear of losing knowledge of their local history arises simultaneously with the fear of losing access to clear water. The environment reminds the inhabitants that it has demands of its own and that there needs to be conversation. It reminds people not to forget, and to engage in nostalgia. In other words, the environment, particularly water as such, has become a moral witness of human actions, both local and global. Nostalgic narration as such is not religious, but it can be recognized to have an ontological function.

References

Anderson, K. and D. C. Jack. 2004. "Learning to Listen: Interview Techniques and Analyses." In *The Oral History Reader*, edited by Perks, R. and A. Thomson, 63–74. 6th ed. London: Routledge.

Anttonen, V. 2014. "Religious Studies as Landscape Studies: Perceptual Strategies and Environmental Preferences in Religion and Mythology." In *New Trends and Recurring Issues in the Study of* Religion, edited by Kovács, A. and J.L. Cox, 113–132. Budapest: L'Harmattan.

———. 2013. "Landscapes as Sacroscapes: Why Does Topography Make a Difference?" In *Sacred Sites and Holy Places*, edited by S. W. Nordeide and S. Brink, 13–32. Turnhout: Brepols.

———. 2003. "Sacred Sites and Markers of Difference—Exploring Cognitive Foundations of Territoriality." In *Dynamics of Tradition: Perspectives on Oral Poetry and Folk Belief*, edited by L. Tarkka, 291–328. Studia Fennica Folkloristica 13. Helsinki: Finnish Literature Society.

Bennett, J. 2010. *Vibrant Matter. A Political Ecology of Things.* Durham, NC: Duke University Press.

Būgiene, L. 2012. "Expression of Cultural Landscape: From Supernatural Place Legends to Everyday Talk." Paper presented at the 6th Nordic-Celtic-Baltic Folklore Symposium, Tartu, Estonia, June 4–7, 2012.

Feldt, S. and Basso, K. H., eds. 1996. *Senses of Place.* Santa Fe, NM: School of American Research Press.

Fingerroos, O. and R. Haanpää. 2006. Muistitietotutkimuksen ydinkysymyksiä. In *Muistitietotutkimus. Metodologisia kysymyksiä*, edited by Fingerroos, O., R. Haanpää, A. Heimo, and U-M. Peltonen, 25–48. Tietolipas 214. Helsinki: Finnish Literature Society.

Fitzgerald, T. 2000. *The Ideology of Religious Studies*: Oxford: Oxford University Press.

Geertz, C. 1973. *The Interpretation of Cultures: Selected Essays.* New York: Basic Books.

Ginzburg, C. 1996. *Johtolankoja. Kirjoituksia mikrohistoriasta ja historiallisesta metodista.* Translated by A. Vuola. Tampere: Gaudeamus.

Honko, L. 1985. "Rethinking Tradition Ecology." *Temenos.* 21(5): 55–82.

Ingold, T. 2000. *The Perception of the Environment: Essays in Livelihood, Dwelling and Skill.* London: Routledge.

Knott, K. 2005. *The Location of Religion. A Spatial Analysis.* London: Equinox.

Kouri, J. 2011. *Lypyrtti-Lypertö: Kylä väylien varrella.* Uusikaupunki: Uudenkaupungin merihistoriallinen yhdistys.

Lassander, M. 2012. "Grappling with Liquid Modernity: Investigating Post-Secular Religion." In *Post-secular Society*, edited by P. Nynäs, M. Lassander and T. Utriainen, 239–267. New Brunswick, NJ: Transaction Publishers.

Latour, B. 2005. *Reassembling the Social: An Introduction to Actor-Network-Theory.* New York: Oxford University Press.

———. 1999. *Pandora's Hope. Essays on the reality of Science Studies.* Cambridge, MA: Harvard University Press.

Law, J. 2006. *After Method: Mess in Social Science Research.* 2nd ed. London: Routledge.

Lund, K. A. and Benediktsson K. 2010. "Introduction: Starting a Conversation with Landscape." In *Conversations with Landscape*, edited by K. Benediktsson and K. A. Lund, 1–12. Farnham: Ashgate.

Massey, D. 2005. *For Space*. London: Sage.

Nordeide, S.W. 2013. "Introduction: The Sacralization of Landscape." In *Sacred Sites and Holy Places*, edited by Nordeide, S.W. and S. Brink, xiii–xxiv. Turnhout: Brepols.

Okely, J. 1992. "Anthropology and Autobiography: Participatory Experience and Embodied Knowledge." In *Anthropology and Autobiography*, edited by Okely, J. and H. Callaway, 1–28. London: Routledge.

Oppenheim, R. 2007. Actor-Network Theory and Anthropology after Science, Technology, and Society. *Anthropological Theory*. [Online] 7(4): 471–493. <http://ant.sagesub.com/content/7/4/471> [Accessed: 31 August 2010].

Portelli, A. 1997. *The Battle of Valle Giulia. Oral History and the Art of Dialogue*. Madison: University of Wisconsin Press.

———. 1991. *The Death of Luigi Trastulli and Other Stories. Form and Meaning in Oral History*. Albany: State University of New York.

Skultans, V. 2006. "Between Experience and Text in Ethnography and Oral History." *Elore* [Online] 13(1): 1–15. <http://ojs.tsv.fi/index.php/elore/issue/view/41> [Accessed 14 October 2013].

Smith, J. Z. 1992 [1987]. *To Take Place. Toward Theory in Ritual*. 2nd edition by J. Neusner, W. S. Green and C. Goldscheider. Chicago Studies in the History of Judaism. Chicago, IL: The University of Chicago Press.

Tilley, C. 1994. *A Phenomenlogy of Landscape. Places, Paths and Monuments*. Oxford: Berg.

Tuan, Y-F. 1977. *Space and Place: The Perspectives of Experience*. London: Edward Arnold.

Tvedt, T. and T. Oestigaard. 2011. "A History of the Ideas of Water: Deconstructing Nature and Constructing Society." In *A History of Water. Series II. Volume 1: Ideas of Water from Ancient Societies to the Modern World*, edited by T. Tvedt and T. Oestigaard. 2nd ed. New York: I.B. Tauris.

Tweed, Thomas. 2006. *Crossing and Dwelling. A Theory of Religion*. Cambridge, MA: Harvard University Press.

Vannini, P. 2009a. "Introduction." In *Material Culture and Technology in Everyday Life. Ethnographic Approaches*, edited by P. Vannini, 3–12. Intersections in Communications and Culture 25. New York: Peter Lang.

———. 2009b. "Material Culture Studies and the Sociology and Anthropology of Technology." In *Material Culture and Technology in Everyday Life. Ehnographic Approaches*, edited by P. Vannini, 15–26. Intersections in Communications and Culture 25. New York: Peter Lang.

Wylie, J. 2007. *Landscape. Key Ideas in Geography*. London: Routledge.

About the Author

Jaana Kouri is a PhD Candidate and part-time teacher in comparative religion at the University of Turku, Finland. She is interested in academic writing, meaning-making processes, nature-venerating spiritualities, oral history and shamanism.

— 13 —

After Dis/enchantment: The Profanity of the Human Sciences

STUART MCWILLIAMS

The sponsoring teleologies of the historiography of magic have tended to affirm a Weberian *Entzauberung* at modernity's core. Some scholars have portrayed this as a necessary and inevitable evolutionary step, while others have lamented the apparent passing of an enchanted premodernity. Many in the arts and humanities, uneasy with triumphalist (and ethnocentric) narratives of progress, have found themselves in a position of "advocacy" for premodern enchantment, whether in a spirit of ethnographic sensitivity or of confessional enthusiasm. This has helped solidify the "two cultures" problem, famously identified by C. P. Snow as one of the principal industrial conditions of contemporary scholarship.

If the natural sciences are sincerely believed to "unweave [the] rainbow" (as John Keats has it), the humanities become counter-positioned on the Romantic side of the dispute, attempting either to re-enchant the world or, perhaps (following this volume), to recognize the latent enchantments of which it has never really been divested.

This chapter contends that the humanities are bound neither to enchant nor disenchant, but rather to act against *reduction*. While metaphysical scientism (or, indeed, Heidegger's "technicity") certainly includes forms of reductivism against which the humanities might argue, it is equally possible for narratives of enchantment and sacrality to be implicated in reductive frameworks of knowing. The

---

Keywords: enchantment, disenchantment, humanities, profane, two cultures, museum

humanist, then, is in the delicate position of putting things, texts and ideas beyond technical and commercial utility, while *also* rendering intelligible and interpretable that which is habitually presented as self-same and absolute, from sacred texts to capital itself.

Introduction

[T]he invincible impression of haziness, inexactitude, and imprecision left by almost all the human sciences is merely a surface effect of what makes it possible to define them in their positivity.

Michel Foucault, *The Order of Things* (1966)

Profane they whose recreation lasts seven days every week.

Thomas Fuller, *The Holy State and the Profane State* (1642)

Whether or not one accepts that modernity has brought—or consists in—a general disenchantment in the Weberian sense, and whether or not one approves of such a transformation, it is certainly the case that the real or hypothetical projects of dis/enchantment seem to demand the taking of a position. Are we disenchanters or (re-)enchanters? As the present volume shows, the dispute is far more complicated than it first appears. Moreover, it does not simply manifest as a "border skirmish" between the magisteria of science and religion. For better or worse, the enchantment controversy also poses a disciplinary question within the academy itself. This essay will consider the implications of this question for the vocation of the humanities. Indeed, it will proceed with the (perhaps tendentious) assumption that every text produced by the humanities is also an implicit manifesto, a claim as to what is the proper use of the precious time allocated to humanists.

Two Cultures; Two Enchantments

In addition to its presumed ties to the Reformation and Enlightenment, the idea of disenchantment has, from its earliest expressions, been associated with the natural sciences (and, in a different but related way, to technology and industry). For Max Weber himself, the project of *Entzauberung* (the elimination of magic) was explicitly "calculatory." Prior to his famous declaration that the "fate of our times is characterized by a rationalization and intellectualization and, above all, by the 'disenchantment of the world'" (Weber 1946, 155), Weber would give the following diagnosis:

> The increasing intellectualization and rationalization [...] means that principally there are no mysterious incalculable forces that come into

play, but rather that one can, in principle, master all things by calculation. This means that the world is disenchanted. One need no longer have recourse to magical means in order to master or implore the spirits, as did the savage, for whom such mysterious powers existed.

(Weber 1946, 139)[1]

Given the close link between disenchantment and calculation, a counter-alignment (voluntary or otherwise) of non-calculatory disciplines with enchantment is perhaps unsurprising. The sense of opposition has been described—and perhaps aggravated—by the "two cultures" model of Charles Percy Snow, whose 1959 lectures of the same name lamented the mutual incomprehension of scientists and "literary intellectuals" (Snow 1959, 23). While Snow was both a scientist and novelist, which lent him the impression of acting as a mediating figure, his principal allegiance to the sciences was never in doubt, and the lectures' harshest critique is reserved for the elitist mystics believed by Snow to have dominated high culture in the first half of the twentieth century.

In the Weberian framework, disciplines that do not calculate are, for better or worse, inclined to become part of the apparatus of mystery. Such a position-taking might take the form of jealous advocacy for the past (especially premodernity) and/or a fresh commitment to the production of "wonder." Whether a humanist actively strives for the re-enchantment of the world or simply stands in place to stem the tide of disenchantment depends on the level of historical optimism with which s/he proceeds. A putative "enchantophilia" along these lines might also, of course, be imposed on the humanities from without as a polemical gesture, so that science's own sense of modernity is bolstered by the consignment of Snow's "literary intellectuals" to a notional antimodern aesthetic cult.[2]

The question of enchantment is clearly a political one within the university and the intellectual sphere at large. Even within the polemics it inspires, however, the central concept is fundamentally disjunctive. Thus, a "science warrior" like Richard Dawkins can mischievously appropriate John Keats's famous expression of Romantic anxiety for the title

---

1. Michael Saler glosses Weber's concept of disenchantment as "the loss of the overarching meanings, animistic connections, magical expectations, and spiritual explanations that had characterized the traditional world, as a result of the ongoing 'modern' processes of rationalization, secularization, and bureaucratization" (Saler 2006, 695).

2. Snow especially regarded literary and aesthetic modernism (with its "hermetic" sensibility) as dangerously regressive. Later, John Carey's *The Intellectuals and the Masses* would strongly criticize these apparently undemocratic, occultist tendencies in modernism. See also note 8 on W. H. Auden's view of the matter.

of his *Unweaving the Rainbow*,[3] while elsewhere he can reclaim the word "magic" in the positive sense of wonder-making (see Dawkins's book for younger readers, *The Magic of Reality*), framing science as the principal means for expanding humanity's sense of awe and intensifying the beauty in its accounts of the world.

Enchantment's disjunctiveness, then, is of a kind that allows it to stand on the one hand for a sense of fullness and meaningfulness in an individual or communal experience of the world,[4] and on the other for ignorance and delusion. The manner in which this multivalent concept has been mapped onto narratives of modernity's arrival is summarized by the literary historian Michael Saler as follows:

> The binary discourse [of disenchantment], which has been the most prevalent, defined enchantment as the residual, subordinate "other" to modernity's rational, secular, and progressive tenets. This marked a departure from the way "enchantment" had been used discursively from at least the Middle Ages, when it signified both "delight" in wonders and the possibility of being "deluded" by them.
>
> (Saler 2006, 695)[5]

It is perhaps unsurprising that the etymology of *enchant* reflects both the derogatory and wondrous senses of the word. The origin is shared

---

3. Do not all charms fly
   At the mere touch of cold philosophy?
   There was an awful rainbow once in heaven:
   We know her woof, her texture; she is given
   In the dull catalogue of common things.
   Philosophy will clip an Angel's wings,
   Conquer all mysteries by rule and line,
   Empty the haunted air, and gnomed mine–
   Unweave a rainbow, as it erewhile made
   The tender-person'd Lamia melt into a shade.

   (Keats, "Lamia" l.229-239)

4. See also Jane Bennett's *The Enchantment of Modern Life* for a positive evaluation of the ethical and political consequences of a certain kind of enchantment. In her later book *Vibrant Matter*, Bennett reaffirms her view that "moments of sensuous enchantment with the everyday world—with nature but also with commodities and other cultural products—might augment the motivational energy needed to move selves from the endorsement of ethical principles to the actual practice of ethical behaviours." (2010, xi)

5. Saler contrasts the "binary" discourse of disenchantment with the "dialectical" version, which consists in critiquing the myths, fantasies and enchantments of modernity itself; for Saler, this tendency begins with Marx, Nietzsche and Freud (Paul Ricoeur's "Masters of Suspicion") and is given its most explicit articulation in Adorno and Horkheimer's *Dialectic of Enlightenment*.

with 'incantation': that is, to enchant is to direct a "chant" at someone or something. To be enchanted is to come under the "spell" of the verbal and the aesthetic. It may be noted here that, historically, greater negative sentiment has accrued to this latter, passive sense. To enchant is an expression of power; to be enchanted is one of submission. Similarly, to disenchant may be liberating, but for oneself to be enchanted is likely to be a matter of regret. A change in voice (between active and passive) subtly but profoundly changes what is meant by enchantment. There is also an ambiguity over the relative roles of humans and nonhumans in the act of enchantment. One may enchant an object or be enchanted by it—compare W. B. Yeats's lines: "We are blest by everything, / Everything we look upon is blest."[6]

Yet to dispense with the risk of beguilement seems also to risk becoming deaf to the "incantations" directed at one. The suspicion on the part of romantics, aesthetes and humanists that the ostensible forces of disenchantment aim at deprecating artistic representation—at enacting an "expulsion of the poets" in the Platonic sense—is a powerful one. It, too, contributes to the solidification of the two cultures problem. Our task here, then, is not to consider enchantment and sacrality as it were "in culture" (the microbiological connotation is apt), but rather as problems which are already immanent in the discourses of the humanities themselves.

The Ambiguous Modernity of the Humanities

The manner in which the human sciences have treated enchantment and sacrality—and the ways in which they have been implicated in advocacy for, or opposition to, values associated with each—has been complicated by the continuities and disjunctures between the two notions. As Bruce Robbins notes, *Entzauberung* (the elimination of magic) was borrowed and adapted by Weber from Schiller's *Entgötterung*, which referred poetically to the flight of the (pagan) gods from Nature. Disenchantment, then, is an expanded version of this nostalgic sense of "de-divinization" (Robbins 2011, 74). Romanticism in its literary and philosophical forms has given art the task of responding to this problem, whether through resistance or elegy.[7] The Romantic imagination is especially given to mixing enchantment and sacrality, speaking of them—and disenchantment/desacraliza-

---

6. Yeats himself was very largely antimodern and enchantophile in his intellectual and aesthetic positions.
7. Interestingly, however, the early Romantics in Germany affirmed the "sobriety" of the Absolute (*Nüchternheit*), a non-transcendence which Walter Benjamin would later find to be troublingly profanatory in itself. See Gasché 1996.

tion—in the same breath.⁸ The human sciences struggle to know whether (or where) to draw a boundary, and moreover whether their own vocation is bound up with a Romantic commitment to the preservation of wonder in the face of scientific reduction.

Until the Enlightenment, one could certainly not have described the human sciences as a whole—as a "project"—even though the discourses of their various disciplines had already been in play for centuries (at least). Thus, it is true to say that the birth of the humanities as such is connected to the invention of a distinctive "science of man" (anthropology in the broad sense) despite the fact that ethnographic writing *avant la lettre* is discernible long before this point.⁹ The clustering of multiple scholarly discourses around the human is also significant in that it is ostensibly made possible by the application of Reason, but it also generates a history of Reason as practised by the rational animal (the subject and object of the new discourse). That which becomes understood as the ultimate expression of rationality in the West—"calculation" as described by Weber—cannot be allowed to manifest fully within the domain of the human sciences without entirely obviating them. Indeed, in Foucault's account of this moment, a retreat or withdrawal of mathematics is noted as a necessary condition for the practice of the new study of the human (taking place, as it were, within the vacuum or remainder):

> [A]rchaeological analysis has not revealed, in the historical *a priori* of the human sciences, any new form of mathematics, or any sudden advance by mathematics into the domain of the human, but rather a sort of retreat of the mathesis, a dissociation of its unitary field, and the emancipation, in relation to the linear order of the smallest possible

---

8. Modernism often shares this tendency. Matthew Mutter notes how W. H. Auden wrestled with the enchantophilia of his poetic predecessors:

   > As a late modernist, Auden had the opportunity to be both tempted by modernist languages of magic and re-enchantment and to achieve critical distance from them. From early in his intellectual development, he was influenced by a variety of magical ontologies, including the neo-pagan blood mysticism of D.H. Lawrence, the Orphic poetics of Rainer Maria Rilke and the tragic occultism of W.B. Yeats. He also read deeply in unconventional anthropology of religion that pursued not so much scientific explanations of the sacred as the sacred itself and in psychoanalytic theories that emphasized the creative unconscious. As Auden developed as a poet, however, he became more and more convinced that magical poetics were based on an untenable response to secular modernity and misguided conceptions of language. "Art," he insisted, "is not Magic... its proper effect, in fact, is disenchanting."
   >
   > (Mutter 2010, 59)

9. Ethnography is, in one sense, as old as Empire itself; consider Tacitus's *Germania* (c.98 CE).

difference, of empirical organisations such as life, language, and labour. In this sense, the appearance of man and the constitution of the human sciences (even if it were only in the form of a project) would be correlated to a sort of 'de-mathematicization'. (Foucault 2002, 381)

While the project of the humanities is in some sense inescapably modern, the activity of its constituent disciplines is not congruent with or reducible to that which is commonly presumed to underwrite modernity as a whole (calculation). This alone demonstrates that, as Bruno Latour has always maintained, modernity is not self-same, nor should we be credulous of the stories and gestures that assert its arrival. While Latour and Foucault are incommensurable in their approaches to the issue (for one, Foucault is himself too credulous of the Enlightenment and the realities of its discourse), both show the necessity of a fundamentally Nietzschean revaluation of modernity's presumed values.[10]

Despite the contradictions and asymmetries of the situation, the superficial persuasiveness of modern narratives of secularization, disenchantment and rationalization has forced humanists into a choice of allegiances. It is tempting to render this choice in terms of the traditional anthropological triad—magic, religion and science—but in truth, modern narratives had already foreclosed the matter. Since Auguste Compte and positivist "Whig history" (which assumes the present to be the fulfilment of the past's promise and a refutation of its errors), these three domains had been plotted on a simple timeline.[11] Since positivist discourse is itself triumphantly coincident with science, the "prior" categories of magic and religion are left on the wrong side of the modern rupture. To operate credulously within this framework is to accept that magic and religion are petrified together, and that advocacy for one is indistinguishable from advocacy for both.

While some have argued against this model—Wittgenstein's *Remarks on Frazer's Golden Bough* is instructive in this regard, as are R. G. Collingwood's essays on culture and enchantment[12]—others have essentially duplicated its logic, even if they have done so in an inverted form. Historians of magic such as Valerie Flint and Brian Easlea have taken on an explicit agenda of advocacy for enchantment (embodied in magic, witch-

---

10. *We Have Never Been Modern* remains the keystone of this revaluation, although the author has now offered an alternative formulation in *An Inquiry into Modes of Existence*. Latour has affirmed the Nietzschean origins of his own philosophy. (Crease et al. 2003, 21.)

11. See Tambiah, *Magic, Religion and the Scope of Rationality*. In his influential *Religion and the Decline of Magic*, the historian Keith Thomas is largely uncritical in his adoption of the three-stage evolutionary narrative critiqued by Tambiah and others.

12. See the posthumous collection *The Philosophy of Enchantment*.

craft and other marginalized practices), which they believe to have been extinguished by modernity.[13] For these writers, the task of the humanities is to seek alternative values in the past (especially premodernity, of course). On first glance this might seem just as Nietzschean as Latour's revaluation of modernity; after all, Nietzsche seems to endorse just such a "counter-present" engagement with the past:

> It is only to the extent that I am a pupil of earlier times, especially the Hellenic, that though a child of the present time I was able to acquire such untimely experiences. That much, however, I must concede to myself on account of my profession as a classicist: for I do not know what meaning classical philology could have for our time if it was not untimely—that is to say, acting counter to our time and, let us hope, for the benefit of a time to come. (Nietzsche 1997, 60)

Yet Nietzsche is not advocating nostalgia, but "untimeliness" *in itself*. Where might one have such untimely experiences today—and in what way might they differ from confessional, affective or nostalgic commitments?

The Museum of the Humanities

If anthropology is a fundamental discipline for the constitution of the humanities as such, there are nevertheless other institutions that serve as necessary conditions. One such is surely the institution of the museum itself. What other place, furthermore, expresses so clearly the multivalent nature of enchantment? A museum attracts its visitors with the promise of wondrous artefacts (the more wondrous the better, and hence the *Wunderkammer* tradition's place as the forerunner to the modern museum),[14] but it withholds these same artefacts from appropriation as cultic objects, at least as conventionally understood. The museum's glass panes suspend the touches (and even kisses) of those for whom an object might, under other circumstances, realize a ritual significance. For the believer, is such an encounter more or less wondrous than one conducted within the context of, for example, conventional liturgy?

Some will clearly view the museum as a tool of secularization, which both disenchants and desacralizes the artefacts it contains. In a 2010 special issue of *Religion and Literature* dedicated to scholars reflecting on

---

13. Flint, *The Rise of Magic in Early Medieval Europe*; Easlea, *Witch-Hunting, Magic and the New Philosophy*. Interestingly, Easlea began as a physicist before moving into the history and sociology of science—a transition partly due to his discomfort with the cultural and spiritual losses entailed by rationalization.

14. There are many excellent studies of these traditions; one of the most intellectually comprehensive is Lorraine Daston and Katharine Park's *Wonders and the Order of Nature, 1150-1750*.

their own faith traditions, the editors express the hope that such a confessional approach—an "uncloseting," as one contributor puts it—might allow the humanities to transcend the status of a museum, to allow for meaningful contact between past and present belief. In a response entitled "Not Just a Museum? Not so Fast," James Simpson draws out the implications of this analogy. Tracking the changing institutional conditions of religious images and their consumption, Simpson acknowledges the power (and partial truth) of narratives of desacralization: "The space of the image shifted from the hot church to the private, though semipublic space of the cool museum, set high in the clouds. But that passage also drained the image of much of its heat and life" (Simpson 2010, 147).

The argument that the museum exists to perform the quintessentially modern task of consigning powerful objects to a sterile Kantian vitrine (in which they are forced to be merely beautiful) is an attractive one. As Simpson notes, however, it offers the museum itself no context save the familiar antimodern teleology. One real, historical purpose of the museum, according to Simpson, has been to forestall religious violence—whether against the person or the image.

> Exhausted by religious violence, and exhausted in particular by the attempt to break images, eighteenth-century northern Europeans invented a new solution for religious artifacts, and especially for religious paintings and sculptures. They stopped smashing them, and instead acknowledged that religious artifacts could be beautiful; they placed those artifacts under the aegis of a new discourse, invented for the purpose, that of aesthetics. In the light of the internecine violence to which the museum was a solution, we can see that the museum, for all its sepulchral silence, is the symptom of a deeply fractured cultural history, otherwise unable to look at objects without reaching for the hammer. The museum reinvented the category of the adiaphora, "things indifferent," things that do not save or damn—things, etymologically, that do not bear weight. The museum permitted the space for artifacts from mutually hostile traditions to be grouped in the same space, just as, for the same reasons, departments of literature embrace texts that would be otherwise at war with each other.
> (Simpson 2010, 143–44)[15]

In his introductory essay to the publication accompanying the exhibition *Iconoclash*, Bruno Latour describes the institution of the museum in a similar way: "Are not museums the temples in which sacrifices are made

---

15. In a contemporary context, one might think of the cultural violence of wahabists and jihadists in the Levant, for whom many archaeological sites and artefacts are idolatrous and require demolition.

to apologize for so much destruction, as if we wanted suddenly to stop destroying and were beginning the indefinite cult of conserving, protecting, repairing?" (Latour 2002, 17). Something important may, then, be retrievable from the idea of the museum. Based on Simpson's account, one might conclude that the "cooling" effect of the museum is such that artefacts are cut off from all kinds of passionate commitments, including the political. When one considers the regularity with which museums are embroiled in political disputes, however, it becomes clear that these passionate commitments are not quite all of the same order; that is, the religious is not homologous to the political.[16] A museum cannot fully liberate (if that is the word) an object from politics—consider the controversy surrounding the Parthenon Marbles—because the museum is itself part of the public sphere. Removing an object from liturgical and devotional use, however, is part of the everyday activity of the museum. It is of course possible that devout visitors might attempt to express their confessional desires. This was the case in the British Museum's much-discussed "Treasures of Heaven" exhibition, which invited such responses; ultimately, however, this exhibition and all other "pseudo-sacred" efforts demonstrate nothing so much as the final impossibility of sacralizing the museum space.[17]

The recontextualizing that occurs in museums is of a type that demands the visitor to "look again" at an artefact. As Latour writes in his introduction to the *Iconoclash* exhibition, "we are gently nudging the public to look for other properties of the image, properties that religious wars have completely hidden in the dust blown up by their many fires and furies" (Latour 2002, 32).

Together with the library (a much older institution, and less con-

---

16. For more on the specific case of religious artefacts and their museological treatment, see Crispin Paine, *Religious Objects in Museums: Private Lives and Public Duties*.

17. At the point of full, monoconfessional sacralization, the museum would simply cease to be a museum. For an example of an attempt to sacralize the humanities via theology, see the Radical Orthodoxy movement led by John Milbank. The movement declares the following as its founding principles:

    "secular modernity is the creation of a perverse theology;
    the opposition of reason to revelation is a modern corruption;
    all thought which brackets out God is ultimately nihilistic;
    the material and temporal realms of bodies, sex, art and sociality, which modernity claims to value, can truly be upheld only by acknowledgement of their participation in the transcendent."

    (Milbank *et al.* 1999, series preface)

    With a new discursive sophistication gained from deep immersion in continental philosophy and literary theory, the movement nevertheless ends where it began, that is, with High Church Anglicanism and traditionalism.

troversial), the museum is constitutive of the human sciences. Part of this constitutive function is what Simpson highlights as the *comparative* structure of the museum; its ability to hold incommensurable traditions in tension. The museum may be said to be secular, but not in the sense that secular*ization* and secular*ism* tend to imply. Its secularity—its worldliness—is that of a discursive space exclusive of revelation. This does not entail a religious artefact being somehow presented as mere matter; such an item's history is folded into its display-worthiness. The act of display undoubtedly creates a (contentious) rupture between the contemporary viewer and the object consigned to the past. However, the museum's comparative structure also allows—even if only in principle—other objects (perhaps incongruous ones, or even ones taken from the contemporary world itself) to form part of the same encounter or visit, so that this rupture is multiplied to the point of its own dubiety. In this way, the museum is emphatically not a mirror of the (disenchanted) modern world; rather, it opens a space in which we might become, in Miguel Tamen's words, "friends of interpretable objects" (Tamen 2001).

Profanation

Perhaps the humanities are not in the business of re-enchantment or resacralization. Perhaps, rather, they share with the museum a dubious secularity founded not on consecration (or desecration), but profanation. Drawing on Roman law, Giorgio Agamben describes the work of profanation as follows:

> And if "to consecrate" (*sacrare*) was the term that indicated the removal of things from the sphere of human law, "to profane" meant, conversely, to return them to the free use of men. The great jurist Trebatius thus wrote, "In the strict sense, profane is the term for something that was once sacred or religious and is returned to the use and property of men."
> (Agamben 2007, 73)

In Agamben's view, the gesture of profanation is distinct from secularization. The latter is a process of simple replacement (often the minimum possible replacement), whereas profanation has a more radical aim:

In this sense, we must distinguish between secularization and profanation. Secularization is a form of repression. It leaves intact the forces it deals with by simply moving them from one place to another. Thus the political secularization of theological concepts (the transcendence of God as a paradigm of sovereign power) does nothing but displace the heavenly monarch onto an earthly monarchy, leaving its power intact.

> Profanation, however, neutralizes what it profanes. Once profaned, that which was unavailable and separate loses its aura and is returned to use. Both are political operations: the first guarantees the exercise of power by carrying it back to a sacred model; the second deactivates the apparatuses of power and returns to common use the spaces that power had seized. (Agamben 2007, 77)

The goal of profanation is "pure means" or "means without end."[18] This might be exemplified in play, sexuality, thinking, language, art and many other activities, as long as these are practised uninstrumentally. While pure means are for Agamben the ultimate expression of humanity, they are always under threat of being "captured" by machinery such as capitalism, which is the systematized instrumental pursual of ends. While this seems to resonate with familiar anti-Enlightenment narratives, Agamben in fact dwells (following Walter Benjamin) on the *cultic* aspects of capitalism. Rather than claiming that commodification brings everything into a secular domain of the "usable," Agamben counterintuitively suggests that capitalism, like conventional religion, is founded on *consecration* and separation. Commodity fetishism is one manifestation of this; the pure and transcendent value of capital itself is another. More important still, however, is capitalism's appetite for consecrating pure means as a means-toward-ends (rendering the profane sacred).

Here Agamben has inverted the usual sense of "use" as a kind of Heideggerian technicity (that is, instrumental use as resource), defamiliarizing this "profane" word so that it can be reunderstood as connoting pure means. In the same essay, "In Praise of Profanation," he performs an analogous inversion with the word 'common'. The word 'profane' itself has also been overturned, and it now has an ambiguous relation to the capitalist profanation described in *The Communist Manifesto*:

> Constant revolutionising of production, uninterrupted disturbance of all social conditions, everlasting uncertainty and agitation distinguish the bourgeois epoch from all earlier ones. All fixed, fast-frozen relations, with their train of ancient and venerable prejudices and opinions are swept away, all new-formed ones become antiquated before they can ossify. All that is solid melts into air, all that is holy is profaned, and man is at last compelled to face with sober senses, his real conditions of life, and his relations with his kind. (Marx and Engels 1992 [1888], 6)

Interestingly, Agamben has an entirely different—and strongly negative—interpretation of the museum's role from that of Simpson. For

---

18. *Means Without End* is also the title of Agamben's short book of essays on politics (Agamben 2000).

Agamben, far from bringing artefacts into common use after the (actual and potential) violence of consecration and iconoclasm, the museum instead operates as part of the machinery of capitalism; that is, it works to *prevent* use.

> The impossibility of using has its emblematic place in the Museum. The museification of the world is today an accomplished fact. One by one, the spiritual potentialities that defined the people's lives—art, religion, philosophy, the idea of nature, even politics—have docilely withdrawn into the Museum. "Museum" here is not a given physical space or place but the separate dimension to which what was once—but is no longer—felt as true and decisive has moved. [...] [E]verything today can become a Museum, because this term simply designates the exhibition of an impossibility of using, of dwelling, of experiencing. [...] [T]he tourists celebrate on themselves a sacrificial act that consists in the anguishing experience of the destruction of all possible use. (Agamben 2007, 83-84)

Agamben thus returns to a conventional Heideggerian understanding of modernity's pathological inauthenticity. In light of Simpson's account, however, it is clear that another conception (albeit an idealistic one) of the museum is possible. The unavoidable problematic that triggers Agamben's anxiety and Simpson's admiration is this: the museum is bound into a tragic irony whereby its efforts to turn objects over to non-instrumental use are already thwarted by the institutional impossibility of making them unreservedly and materially available for visitors to touch, hold, and (mis)use.

The humanities have the freedom—if they accept it—to conduct the profanatory work of Simpson's museum without the apparatus of decontamination which Agamben finds unacceptable. That is to say, humanists can be curators without being custodians.

Conclusion

Critical curation is not free from political responsibilities. In part, its obligations derive from the fragility of its intellectual and institutional constituents. As such, Agamben's warning about the vulnerability of pure means is timely. The humanities, which historically have embodied or cultivated countless of these means without ends, have not escaped the notice of the consecrators. The new neoliberal university aims to exclude that which is unproductive, unsustainable, and that which lacks "impact."[19] Not only do the humanities conduct profanatory work (bring-

---

19. See Helen Small's *The Value of the Humanities* for a critical account of this transformation. A recent and thorough examination of the neoliberal "revolution" can be found in Wendy Brown's *Undoing the Demos*.

ing that which has been separated into common use), they themselves are profane because they are directed at nothing in particular—which is not the same as being without direction or movement. Such endlessness is not tolerated by the established faith:

> If the apparatuses of the capitalist cult are so effective, it is not so much because they act on primary behaviours, but because they act on pure means, that is, on behaviours that have been separated from themselves and thus detached from any relationship to an end. In its extreme phase, capitalism is nothing but a gigantic apparatus for capturing pure means, that is, profanatory behaviours. Pure means, which represent the deactivation and rupture of all separation, are in turn separated into a special sphere. (Agamben 2007, 87-88)

The new rationalized university does not disenchant; it takes the unacceptable profanity of the human sciences and strives to transform them into new and unprofanable activities with measurable ends. Perhaps, as Agamben claims, "the profanation of the unprofanable is the political task of the coming generation" (Agamben 2007, 92). The work of those who engage in such an effort will doubtless be seen as mere recreation—and that, after all, is only for Sundays.

References

Adorno, T. W. and M. Horkheimer. 1997. *Dialectic of Enlightenment*. Translated by John Cumming. London: Verso.

Agamben, G. 2007. *Profanations*. Translated by Jeff Fort. New York: Zone Books.

———. 2000. *Means without End: Notes on Politics*. Translated by V. Binetti and C. Casarino. Minneapolis: University of Minnesota Press.

Brown, W. 2015. *Undoing the Demos*. New York: Zone Books.

Carey, J. 1992. *The Intellectuals and the Masses: Pride and Prejudice among the Literary Intelligentsia, 1880-1939*. London: Faber and Faber.

Collingwood, R. G. 2005. *The Philosophy of Enchantment: Studies in Folktale, Cultural Criticism, and Anthropology*, edited by D. Boucher, W. James and P. Smallwood. Oxford: Oxford University Press.

Crease, R. *et al.* 2003. "Interview with Bruno Latour." In *Chasing Technoscience: Matrix for Materiality*, edited by D. Idhe and E. Selinger, 15-26. Bloomington: Indiana University Press.

Daston, L. and K. Park. 2001. *Wonders and the Order of Nature, 1150-1750*. New York: Zone Books.

Dawkins, R. 1999. *Unweaving the Rainbow: Science, Delusion and the Appetite for Wonder*. London: Penguin.

Easlea, B. 1980. *Witch Hunting, Magic and the New Philosophy: An Introduction to Debates of the Scientific Revolution 1450-1750.* Brighton: Harvester Press.

Flint, V. 1991. *The Rise of Magic in Early Medieval Europe.* Oxford: Clarendon Press.

Foucault, M. 2002. *The Order of Things: An Archaeology of the Human Sciences.* Translated by A. M. Sheridan Smith. London: Routledge.

Gasché, R. 1996. "The Sober Absolute: On Benjamin and the Early Romantics." In *Walter Benjamin: Theoretical Questions*, edited by D. S. Ferris, 50–74. Stanford, CA: Stanford University Press.

Keats, J. 2001. "Lamia." *John Keats: Major Works*, edited by Elizabeth Cook, 305–322. Oxford: Oxford University Press.

Latour, B. 2002. "What Is Iconoclash?" In *Iconoclash: Beyond the Image Wars in Science, Religion and Art*, edited by B. Latour and P. Weibel, 16–40. Cambridge, MA: MIT Press.

———. 1993. *We Have Never Been Modern.* Translated by C. Porter. Cambridge, MA: Harvard University Press.

Marx, K. and F. Engels. 1992 [1888]. *The Communist Manifesto*, edited by D. McClellan. Oxford: Oxford University Press.

Milbank, J., C. Pickstock and G. Ward, eds. 1999. *Radical Orthodoxy: A New Theology.* London: Routledge.

Mutter, M. 2010. "The Power to Enchant that Comes from Disillusion." *Journal of Modern Literature* 34(1): 58–85.

Nietzsche, F. 1997. "On the Uses and Disadvantages of History for Life." In *Untimely Meditations*, edited by D. Breazeale, 57–124. Translated by R. J. Hollingdale. Cambridge: Cambridge University Press.

Paine, C. 2013. *Religious Objects in Museums: Private Lives and Public Duties.* London: Bloomsbury.

Robbins, B. 2011. "Enchantment? No Thank You." In *The Joy of Secularism*, edited by G. Levine, 74–94. Princeton, NJ: Princeton University Press.

Saler, M. 2006. "Modernity and Enchantment: A Historiographic Review." *The American Historical Review* 11(3): 692–716.

Simpson, J. 2010. "Not Just a Museum? Not So Fast." *Religion and Literature* 42(1–2): 141–161.

Small, H. 2013. *The Value of the Humanities.* Oxford: Oxford University Press.

Snow, C.P. 1959. *The Two Cultures and the Scientific Revolution.* Cambridge: Cambridge University Press.

Tacitus. 2009. *The Agricola and the Germania*, edited by J. Rives. Translated by H. Mattingly. New ed. London: Penguin.

Tambiah, S. J. 1990. *Magic, Science, Religion and the Scope of Rationality*. Cambridge: Cambridge University Press.

Tamen, M. 2001. *Friends of Interpretable Objects*. Cambridge, MA: Harvard University Press.

Weber, M. 1991. "Science as a Vocation." In *Max Weber: Essays in* Sociology, edited and translated by H. H. Gerth and C. Wright Mills, 129–56. Oxford: Routledge.

Wittgenstein, L. (1967) 2010. *Remarks on the Golden Bough*. Translated by A. C. Miles and R. Rhees. Bishopstone: Brynmill Press.

Yeats, W.B. 1997. "Dialogue of Self and Soul." In *W.B. Yeats: The Major Works*, edited by E. Larrissy, 122–124. Oxford: Oxford University Press.

About the Author

Stuart McWilliams teaches English Literature at Åbo Akademi University, Finland. Previously, he was a research fellow at the University of Edinburgh's Institute for Advanced Studies in the Humanities. His research interests include literary medievalism and the critical history of enchantment. He is the author of the monograph *Magical Thinking: History, Possibility and the Idea of the Occult* (Bloomsbury, 2013).

— 14 —

Epilogue: When Things Talk Back

KOCKU VON STUCKRAD

This is a great book. It is an honor to be asked to reflect on the contributions of a volume like this, a work that provides so many stimulating and innovative perspectives on the study of religion in the twenty-first century. It is humbling too, as in many ways the authors' expertise in this volume by far exceeds my own knowledge of the themes addressed herein. Hence, the only thing I can offer in this brief epilogue is to point out, what from my perspective strikes me as important here, and where I see relevant questions for future research.

My own scholarly background is made up of theoretical approaches that have been developed in cultural studies, critical historiography, the sociology of knowledge, as well as pragmatist and relativist approaches in philosophy. For me, these intellectual traditions come together in discourse research, which for some time has been one of my scholarly habitats (von Stuckrad 2014; von Stuckrad 2015; Wijsen and von Stuckrad 2016). Discourse research has emerged from disciplinary contexts as varied as literature studies, cultural studies, philosophy, historiography, sociology, political science, and anthropology. It is interdisciplinary at its core (see Angermuller, Nonhoff et al. 2014; Angermuller, Maingueneau, and Wodak 2014). Interdisciplinarity—in contrast to multidisciplinarity—means that the approaches and research results from various disciplines do not just exist side by side, but that they are brought into critical dialogue with one another (Kocka 1987; Joas and Kippenberg 2005). Claims in historiography are contrasted with insights from sociology, anthropological claims are compared to conclusions from literature studies, and so forth. This is exactly what the editors of this volume have in mind in saying: "Instead of concluding that the issue is merely a matter of happily co-existing perspectives, [...] we think that understanding often develops through the productive agonism of bringing different perspectives together" (Introduction, 2).

From a discursive point of view, interdisciplinarity also includes the natural sciences. We can describe the practices and procedures of the natural sciences as materializations of discourses; and in turn, these practices stabilize and legitimize the assumptions that have made them possible. Hence, discursive structures organize the attribution of meaning to things and provide shared assumptions with regard to accepted and unaccepted knowledge. Discourse research is not so much interested in generic borders between the natural sciences and the social or cultural sciences (it is interested in the *social construction* of those borders, but that is a different issue entirely). We can acknowledge the different methodologies of the natural sciences and the humanities in their attempt to produce accepted knowledge. However, in both systems of knowledge the same discursive structures are operative (Latour and Woolgar 1986; Edwards, Ashmore, and Potter 1995; Parker 1998; Potter and Hepburn 2008, 287–288; Nikander 2008, 413).

In this theoretical frame, the concept of "relationality" is salient. It is only in relation to something else that things assume meaning; it is this position in a network of communication and meaning-making that determines the order of knowledge a discourse community follows (on a relational approach to religion and science see Vollmer and von Stuckrad 2016). Relationality also links the epistemological levels of a discourse to its social and practical levels. Moreover it makes clear that communities need the construction of *difference* to determine their identity. As the editors point out: "Magic, enchantment and eventually even religion are terms that have been used to separate the modern from the pre-modern, two groups of people whose identity (for moderns) hinged on their stance to these concepts via a logic of progress" (Introduction, 12). While this volume is particularly informed by anthropological and sociological approaches, such a description of identity-work has been discussed in historiography, as well. Charles Zika, for instance, even called the underlying dynamic "exorcism."

> The religious, the violent, the evil, the irrational, the demonic—these are some of the contemporary demons, alive and well at the turn of the twenty-first century, which we consistently endeavour to exorcise from the common sense of our experience. And one of the fundamental techniques we employ is to ensure their distance. We exorcise them to the geographical, cultural and chronological margins—to the underdeveloped, the poor, the disadvantaged, the colonized; to the primitive, the

savage, the uncivilised; to the medieval imaginary of magic and mysticism and dark age barbarism. [...] From the cusp of the twenty-first century, it is difficult to understand the survival of a common sense belief in modernity as rational and enlightened, beyond ideology and unencumbered by religious zeal, graced by decorum and civilised behaviour. The most terrible of wars, a frightening expansion of destructive technologies, genocide and ethnic cleansing, all do little to dissuade us; and geared up to fight the long war on terrorism, our political leaders draw on the same cultural arsenal of "civilisation" for its legitimation.

(Zika 2003, 4)

Zika's comment underscores the fact that scholars are acting in a discourse community within the academy, but also as social actors with moral and political positions. And these positions and "positionings" are flexible and dependent on structures—hence this volume's insistence on *dynamic* relationality. The focus on the dynamic nature of relationality is an important contribution to ongoing discussion. This is because it opens up the network of relations to historical change and to new elements that gain attention.

One of those previously underestimated elements is the role nonhuman actors play in the process. Nonhuman actors play a role in the formation of meaning, as well as—in discursive language—in the constitution of discourse communities. "New materialism" is interested in these levels of discursive communication (see Coole and Frost 2010; Johnston 2016; Ioannides 2016), and several chapters in the present volume discuss its implications and challenges. To highlight what is new and innovative in this approach, a brief look at animal studies can help. As Jonathan K. Crane explains, "animal studies draws on history, anthropology, economics, philosophy, religious studies, political science, law, biology, psychology, and others. The field's diversity reflects the complexity of the subject matter" (Crane 2016, 20). Animal studies are part of a larger discourse that addresses the position of the human species in a global environmental setting. This discourse is often presented with religious overtones that link environmental concerns with the veneration of nature as a living being (on the "Gaia hypothesis" and the global "greening of religion" see Taylor 2010). We can note that the establishment of this field of research is both the materialization of a discursive change and the stabilization of the exact changes that gave birth to the field.

Since the publication of Peter Singer's now classic *Animal Liberation: A New Ethics for our Treatment of Animals* in 1975, the field of bioethics and animal studies has gained increased momentum. In a critical response to Aristotelian, Cartesian, and Kantian understandings of animals as "machines" Singer attacked the privileging of humans over animals.

This also led Singer to popularize the term "speciesism" to frame the privileged positions humans were afforded. The strongholds of belief in the extraordinary status of the human beings have, thus, fallen one by one. Today, it is hard to escape the conclusion that the human animal is not fundamentally different from other animals. Nonhuman animals have language, personality, agency, a theory of mind; they clearly possess a rich social life with individual characters; they engage in ritual and interspecies communication (representative of the current discussion are Cavalieri 2004; Calarco 2008; Safina 2015). Paola Cavalieri recently moved a step further and proclaimed "the death of the animal," i.e., the end of the distinction between humans and other animals (Cavalieri 2012). Similarly, Jonathan K. Crane notes that the "spiraling anthropocentrism that has long reigned in animal studies is increasingly found wanting, if not suffocating" (Crane 2016, 10). Leaving such anthropocentrism behind, Crane is part of a group of scholars who not only attribute agency and personality to nonhuman animals, but also see them as ethical agents in an interspecies dialogue.

Such an approach is in line with animism. Much like "paganism," animism is a concept that was discarded by theologians and scholars of religion well into the twentieth century. Recently however, the positive adoption of animism by religious practitioners has been shared in a discourse community with scholars of religion. Following Graham Harvey's definition we can regard animists as "people who recognize that the world is full of persons, only some of whom are human, and that life is always lived in relationship to others. Animism is lived out in various ways that are all about learning to act respectfully (carefully and constructively) towards and among other persons" (Harvey 2005, xi). In this "new animism," relationship and, more abstractly, relationality are key terms because they emphasize the relative meaning that persons and actions achieve in a communicative network. This opens up new directions of research, as the editors of the present volume note in their introduction, as well: "What we, the editors, learned while co-composing this book, is that the point is not that everything is agentic; the point is that *how* something is agentic emerges as an effect of entangled networks of relational dynamics" (Introduction, 20, emphasis original). Consequently, this volume takes up the challenges of new materialism, pushing the limits of discourse even further than communication between human animals and nonhuman animals. It is an interesting move to link those considerations to a specific interpretation of Bruno Latour's Actor-Network-Theory (ANT; see Latour 2005):

> The revolutionary claims that emerged from decades of ANT research were not that scientific facts had been revealed to be socially con-

structed, but rather, that even the highest, hardest and strongest of objects in the modern world (facts) were the emergent results of complex compositions that involved the agency of nonhuman actors. In other words, that said practices could not be adequately explained while maintaining a divide between "the social" and "the natural." [...] Once this realization sunk in, that the hard sciences actually needed to acknowledge the influence of nonhuman agency in order to legitimate their practices, the great divide between fact and fetish no longer appeared as given. To underline this ambivalence, Latour eventually coined the term "factish" (see Latour 2010, 2011). (Introduction, 8–9)

Hence, agency is here extended beyond human and nonhuman animals to include "things" and "facts" as well. Science—and the laboratory life Latour and Woolgar examined—provides many examples of this, but it may be even more interesting to look at literature at this point. Poetry is full of examples that attribute agency to nonhuman animals and also to objects in nature, such as trees and plants. But repeatedly, we also see the inclusion of seemingly "inanimate" objects in a relational network of agents. Billy Collins' poem "The Iron Bridge" can illustrate this:

> I am standing on a disused iron bridge
> that was erected in 1902
> according to the iron plaque bolted into a beam,
> the year my mother turned one.
> Imagine—a mother in her infancy,
> and she was a Canadian infant at that,
> one of the great infants of the province of Ontario.
> But here I am leaning on the rusted railing
> looking at the water below,
> which is flat and reflective this morning,
> sky-blue and streaked with high clouds,
> and the more I look at the water,
> which is like a talking picture,
> the more I think of 1902
> when workmen in shirts and caps
> riveted this iron bridge together
> across a thin channel joining two lakes
> where wildflowers blow along the shore now
> and pairs of swans float in the leafy coves.
> 1902—my mother was so tiny
> she could have fit into one of those oval
> baskets for holding apples,
> which her mother could have lined with a soft cloth

and placed on the kitchen table
so she could keep an eye on infant Katherine
while she scrubbed potatoes or shelled a bag of peas,
the way I am keeping an eye on that cormorant
who just broke the glassy surface
and is moving away from me and the bridge,
swiveling his curious head,
slipping out to where the sun rakes the water
and filters through the trees that crowd the shore.
And now he dives,
disappears below the surface,
and while I wait for him to pop up,
I picture him flying underwater with his strange wings,
as I picture you, my tiny mother,
who disappeared last year,
flying somewhere with your strange wings,
your wide eyes, and your heavy wet dress,
kicking deeper down into a lake
with no end or name, some boundless province of water.

(Collins 2002, 169–170)

The image is a "talking picture" that translates the agency of the bridge, the water, the clouds, the wildflowers, the swans, and the cormorant into a dynamic network of communication with human agents, both living and deceased.

Many authors in this volume have highlighted such an understanding of relationality and have tested it in various ways. Anne-Christine Hornborg, for instance, argues that "material objects that are employed in rituals are not merely passive carriers of attached cultural meanings"; rather, they are "ritual agents" who "achieve important performative functions in the field of transformations" (Hornborg, this volume, 27). Jay Johnston, too, has much to contribute to new materialism. Building her argument on poststructural philosophy, European art historical discourse, and what is known as the Western esoteric tradition, Johnston proposes an "Esoteric Aesthetics." Johnston's proposition "enables a further reformulation and re-thinking of aesthetic relations *per se*: an approach which has potentially radical implications for the concept of subjectivity, artistic agency and interpretations of the *role* of image or object *and* the viewer" (190–191, emphasis original). In an analysis of relational dynamics, things such as a magical amulet, a statue, and an image are considered both objects and subjects, subjects that perform their agency independently from human agency.

Discourse theory makes these poststructuralist extensions of its analytical tools possible, because it allows for the inclusion of non-linguistic and non-rational ways of communication. A discourse community consists of more than human actors and may include dynamic objects, as well. That is also why poets and fiction writers, as well as politicians, lawyers, film-makers, and many others, along with their material productions, are part of a discourse community. Naturally this also makes the actors and their products worthy of attention of the discourse researcher. When it comes to agency, though, we should not forget that agency is usually *attributed* to other actors; agency is not just there. It is *we* who attribute agency to nonhuman animals or, as in new materialism, to things like images, stones, or an iron bridge. Empirical data seems to suggest that nonhuman animals, too, attribute agency to other animals and presumably even to objects (similar to human toddlers who attribute agency to stuffed animals and other objects). It will be harder to prove, however, that agents such as images, stones, and an iron bridge attribute agency to other members of the discourse community.

One of the most interesting arguments of the present volume is that it addresses this challenge to new materialism directly. Several chapters—notably by Johnston, Linda Annunen and Peik Ingman, Amy Whitehead, and to some extent Hornborg—seem to agree that we can sidestep the attribution of agency by saying that agency is something that emerges in encounters. From that point of view, an iron bridge may not be able to attribute agency to others, but it could participate in encounters that distribute agency. In this way, new materialism multiplies perspectives on what agency means, and that is a major step forward.

Let me close with the wish that this book may be an agent that will illuminate the entangled networks of relational dynamics.

References

Angermuller, J., D. Maingueneau, and R. Wodak, eds. 2014. *The Discourse Studies Reader: Main Currents in Theory and Analysis.* Amsterdam and Philadelphia: John Benjamin's Publishing Company.

Angermuller, J., M. Nonhoff, E. Herschinger, F. Macgilchrist, M. Reisigl, J. Wedl, D. Wrana and A. Ziem, eds. 2014. *Diskursforschung: Ein interdisziplinäres Handbuch,* 2 vols. Bielefeld: Transcript.

Calarco, M. 2008. *Zoographies: The Question of the Animal from Heidegger to Derrida.* New York: Columbia University Press.

Cavalieri, P. 2012. *The Death of the Animal: A Dialogue.* New York: Columbia University Press.

———. 2004. *The Animal Question: Why Nonhuman Animals Deserve Human Rights.* Oxford: Oxford University Press.

Collins, B. 2002. *Sailing Alone Around the Room: New and Selected Poems.* New York: Random House.

Coole, D. and S. Frost, eds. 2010. *New Materialisms: Ontology, Agency, and Politics.* Durham, NC: Duke University Press.

Crane, J. K. 2016. "Beastly Morality: A Twisting Tale." In *Beastly Morality: Animals as Ethical Agents*, edited by Jonathan K. Crane, 3–27. New York: Columbia University Press.

Edwards, D., M. Ashmore, and J. Potter. 1995. "Death and Furniture: The Rhetoric, Politics and Theology of Bottom Line Arguments against Relativism." *History of the Human Sciences* 8: 25–49.

Harvey, G. 2005. *Animism: Respecting the Living World.* Kent Town: Wakefield Press.

Ioannides, G. 2016. "The Matter of Meaning and the Meaning of Matter: Explorations for the Material and Discursive Study of Religion." In *Making Religion: Theory and Practice in the Discursive Study of Religion*, edited by F. Wijsen and K. von Stuckrad, 51–73. Leiden: Brill.

Joas, H. and H. G. Kippenberg, eds. 2005. *Interdisziplinarität als Lernprozeß: Erfahrungen mit einem handlungstheoretischen Forschungsprogramm.* Göttingen: Wallstein.

Johnston, J. 2016. "Slippery and Saucy Discourse: Grappling with the Intersection of 'Alternate Epistemologies' and Discourse Analysis." In *Making Religion: Theory and Practice in the Discursive Study of Religion*, edited by F. Wijsen and K. von Stuckrad, 74–96. Leiden: Brill.

Kocka, J., ed. 1987. *Interdisziplinarität: Praxis – Herausforderung – Ideologie.* Frankfurt am Main: Suhrkamp.

Latour, B. 2011. "Fetish-Factish." *Material Religion* 7(1): 42-49.

———. 2010. *On the Modern Cult of the Factish Gods.* Translated by H. MacLean and C. Porter. Durham, NC: Duke University Press.

———. 2005. *Reassembling the Social: An Introduction to Actor-Network-Theory.* Oxford: Oxford University Press.

Latour, B. and S. Woolgar. 1986. *Laboratory Life: The Construction of Scientific Facts.* Princeton, NJ: Princeton University Press.

Nikander, P. 2008. "Constructionism and Discourse Analysis." In *Handbook of Constructionist Research*, edited by J. A. Holstein and J. F. Gubrium, 413–428. New York: The Guilford Press.

Parker, I. ed. 1998. *Social Constructionism, Discourse and Realism.* London: Sage.

Potter, J. and A. Hepburn. 2008. "Discursive Constructionism." In *Handbook of Constructionist Research*, edited by J. A. Holstein and J. F. Gubrium, 275–293. New York: The Guilford Press.

Safina, C. 2015. *Beyond Words: What Animals Think and Feel*. 2nd ed. New York: Henry Holt and Company.

Singer, P. 1975. *Animal Liberation: A New Ethics for our Treatment of Animals*. New York: New York Review/Random House.

Taylor, B. 2010. *Dark Green Religion: Nature Spirituality and the Planetary Future*. Berkeley: University of California Press.

Vollmer, L.J. and K. von Stuckrad. 2016. "Science." In *Oxford Handbook of Religion*, edited by S. Engler and M. Stausberg. Oxford: Oxford University Press.

Von Stuckrad, K. 2016. "Religion and Science in Transformation: On Discourse Communities, the Double-Bind of Discourse Research, and Theoretical Controversies." In *Making Religion: Theory and Practice in the Discursive Study of Religion*, edited by F. Wijsen and K. von Stuckrad, 203–224. Leiden: Brill.

———. 2015. "Discourse." In *Vocabulary for the Study of Religion*, edited by R.A. Segal and K. von Stuckrad, 3 vols. Vol. I: 429–438. Leiden: Brill.

———. 2014. *The Scientification of Religion: An Historical Study of Discursive Change, 1800–2000*. Berlin: De Gruyter.

Wijsen, F. and K. von Stuckrad, eds. 2016. *Making Religion: Theory and Practice in the Discursive Study of Religion*. Leiden and Boston: Brill.

Zika, C. 2003. *Exorcising Our Demons: Magic, Witchcraft, and Visual Culture in Early Modern Europe*. Leiden: Brill.

About the Author

Kocku von Stuckrad is Professor of Religious Studies at the University of Groningen, the Netherlands. He has published extensively on topics related to the history of religion in Europe, method and theory in the study of religion, discursive study of religion, the diversity of knowledge systems, esoteric and mystical traditions in European intellectual history, the history of astrology, religion and (philosophies of) nature, as well as on religion and secularity. He served as President of the International Society for the Study of Religion, Nature, and Culture (ISSRNC) and was a founding board member of the European Society for the Study of Western Esotericism (ESSWE). Currently, he is President of the Dutch Association for the Study of Religion. He was co-chair of the Critical Theory and Discourses on Religion Group and is currently the co-chair of the Religion in Europe Group of the American Academy of Religion.

Index

A

accountability 98
Actor-Network Theory (ANT) 8, 9, 15, 24, 78, 87, 88, 89, 171, 209, 231, 233, 244, 270
affect 16–18, 31, 57, 86, 88, 97, 128, 130, 197, 202
affordance 88, 94, 99
Agamben, Giorgio 19, 167, 178, 261–264
agency 2, 3, 8, 9, 14, 15, 17, 19, 20, 27, 28, 30, 31, 33, 35, 38, 41, 49, 58, 59, 61, 65–73, 75, 77– 80, 89, 93, 115, 127, 130, 131, 135–137, 139, 146, 159, 160, 171, 208, 215, 218, 231, 232, 236, 237, 239, 242–246, 270–273
  material agency 189, 190–199, 202, 204
agnosticism 87, 109, 110, 116, 117, 120, 123
Ahearn, Laura 66, 67, 78
Alcalá 46–49, 52–55, 57, 59–61
Andalusia 45, 46
angels 125, 126, 128–140, 143, 151, 175, 177, 178, 180, 195
animism 20, 25, 27, 28, 43, 53, 55, 59, 60, 63, 87, 270
  neo- or new animism 28, 45, 48, 53, 55, 270
antibiosis 165, 173
Asad, Talal 3, 33, 209

authenticity 79, 145, 150, 158
autoethnography 231

B

Balagangadhara, S. N. 209
Bambara people 30
Barad, Karen 98
Baudrillard, Jean 209, 210
Bauman, Zygmunt 224
Beck, Ulrich 224
belief(s) 8, 9, 18, 51, 55, 57, 60, 69, 80, 88, 94–96, 101, 109, 110, 112–118, 120, 122, 123, 152, 155, 173, 176, 179, 200, 204, 221, 225, 226, 259, 269, 270
Belting, Hans 190, 196
Bender, Courtney 127
Benjamin, Jessica 166, 167, 180–182, 184
Bennett, Jane 126, 138, 139, 254
Berger, Peter 7
Berlant, Lauren 97
Bird-David, Nurit 27, 28, 57
blame 85, 96–98
blaming 96
Bourdieu, Pierre 4
Buber, Martin 48, 49
Byrne, Lorna 129, 132, 135

C

Callon, Michel 87
Catholicism 32, 34, 39, 45, 47, 58, 146, 147, 150–152, 155–159
camaristas 47, 48, 51, 53, 55, 56, 58, 62
Canada 28, 43
Cape Breton Island 34, 43
capitalism 170, 262–264,
Carveth, Donald 97, 98
Christianity 24, 35, 39, 50, 113, 128–130
Church of Jesus Christ of Latter Day Saints (LDS) 91
Collins, Billy 271, 272
commensalism 165, 172
complementarity 166, 167, 178, 184, 185
complexity 1, 18, 207, 208, 213, 227
composition 1, 15, 72, 79, 85, 86, 89, 95, 96, 98, 99, 101, 110–112, 119, 135, 171, 218
compositionism 112
conceptionalization 67, 77, 78, 80, 197, 232, 236, 239
consecration 261–263
control 13, 14, 19, 52, 72, 74, 76, 77, 80, 85, 86, 88, 89, 91–93, 99, 101, 102, 113, 127, 151, 169, 170, 175, 183, 207, 219, 220–223, 225, 226
Cree people 56, 57
Csordas, Thomas 126, 137
Curry, Patrick 45, 48, 49–53, 55, 61

D

Dawkins, Richard 253, 254
de Castro, Viveiros 31, 59
Deleuze, Gilles 17, 190
desacralization 259
discourse research 267, 268, 273
Disenchantment 12, 13, 50, 85, 86, 91, 93, 103, 110, 127, 251–256
Douglas, Mary 212, 221
Durkheim, Emile 4, 5, 54, 227

E

Eccles, Janet 129
ecology 43, 179, 235, 239, 244, 245
embodiment 16, 125, 143
empowerment 15, 66, 68, 87, 134, 226
enchantment 3, 10–12, 16–18, 20, 28, 45, 48–62, 85–87, 89–91, 96, 98, 99, 101–103, 125–128, 130, 131, 136, 137–139, 203, 251–255, 257, 258, 266, 268
enlightenment, the 50, 86, 256, 257
environment 29, 43, 54, 56, 191, 202, 231, 233, 235–238, 240, 241, 243–246, 269
   social environment 117, 147, 157, 209
esoteric aesthetics 189, 191, 192, 202, 203, 272
ethnomethodology 207, 209, 230
Evangelical Lutheran Church of Finland 69, 125, 128–130, 140
experience 15, 18, 30, 32, 33, 38, 40, 45–48, 50–52, 54, 55, 57, 60–62, 67, 68, 71, 72, 75–77, 79, 80, 96, 97, 99, 100, 102, 120, 127, 128, 130–135, 138, 139, 149, 150, 153, 159, 160, 175, 177, 181, 183, 184, 189, 190, 192–194, 197, 198, 202–204, 210, 215, 217–221, 225, 232, 237–241, 245, 254, 258, 263, 268
externalization 65, 145, 153

F

factish 9, 51, 89, 115, 116, 176, 177, 271
Faivre, Antoine 139, 197
fate 65, 69, 72–74, 79, 81, 169, 252
Fátima 145, 146, 148–161
fetishism 7, 12, 114, 116, 262
Finland 2, 66, 71, 125, 129, 130, 140, 231, 266
Fitzgerald, Timothy 3, 10, 209, 212, 213, 245
Freedberg, David 190, 196
freedom 74, 75, 80, 87, 89, 90, 92, 93, 134, 222, 263
free will 65–67, 78, 114
Fuller, Thomas 252

G

Geertz, Clifford 33, 225, 226, 239
Gell, Alfred 59, 62, 190, 194
Gellner, Ernest 223
Giddens, Anthony 74, 76
Goldsworthy, Andy 189, 190, 192, 201, 202, 204
governance 145, 152, 163
Grosz, Elisabeth 94, 126
guilt 85, 97, 98, 183

H

Hallowell, Irving 28–30, 56
Hanegraaff, Wouter 196

Index

Haraway, Donna 7, 19
Harvey, Graham 11, 20, 45, 48, 53, 55, 56, 61, 73, 270
Heidegger, Martin 234, 251
Hertzberg, Lars 95, 96
Hodder, Ian 13, 14
Honko, Lauri 235, 236, 241
humanities 251, 253, 255, 257, 258, 260, 263, 268
homosexuality 102

I

iconoclash 165–167, 174, 177, 260
iconoclasm 115, 165–168, 170, 175, 179, 180, 182, 185
infra-language 6, 9, 10, 19
interdisciplinarity 267, 268
interrituality 39
intersubjectivity 189
impasse 165–167, 174, 177, 180
improvisation 207, 208, 213, 218, 222, 223, 230
Ingold, Tim 29, 30, 45, 48, 57, 58–61, 232, 234, 236–238, 241, 243, 245
instruction 199, 200, 213–218

J

Jesus 37, 48, 149, 150, 174
Joy, Morny 20, 126, 139

K

Kant, Immanuel 18, 192, 194, 259
Keane, Webb 113, 114
Keats, John 103, 251, 254
kekunit ritual 28, 34, 36, 37, 39, 40
King, Richard 209
Kinsley, David 224, 225
Klein, Melanie 98, 181
Koberg, Albert 164
Kohrs-Campbell, Karlyn 67

L

Lacan, Jacques 181, 182
Lagerspetz, Olli 4, 5, 11, 95, 96
landscape 201, 202, 232, 235–237, 241, 243, 245
Lassander, Mika 233, 239, 244
Latour, Bruno 4, 6–13, 48, 51, 61, 78, 79, 86–92, 109–124, 128, 133, 146, 159, 160, 165, 166, 168, 170, 173, 174, 176, 181, 194, 208–212, 223, 227, 232–235, 238, 239, 242, 246, 257–260, 268, 270, 271
law of the father 181
Leach, James 59
legitimation 145, 152, 154, 155, 158
letting go 76, 85–87, 90, 91, 95, 98, 99, 103
Levinas, Emmanuel 98
Luckmann, Thomas 7
Luhmann, Niklas 77
Lynch, Gordon 136
Lypyrtti 231–235, 240, 243, 244, 246

M

magic 10, 13, 49, 50, 52, 59, 60, 81, 125, 127, 128, 130, 137, 138, 169, 183, 191, 195, 198, 200, 201, 204, 207, 221, 224, 251, 253–258, 268, 272
Mali 30
Martin, Craig 14
Marx, Karl 113, 254, 262
Massey, Doreen 233, 238
Massumi, Brian 17
mastery 13, 51, 85–88, 90, 91, 94, 95, 97, 101, 103, 117
Masuzawa, T. 3
materiality 35, 37, 45, 63, 126, 135, 191, 193–196, 202, 204
Mauss, Marcel 182
McCutcheon, Russell 3, 5–10, 14
McGuire, Meredith 136
McWilliams, Stuart 14
meaning 5, 14, 27, 32, 33, 38–40, 55, 67, 68, 114, 115, 126, 130, 136, 177, 189, 195–197, 207, 209, 218, 230, 232, 233, 236, 238–240, 242, 243, 245, 253, 258, 268–270, 272
  meaning-making 7, 8, 14, 232, 238, 249, 268
metaphor 10, 51, 60, 125, 126, 135, 139, 159, 210, 243
Miller, Adam S. 91
Miles, Margaret 58
Mi'kmaq people 28, 33, 34, 35, 38–40, 43
Moberg, Jessica 37
modernity 9, 10, 14, 20, 45, 48, 51, 52, 72, 77, 85–87, 112–114, 117–119, 165, 166, 168, 184, 207, 224, 227, 228, 251–258, 260, 263, 269

Morton, Timothy 15
museum 16, 251, 258-261, 263

N

negligence 165, 168, 177, 182
New Age 69, 129
new materialism 11, 195, 269, 270, 273
Nietzsche, Friedrich 254, 257, 258
Nongbri, B. 3
nostalgia 14, 231, 240, 243, 258
Nye, Malory 11
Nynäs, Peter 2, 20

O

Object relations theory 183, 186, 192, 203
occidentalism 86
Ojibwa people 28-30
ontology 28, 60, 78, 81, 91, 98, 189, 192, 197
oral history 231, 232, 240, 244, 249
ordering practices 3, 207, 208, 212
  ordinary ordering practices (OOP) 212, 213
orientalism 86
Orsi, Robert 5-9, 54, 126, 130

P

Paine, Crispin 16, 260
Paden, William E. 1
Peirce, Charles 31
Pels, Peter 50, 60,
performativity 27
person 20, 27-34, 36, 39-41, 53, 55-58, 61, 67, 77, 78, 90, 96, 114, 129, 130, 170, 174, 194, 242
pharmakon 165, 168, 169
place 2, 35, 37, 41, 43, 46, 49, 51, 52, 54, 56, 57, 72, 105, 132, 134, 145, 146, 151-153, 155, 159, 160, 204, 231-246, 258, 263
Platonism 50
poetry 271
post-colonialism 3, 124
Post-secular culture and a changing religious landscape in Finland project (PCCR) 2, 20, 66, 128
predictability 97
profanation 19, 165, 168, 261, 262, 264
profane 18, 19, 36, 50, 61, 149, 251, 252, 261, 262
Protestantism 50, 58, 113

Prothero, Stephen 5
purification 35, 112-116, 122, 145, 154, 158, 209, 210, 211

Q

queer 99, 102, 105, 165, 167

R

Rappaport, Roy 28, 32, 33, 35, 39
relational epistemology 27, 57
relationality 3, 52, 57, 166, 268-270, 272
reliance 85, 95, 96, 99
religion
  concept of 1-4, 11, 13, 20, 28, 50, 53, 55, 69, 88, 102, 109-113, 116-123, 125-127, 174, 208
  discursive study of 268, 269, 275
  liberal religion1 30
  lived religion 24, 143
  materiality of 196
  marketization of 137
  phenomenology of 194
  post-secular approach to the study of 139
  religious belief 109, 112, 113, 115
  secularist studies of 139
  study of 207-213, 223
  vernacular religion 45, 46, 49, 52, 54, 55
re-enchantment 201, 256, 261
rethoric 65, 70, 73, 240
risk 5, 11, 14, 35, 72, 97, 99, 101, 121, 139, 154, 171-173, 178-180, 182, 215, 221, 223, 224, 255
ritual 3, 10, 15, 16, 18-20, 27-41, 47, 52, 55, 58, 63, 105, 125, 127, 130-135, 143, 145, 146, 148, 150, 153, 159, 160, 191, 192, 195, 196, 198-200, 204, 206, 220, 221, 225, 258, 270, 272
ritual objects 27, 31-33, 35, 37-41

S

sacrilege 19, 165, 167, 168, 177, 179, 185
sacralization 3, 10-12, 16, 19, 20, 24, 37, 145, 165, 167, 168, 235, 243, 260
resacralization 261
Schiller, Friedrich 255
Scott, Colin 49, 56, 57, 61
secularism 109, 261

Index

secularization 117, 119, 120, 127, 130, 230, 253, 257, 258, 261
Sedgwick, Eve 16, 94, 95, 178
Shiva 31
Simpson, James 259, 260, 263
Singer, Peter 269, 270
Smith, Jonathan Z. 3, 240, 242
Snow, Charles Percy 253
social construction 6, 7, 212, 268
Spain 46, 49, 147, 156
Starhawk 184
Stengers, Isabelle 19, 116, 168, 169, 171, 172, 177, 179, 180, 184
strategy 18, 112, 222, 224, 226
Strauss, Sarah 73, 80
Stringer, Martin 13
subjunctive mode 125, 127, 135
Sund, Ann-Helen 185

T

Tarde, Gabriel 4
Taves, Ann 5, 127, 139
textualization 231, 232, 245, 246
thirdness 166, 181
Thrift, Nigel 17
time 16, 54, 56, 58, 146, 161, 195, 231, 240
transformation 13, 27, 31–33, 36, 38, 73, 97, 109, 116, 118, 120, 121, 139, 146, 160, 180, 242, 252, 272,
  transformation talk 118–120
translation 5, 6, 9, 87, 88, 96, 112, 117, 118, 180, 197–199, 209, 211, 233, 238, 243
trust 40, 85, 95–99, 102
Turku 24, 66, 68, 70, 249
Turner, Victor 31–33, 38, 225
Tweed, Thomas 5, 13, 235, 240, 245
two cultures 251, 252, 255
Tylor, Edward 28, 59

U

uncanny 2, 15, 61
uncertainty 103, 132, 157, 219, 223, 234, 262
  managing uncertainty 207, 208, 222, 226
unpredictability 85, 89, 97, 207, 208, 220, 224

V

Valkealahti, Pekka 185
Vannini, Phillip 233, 239, 244, 245
Vincett, Giselle 129
Virgin Mary 45, 47, 49, 60, 146, 149, 151, 153, 158
von Stuckrad, Kocku 20, 196, 197, 267, 268

W

Walker Bynum, Caroline 194
water 1, 35, 77, 146, 201, 202, 231, 232, 234, 240, 241, 243, 244, 246, 271, 272
Weber, Max 50, 53, 94, 96, 130, 158, 169, 227, 252, 253, 256
West African drumming practices 99–101
Westermarck, Edvard 4, 5
Whitehead, Amy 18
Winch, Peter 4, 5, 11
Wittgenstein, Ludvig 196, 257
women 37, 39, 47, 58, 70, 125, 128–139, 143, 184, 242

Y

yoga 17, 65, 66–82, 130

Z

zero-sum game 86, 88, 89, 92, 99, 103
Zika, Charles 268, 269

www.ingramcontent.com/pod-product-compliance
Lightning Source LLC
Chambersburg PA
CBHW052104230426
43671CB00011B/1923